SAMUEL ADAMS

SAMUEL ADAMS

FATHER
of the
AMERICAN
REVOLUTION

MARK PULS

First published in 2006 by
PALGRAVE MACMILLAN™
175 Fifth Avenue, New York, N.Y. 10010 and
Houndmills, Basingstoke, Hampshire, England RG21 6XS.
Companies and representatives throughout the world.

PALGRAVE MACMILLAN is the global academic imprint of the Palgrave
Macmillan division of St. Martin's Press, LLC and of Palgrave Macmillan Ltd.
Macmillan® is a registered trademark in the United States, United Kingdom and
other countries. Palgrave is a registered trademark in the European Union and other
countries.

ISBN-13: 978-1-4039-7582-9
ISBN-10: 1-4039-7582-5

Library of Congress Cataloging-in-Publication Data is available from the Library of
Congress.
Puls, Mark, 1963–
    Samuel Adams : father of the American Revolution / by Mark Puls.
      p.   cm.
    Includes bibliographical references.
    ISBN 1-4039-7582-5 (alk. paper)
    1. Adams, Samuel, 1722–1803.   2. Politicians—United States—Biography.
3. United States. Declaration of Independence—Signers—Biography.   4. United
States—Politics and government—1775–1783.   I. Title.
E302.6.A2P85   2006
973.3092—dc22
[B]

                                                                    2006044782

A catalogue record of the book is available from the British Library.

Design by Letra Libre, Inc.

First edition: October 2006
10 9 8 7 6 5 4 3 2 1
Printed in the United States of America.

To my parents, Gerald and Sheron Puls,
who taught me all of life's lessons

Without the character of Samuel Adams, the true history of the American Revolution can never be written. For fifty years his pen, his tongue, his activity, were constantly exerted for his country without fee or reward.

—John Adams

CONTENTS

Acknowledgments   xi

Timeline of the Life of Samuel Adams   1
Who Is Who in *Samuel Adams: Father of the American Revolution*   3
Introduction   13
1. The Education of a Radical   19
2. Civil Disobedience   35
3. A Bundle of Sticks   45
4. The True Sentiments of America   65
5. All the King's Men   77
6. Persecution   91
7. The Boston Massacre   99
8. Standing Alone   113
9. The Fuse of a Revolution   133
10. Portents of War   149
11. Revolution   165
12. Independence   179
13. The Trials of War   191
14. A Constitution   211
15. Twilight   223
Epilogue: Patriarch of Liberty   233

Notes   239
Bibliography   261
Index   267

Photosection appears after page 116.

ACKNOWLEDGEMENTS

No book is written without help from many people. I would like to thank Melvin Claxton, Matthew Puls, Michael Puls, Leslie Rivas-Lynch, Denise Edwards, Steven Haines, and Jeremy Pearce for their steadfast encouragement and support. I also am indebted to Alessandra Bastagli, Editor at Palgrave Macmillan, for her guidance, and to Mel Berger of the William Morris Agency for his belief in this work. Also, I would like to thank Billie Rae Bates for helping prepare the manuscript. I also appreciated the assistance of Carrie F. Supple of the Massachusetts Historical Society and Erin M. A. Schleigh of the Museum of Fine Arts, Boston.

TIMELINE OF THE LIFE
OF SAMUEL ADAMS

1722: Born on September 16 in Boston.

1740: Graduates from Harvard.

1748: Begins public writing career.

1749: Marries Elizabeth Checkley.

1751: His son, Samuel, is born.

1756: His daughter, Hannah, is born. He is elected as a tax collector.

1757: His wife dies.

1764: Marries Elizabeth Wells. Launches protest over Sugar Act, makes call for a colonial congress; publicly questions Parliament's authority in America; convinces local businesses to boycott British goods; drafts Massachusetts' statement on colonial rights.

1765: Steps up boycott; orchestrates the call for the Stamp Act Congress; is elected to the Massachusetts House of Representatives.

1766: Elected clerk of House; Stamp Act is repealed.

1768: Writes statement on colonial rights, published in England as "The True Sentiments of America." Launches boycott in protest of Townshend Acts; writes circular letter, which unites colonial resistance to British taxes. British military occupation of Boston begins.

1770: Adams wins concessions from British to lift military occupation after the Boston Massacre.

1771: Begins series of influential newspaper articles detailing "the cause of American freedom" to rouse resistance in the colonies.

1772: Creates committee-of-correspondence network of colonial leaders to coordinate resistance.

1773: Discloses letters of Massachusetts Governor Thomas Hutchinson; writes statement of "Rights of Colonists," which is published as a pamphlet; orchestrates the Boston Tea Party. In a series of newspaper articles, becomes the first American public figure to call for the Continental Congress; for independence from England, and for a Bill of Rights.

1774: Elected delegate to the first Continental Congress; wins support for the Suffolk Resolves, which calls for colonists to ignore Britain's Coercive Acts, train militia, and withhold taxes from royal governments.

1775: Revolutionary War begins in April when British troops try to arrest Adams and John Hancock at Lexington. Attends second Continental Congress; orchestrates George Washington's nomination as commander-in-chief of the American Army.

1776: Wins support for the Declaration of Independence and for the drafting of the Articles of Confederation.

1777: Becomes the leading figure in Congress prosecuting the war.

1779: Attends the Massachusetts state constitution convention.

1781: Adams signs the ratified Articles of Confederation and retires from Congress; is elected president of the Massachusetts senate.

1788: Attends the Massachusetts ratifying convention for the U.S. Constitution.

1789: Elected lieutenant governor of Massachusetts.

1794: Elected governor of Massachusetts.

1797: Retires from public life.

1803: Dies on Sunday, October 2, 1803.

WHO IS WHO IN
SAMUEL ADAMS:
FATHER OF THE
AMERICAN REVOLUTION

Adams, Elizabeth Checkley: Adams' first wife and mother of his two children, Samuel and Hannah.

Adams, Elizabeth Wells (Betsey): Adams' second wife.

Adams, Hannah: Adams' daughter; born in 1756.

Adams, Henry: Adams' great-grandfather.

Adams, John (the elder): Adams' grandfather.

Adams, John: Adams' second cousin. Delegate to the Continental Congress; U.S. diplomat to France and Europe; U.S. ambassador to England; first U.S. vice president; second U.S. president.

Adams, Joseph: Adams' brother; born in 1728.

Adams, Mary Fifield: Adams' mother.

Adams, Mary: Adams' sister; born in 1717.

Adams, Samuel (Deacon): Adams' father; merchant; popular Whig party leader.

Adams, Samuel (son): Adams' son; born in 1751.

Allan, Ethan: Vermont leader of Green Mountain Boys; Continental brevet colonel; militia major general. Led capture of Ticonderoga.

Ames, Fisher: Dedham, Massachusetts member of the Massachusetts Ratifying Convention in 1788; member of Congress in 1789.

Arnold, Benedict: Continental general. Aided Ethan Allan in capture of Ticonderoga; became a traitor to America by offering the British to sellout his command for 10,000 pounds sterling.

Attucks, Crispus: Free sailor of African and Native American descent slain during the Boston Massacre.

Baltimore, Lord (Cecilius Calvert): English lord; proprietor of colonial Maryland.

Belcher, Jonathan: Royal Governor of Massachusetts during the land-bank controversy.

Bernard, Francis: Royal Governor of Massachusetts, 1760–1769.

Botetourt, Lord (Norbonne Berkeley): Royal governor of Virginia, 1768–1770.

Bowdoin, James: Boston Whig leader; writer; member of colonial legislature. Elected to Continental Congress but prevented due to health issues; became Massachusetts' governor in 1785.

Brown, John: Providence, Rhode Island merchant; delegate to the Continental Congress.

Burgoyne, John: British general who defeated American General Horatio Gates at Saratoga.

Burke, Edmund: English political writer; member of Parliament; private secretary to the Marquis of Rockingham.

Bute, John Stuart: British prime minister, 1762–1763.

Checkley, Elizabeth: *See* Adams, Elizabeth Checkley.

Checkley, Samuel: Adams' father-in-law. Pastor of Old South Congregational Church.

Choiseul, Etienne Francois: French minister of war.

Church, Benjamin: Physician; Whig leader; member of Boston Committee of Correspondence; member of Massachusetts provincial congress; first major traitor to American cause.

Clark, Jonas: Lexington clergyman; Pastor of First Parish Congregationalist Church.

Clarke, Richard: Tea consignee for the East India Company.

Conway, Thomas: Foreign mercenary and brigadier general who led Congressional effort to replace George Washington with Horatio Gates as command-in-chief of Continental Army.

Cook, Elisha: Friend of Adams' father. Popular Whig leader.

Cooper, Samuel: Boston clergyman; patriot leader.

Copley, John Singleton: Master portrait painter and artist from Boston.

Corner, John: British naval officer.

Cornwallis, Charles: British general; surrendered to American and French forces at Yorktown.

Cromwell, Oliver (1599–1688): English military and political leader who led successful rebellion against the monarch; became semiautocratic lord protector.

Cushing, Thomas (the elder): Adams' first employer. Merchant; father of Whig leader Thomas Cushing.

Cushing, Thomas (the younger): Merchant; Whig leader; speaker of the Massachusetts Colonial legislature; delegate to Continental Congress.

Dalrymple, William: British military officer. Led troops that occupied Boston from 1768–1770.

Dana, Francis: Boston attorney and member of the Sons of Liberty. Delegate to the Continental Congress; diplomat to France and Europe during the revolution; chief justice of the Massachusetts Supreme Court.

Dartmouth, Lord (William Legge): British secretary of state for the American colonies, 1772–1775.

Deane, Silas: Connecticut delegate to the Continental Congress; American diplomat to Europe during the revolution.

DeBerdt, Dennys: London agent for Massachusetts, 1765–1770.

Devens, Richard: Charleston, Massachusetts Whig patriot.

Dickinson, John: Philadelphia author of *Letters from a Pennsylvania Farmer* in support of colonial rights; attorney; delegate to the Continental Congress; militia officer.

Du Chatelet, Count: French ambassador to London during the Townshend Acts controversy.

Duchè, Jacob: Assistant rector of the United Parishes of Christ's Church and St. Peter's in Philadelphia.

Dunmore, Lord (John Murray): Earl of Dunmore; royal governor of Virginia.

Edes, Benjamin: Printer and publisher of the *Boston Gazette;* founding member of the Sons of Liberty.

Edwards, Jonathan: Popular evangelist and clergyman.

Fenton: British colonel who tried to bribe Adams for his support of English policies.

Fifield, Richard: Adams' father-in-law. Leading businessman in Boston.

Flucker, Thomas: Messenger for General Thomas Gage.

Folsom, Nathaniel: New Hampshire militia officer; delegate to the Continental Congress.

Franklin, Benjamin: Philadelphia printer; London agent for colonies; delegate to the Continental Congress; diplomat to France and Europe; member of the U.S. Constitutional Convention.

Franklin, William: Son of Benjamin Franklin. Royal governor of Pennsylvania; Loyalist.

Gadsden, Christopher: Charleston, South Carolina merchant; member of the colonial legislature; delegate to the Continental Congress.

Gage, Thomas: British general in charge of English forces in North America, 1763–1775; royal military governor of Massachusetts, 1774–1775.

Galloway, Joseph: Philadelphia attorney, Loyalist; member of Pennsylvania colonial legislature; delegate to the Continental Congress.

Gates, Horatio: Major General in Continental Army. Defeated British forces under General John Burgoyne at Saratoga.

George III, King (George William Frederick): King of Great Britain and Ireland.

George IV: Son of King George III. Prince of Wales.

Gerry, Elbridge: Whig leader from Marblehead, Massachusetts; delegate to the Continental Congress.

Gill, Jonathan: Printer and publisher of *Boston Gazette;* founder of the Sons of Liberty.

Gordon, William: Historian; author of *History of the American Revolution.*

Gray, John: Co-owner of Boston rope manufacturing plant.

Greenleaf, Benjamin: Whig leader in Massachusetts; member of the colonial legislature.

Greenleaf, Stephen: Suffolk County Sheriff.

Grenville George: In 1763, became first Lord of the Treasury and Chancellor of the Exchequer. Author of the Grenville Acts.

Gridlely, Jeremiah: Boston attorney.

Habersham, James: Savannah, Georgia merchant; government leader; Loyalist.

Hamilton, Alexander: New York attorney; General Washington's aide-de-camp; Continental officer; co-author of *The Federalist;* attended U.S. Constitutional Convention in Philadelphia; first U.S. Secretary of the Treasury.

Hancock, John: Boston Whig leader; member of the Massachusetts colonial legislature; head of the Massachusetts militia; president of the Massachusetts provincial congress; member and president of the Continental Congress; governor of Massachusetts.

Hancock, Thomas: Uncle of John Hancock. Boston's wealthiest merchant.

Hawley, Joseph: Whig leader and lawyer from Northampton, Massachusetts; member of the colonial legislature.

Henry, Patrick: Member of the Virginia colonial legislature; delegate to the Continental Congress.

Hillsborough, Lord (Wills Hill): British Secretary of State for the American colonies.

Hollis, Thomas: British publisher; advocate of American rights.

Hood, Samuel: British admiral. Head of British naval squadron in America from 1768–1770.

Hughes, John: Friend of Benjamin Franklin. Philadelphian stamp master; Quaker.

Hutchinson, Thomas: Tory leader in Massachusetts; chief justice; royal lieutenant governor; royal governor.

James I, King: King of England, Ireland, and Scotland (1566–1625).

Jay, John: New York attorney; delegate and president to the Continental Congress; colonel in the state militia; diplomat to Spain; negotiated 1783 peace treaty with England; appointed as minister to England; first chief justice of the U.S. Supreme Court; negotiated controversial 1795 Jay Treaty with Britain.

Jefferson, Thomas: Member of Virginia House of Burgesses; member of Continental Congress; Massachusetts governor; U.S. ambassador to France; second U.S. vice president; third U.S. president.

Killroy, Matthew: British soldier who fired musket at Boston Massacre.

King, Rufus: Newbury Port, Massachusetts House leader; member of the Continental Congress. Attended the U.S. Constitution convention in Philadelphia in 1787 and the Massachusetts Ratifying Convention 1788.

Knox, Henry: Boston bookseller present at the Boston Massacre. Artillery officer; Continental general and confidante of George Washington; Secretary of War under the confederation; proponent of the U.S. Constitution; first U.S. Secretary of War.

Lee, Arthur: Brother of Virginian Richard Henry Lee. Adams' correspondent in London.

Lee, Richard Henry: Whig leader and close political ally of Samuel Adams. Member of Virginia House of Burgesses; member of Continental Congress; member of U.S. Senate.

Legge, William: *See* Dartmouth, Lord.

Leonard, Daniel: Boston Tory; Loyalist; attorney; writer; member of the Massachusetts' colonial council.

Lincoln, Benjamin: Farmer and Continental general from Hingham, Massachusetts. Commanded troops sent against Shays' Rebellion.

Locke, John: English political writer.

Lynch, Thomas: South Carolina planter; member of the Stamp Act Congress; member of colonial legislature; delegate to the Continental Congress.

Madison, James: Virginia delegate to the Continental Congress in 1779; attended the U.S. Constitutional Convention in Philadelphia; co-author of *The Federalist* and proponent of the U.S. Constitution; U.S. Secretary of State under Thomas Jefferson; fourth U.S. President.

Mansfield, Lord (William Murray): Member of the British House of Lords.

Mather, Cotton: Massachusetts political and religious leader; clergyman.

Mather, Dr. Reverend: Boston clergyman.

Mauduit, Israel: Ally of British Prime Minister John Stuart Bute.

Mauduit, Jasper: Brother of Israel Mauduit. London agent for Massachusetts.

McKean, Thomas: Attorney; Delaware delegate to the Continental Congress.

Meserve, George: New Hampshire stamp master.

Montagu: *See* Sandwich, Lord.

Montesquieu: French political writer, author of *The Spirit of the Laws.*

Montgomery, Hugh: British soldier who fired musket at Boston Massacre.

Murray, John: *See* Dunmore, Lord.

North, Lord Frederick: British prime minister, 1770–1782.

Oliver, Andrew: Brother-in-law of Thomas Hutchinson. Stamp master; Whig leader; royal lieutenant governor of Massachusetts.

Otis, James: Close political ally of Adams. Massachusetts advocate general; Whig leader; member of Stamp Act Congress; member of Massachusetts Colonial legislature.

Paine, Robert Treat: Boston Whig leader; clergyman; attorney; judge; defended troops after the Boston Massacre; member of Massachusetts provincial assembly; delegate to the Continental Congress.

Paine, Thomas: English journalist and pamphlet writer; author of *Common Sense* and *The Crisis.*

Parker, John: Massachusetts militia captain of Minutemen in Lexington.

Paxton, Charles: Political ally of Massachusetts' Royal Governor Francis Bernard; friend of Charles Townshend; customs official in Boston.

Penn, William: English lord; proprietor of colonial Pennsylvania.

Pitcairn, John: British major who led troops at Lexington and Concord.

Pitt, William: Earl of Chatham. Member of the House of Commons and then House of Lords; British prime minister; opposed the Stamp Act; known "the Great Commoner."

Preston, Thomas: British captain; led troops at Boston Massacre.

Purviance, Jr., Samuel: Member of the Cecil County, Maryland committee of correspondence.

Quincy, Josiah: Massachusetts' attorney; Whig leader; provided legal defense for troops after the Boston Massacre.

Randolph, John (1727–1784): Distant cousin of Thomas Jefferson. Loyalist; royal attorney general of Virginia; fled to England with Lord Dunmore.

Randolph, John (1773–1833): U.S. Congressman.

Randolph, Peyton: Virginia attorney; delegate and first president of the Continental Congress.

Reed, Joseph: Philadelphia attorney; delegate to the Continental Congress; Continental officer; military secretary to George Washington;

adjutant general of the American Army; met with British general Sir
William Howe at Staten Island for peace talks in 1776.

Revere, Paul: Boston silversmith; engraver; courier for Whig leadership;
proponent of U.S. Constitution.

Rivington, James: Loyalist publisher of *Rivington's Royal Gazette;* American spy and secret agent for George Washington.

Rockingham, Marquis of (Charles Watson-Wentworth): British prime
minister, 1765–1766.

Rodney, Caesar: Delaware delegate to the Continental Congress; militia
general.

Rotch, Francis: Owner of merchant ship *The Dartmouth,* which carried
East India Company tea to Boston.

Ruggles, Timothy: Tory leader in Massachusetts colonial legislature.

Rush, Benjamin: Philadelphia surgeon; delegate to the Continental
Congress; Continental surgeon general.

Rutledge, Edward: Younger brother of John Rutledge. Attorney; South
Carolina delegate to the Continental Congress.

Rutledge, John: Attorney; member of the colonial legislature in South
Carolina; delegate to the Continental Congress.

Sandwich, Lord (John Montagu): First Lord of the British Admiralty.

Sayre, Stephen: London merchant; worked informally on behalf of
Massachusetts.

Scott, James: Captain of John Hancock's merchant ship *The Hawley.*

Sewall, Jonathan: Attorney; Royal advocate general of Massachusetts.

Shays, Daniel: Continental officer from Hopkinton, Massachusetts;
militia soldier; veteran of Bunker Hill; led revolt of indebted
farmers by seizing courts and the federal arsenal at Springfield.

Sherman, Roger: Connecticut delegate to Continental Congress; served
on committee to draft the Declaration of Independence.

Shirely, William: Royal Governor of Massachusetts in the 1750s.

Singletary, Amos: Sutton, Massachusetts farmer; attended the Massachusetts Ratifying Convention in 1788.

Smith, Adam: English intellectual; economist; author of *Wealth of
Nations.*

Smith, James: British naval official.

Smith, Jonathan: Berkshire, Massachusetts farmer; attended the Massachusetts Ratifying Convention in 1788.

Sullivan, John: Attorney; New Hampshire delegate to the Continental Congress; Continental general.

Thacher, Oxenbridge: Whig leader; Boston member of the Massachusetts Colonial legislature.

Thomson, Charles: Philadelphia merchant; radical. Delegate to the Continental Congress, where he served as secretary; member of Confederation Congress.

Townshend, Charles: British official; Chancellor of the Exchequer.

Trumbull, Jonathan: Connecticut royal governor who supported colonists; the only pre-independence governor to continue in office through the revolution.

Voltaire: French writer of the Enlightenment.

Warren, James: Militia general; President of Massachusetts Provincial Assembly.

Warren, Joseph: Physician; Boston Whig leader; co-author on appeal for Committees of Correspondence and Suffolk Resolves; head of Boston's Committee of Safety; American general.

Warren, Mercy Otis: Sister of James Otis; wife of James Warren. American historian; playwright.

Washington, George: Member of Virginia House of Burgesses; lieutenant general and later commander-in-chief of American Army; proponent of U.S. Constitution; first U.S. president.

Waters, Daniel: Charleston, Massachusetts militia leader, later a naval officer and privateer.

Watson-Wentworth, Charles: *See* Rockingham.

Webster, Daniel: U.S. Senator for Massachusetts; U.S. Secretary of State.

Wedderburn, Alexander: British solicitor general.

Wells, Elizabeth: *See* Adams, Elizabeth Wells.

Wells, Thomas: Brother of Adams' second wife; later Adams' son-in-law. Married to his daughter Hannah.

Whately, Thomas: British joint secretary of the treasury.

Whitefield, George: Clergyman and evangelist.

Wilson, James: Philadelphia attorney; urged loyalty to the king but not to Parliament in what became known as the "dominion theory."

Witherspoon, John: Scotland-born educator; clergyman in New Jersey; president of College of New Jersey (later Princeton University); delegate to the Continental Congress.

INTRODUCTION

The gray-haired man led the children through Boston's winding streets to the town common square. He gripped their fingers gently, like a careful guide. The children included his young kinsman, John Quincy Adams. The middle-aged patriot, Samuel Adams, drew the children to the edge of the square to watch the imposing sight of British soldiers marching to the staccato beat of a military cadence through the heart of Boston.

He lifted his hand, which trembled from a lifelong affliction of palsy. His fingers danced as if discharging the electric impulses of rising agitation as he pointed to the red-clad infantrymen. In a solemn voice, he warned the children that these troops, which occupied Boston in 1774, threatened their freedom. He looked into their eyes to make certain they understood. He wanted them, even at an early age, to cherish the blessing he believed their forefathers had left them in leaving England more than a century and a half earlier. He made liberty seem a tangible thing, a sort of wonderful treasure that needed constant protection. This was the lesson he hoped to instill.

By the time the American Revolution began with the shots at Lexington in 1775, Samuel Adams had already spent a decade working to the convince colonists young and old alike that independence could only be secured with a break from England. To British Loyalists, Adams was the leading antagonist in Anglo-American relations. To colonial patriots, he was the embodiment of the spirit of liberty. As Britain tried to extend its authority in America in the 1760s and 1770s by installing a puppet government, Adams believed that colonists would eventually face two choices: submission or independence. He once wrote that "Shakespeare tells us, there is a tide in human affairs, an opportunity which wise men carefully watch for."[1] Sensing that tide, he took it upon himself to prepare America for the opportune moment he believed was coming by encouraging the colonies to unite, to defend their liberties, to establish new state governments, to form a national Congress, and to be ready to declare national sovereignty.

This was an audacious dream in 1765 when Adams first began to advocate independence among his political friends in Boston. Britain was the most powerful empire Europe had seen since the fall of Rome, and he was a near-penniless colonial assemblyman on the outer edges of the civilized world. Yet Adams possessed extraordinary gifts of political vision and ingenuity. As Woodrow Wilson once observed of Samuel Adams: "He was the sort of man and orator whose ascendancy may mean revolution almost when he chooses."

When in 1768 the British sent a battleship and regiments to Boston in response to Adams' strategies of civil disobedience, he shed any remaining doubts over his course of action and pledged within himself to precipitate a revolution. He believed, however, that years of groundwork were needed to solidify the disparate colonies and crystallize a national consciousness centered on liberty. Leading up to the Revolution, Adams worked incessantly to convince Americans to become keenly aware of their civil rights and to ardently defend them.

Of the major founding fathers, only Samuel Adams advocated independence before Lexington. In the critical prewar years, it was Adams who mapped out what became known as American values about liberty, self-government, and natural human rights. His arguments were later echoed in the Declaration of Independence. Thomas Jefferson called him the "Patriarch of Liberty."

Despite his many achievements and their lasting impact, his legacy goes largely unheralded in recent years, even during a wave of interest about the Founding generation. While Adams was hailed as the "Father of the American Revolution" in his own time, his role in birth of the nation has been overshadowed by founders who went on to become U.S. Presidents or by men who rose to prominence during the inaugural federal government. Biographers and historians have often assigned more significant places to men who had little influence before the Revolution in shaping the birth of the nation or forging its foundational ideals.

Adams' legacy suffers in large part because he was no longer involved in national politics by the time by the time George Washington became the nation's first president in 1789. Adams, a decade older than Washington, thirteen years older than John Adams, and nineteen years older than Jefferson, believed his goals had been accomplished with independence and was content to watch a younger generation step to the helm. His absence from national politics after the 1780s, however, does not diminish his unparalleled contribution to the founding of America.

For his part, Adams was indifferent about his place in history. He left no memoirs, no autobiography, and chose not to write letters for posterity's sake, as did many leaders of his generation. He made no attempt to collect his writings and letters, and in an effort to protect friends, destroyed many correspondences that would have documented his role in shaping critical events. The record of his early life is frustratingly sparse.

Since Adams' death in 1803, the assessments of his contributions to American history have undergone several revisions, based in part on views of the Revolution itself. Nineteenth-century historians such as George Bancroft, in his 1882 exhaustive, six-volume *History of the United States from the Discovery of the American Continent*—which is generally thought of as the best history of the revolution ever written—saw Adams as the major figure in American movement leading up to the war: "No one had equal influence over the popular mind."[2] James K. Hosmer's 1888 biography, *Samuel Adams,* ranked his subject second only to George Washington in importance to the founding of the United States.

Since then, Adams' reputation has suffered from several Revolution-era propaganda pieces that have been erroneously attributed to him, most notably "The Horrid Massacre in Boston," written by James Bowdoin; a piece signed "An American" that is included in the 1904 collection *The Writings of Samuel Adams,* edited by Harry Alonzo Cushing; as well as a speech dated August 1, 1776, contained in *The World's Famous Orations* by William Jennings Bryan and Francis W. Halsey, published in 1906.

Until the 1920s, historians treated Adams in the same generally positive light accorded the other Founding Fathers. A revision of his record began with Ralph V. Harlow's 1923 *Samuel Adams—Promoter of the*

American Revolution: A Study in Psychology and Politics, which portrayed Adams as a propagandist and zealot, a view furthered by John C. Miller's 1936 *Samuel Adams: A Pioneer in Propaganda.*

In recent years, Samuel Adams has been treated by historians as a propagandist who stoked the passions of the poor and built resentment against the British to further his own career. Scholars such as Russell Kirk dismissed Adams as a "well-born demagogue" in his 1974 *The Roots of American Order.*

But the historical record and an examination of Adams' writings tell a very different story. Adams and the other colonists involved in the civil rights struggle were not an unthinking mob, but highly reflective people who stated their case with reasoned arguments in pamphlets, letters, petitions, and newspaper articles. In his writings, Adams placed his faith in a logical persuasion, devoid of feckless emotional appeals, in the same manner of modern newspaper columnists. His readers were highly literate, and well versed in the allusions to ancient Latin and Greek writers and examples from antiquity from which he drew analogies. His crusade eventually drew in intellectuals such as John Adams, Thomas Jefferson, and Benjamin Franklin, as well as affluent men such as George Washington and John Hancock. Mob violence was common in England during the eighteenth century, but these protests never achieved any specific political goals. It's highly unlikely that the successful colonial resistance in the prewar years as well as the Revolution itself and the creation of an independent nation would have occurred without the involvement of the educated and affluent.

Adams' political foresight and broad understanding of political power often made him appear radical and belligerent in comparison to the caution of other colonial leaders. But Adams was not trying to change society; he was attempting to preserve rights he believed the colonists already possessed. He believed early on in the struggle with England that American liberty could only be secured through independence while several prominent patriots held out hope for reconciliation until 1775 and 1776. Lawyers such as John Adams and Thomas Jefferson viewed the conflict in strictly legal terms, believing that American grievances could be resolved by negotiating a British agreement on their constitutional rights. But Adams saw the struggle in a much broader scope, and doubted that any imperial power would give up a piece of its empire at the negotiating table. He realized that such a concession would threaten stability throughout Britain's empire and would not likely come without a war. He also understood the economic issues, believing that England saw America as a trade rival rather than a partner and had a vested interest curtailing its commercial freedom.

The questions over Samuel Adams' career, his writings, and place in history are central to those concerning the justification for the Revolution itself and whether the war with England could have been avoided. It is unlikely that the break with England in 1776 would have occurred without him. For this reason, this book focuses on Adams' writings and tactics, and attempts to explain how a man with very little means except for his words and political genius could orchestrate a revolution, lay the foundations for an independent nation, and split what was then the world's greatest empire.

1

THE EDUCATION OF A RADICAL

As a child, Samuel Adams would climb the outdoor stairway to the rooftop observatory of his family's home. From his perch there, the boy could see the expanse of the Boston Harbor, dotted with ships that arrived and then disappeared over the horizon of the Atlantic.

To the young boy, it seemed like the center of the universe. Boston was then the largest town in North America, a bustling trade port with commercial ties that reached around the globe. Young Samuel could see, moored along the wharves, merchant ships that brought timber, tobacco, tar, rice, and tea from colonies to the south. Wheat came shipped from Maryland, imported luxuries were brought from England and smuggled from European ports, and the West Indies sent sugar and molasses to supply the rum trade. News from England took two months to cross the ocean.

Along the docks, fishing boats for harvesting cod and herring were docked in the early mornings and late afternoons. He could watch the fishermen unload their bounty, while their wives and children gathered to begin the process of salting the fish for market. He could see the forty-ton whale boats that brought back the oil that illuminated Boston homes.

Shipyards were also part of the panorama, employing a host of tradesmen from shipwrights, to carpenters, to caulkers and rope makers. The muscular artisans shaped tough oak into formidable hulls that could withstand storms and the battering of the sea. Taverns thrived along the

wharves. On the streets of Boston, accents from strange lands mixed in
the salt air.

Samuel Adams felt a deep connection to his hometown. His parents
told him that their family hailed from some of the earliest settlers of the
Bay Colony. He was fascinated by stories of his ancestors—how they
sailed from England the previous century to help build a new society.
His forebears loomed larger than life in his eyes, courageous, principled,
and willing to withstand the hardships of an untamed land to build a
better life for their descendants—for his sake.

Samuel's parents told him that his family had been part of the great
Puritan migration that began at Plymouth and spread to the rest of
Massachusetts to build a City of God. He was moved by stories of his
great-grandparents' flight from religious persecution as Protestants under
Charles I of England. The king had married a Catholic queen, Henrietta
Maria, and changed the liturgy of the Church of England to make con-
cessions to Roman Catholics. The Puritans, including Adams' ancestors,
wanted to return to what they viewed as a "purer" form of worship.
Samuel listened intently to the history of his great-grandfather's family.
They had braved the raging North Atlantic out of religious conviction,
to sail to an untamed land to settle and worship in freedom.[1]

Samuel cherished his heritage and understood that his ancestors
made a great sacrifice for the freedom he enjoyed. He felt a great debt
and a need to be worthy of his forebears' example. His world was the reward of their sacrifices. He was descended from Henry Adams, progen-
itor of eighty-nine grandchildren in America. Henry left Barton St.
David in Somersetshire, England, with his wife, Edith Squire, and nine
children. They settled in Braintree (renamed Quincy), Massachusetts, in
1638. Each of his sons settled outside Braintree with the exception of
Joseph Adams, grandfather of John Adams, the future president.[2]

Samuel Adams' grandfather, John Adams the elder, a sea captain, settled in Boston. Samuel's father, who was also named Samuel, was born in
the town in 1689. At an early age, his father felt a burning ambition to
rise to the elevated circle of distinguished men in town. He was the son
of a sailor, however, and his family could not afford to send him to Harvard. He lacked the gentleman's education that set apart the town's leading men, who could discuss Homer in Greek or Virgil in Latin. He did

not speak the languages of the educated that was critical to social standing. Yet Adams noticed the proud merchants who paraded in fine silk attire carrying finely carved canes through Boston's crooked streets and bustling markets. The town's port allowed many men to become wealthy. Adams realized that he had a better chance at prosperity as a merchant than by following his father's example at sea. After deciding to try his hand in business, he opened a malt shop and worked as a merchant.

He also began a courtship with Mary Fifield, the only daughter of Richard Fifield, a leading businessman in town. A devoutly religious woman with an artistic bent, Mary stitched intricate designs on finely woven linen.

Samuel's father valued industry, and worked hard at making his business a success. At an early age, he was already turning a profit and amassing substantial holdings. At twenty-three, he could afford to buy an impressive home on a sprawling parcel along the waterfront on Purchase Street. The house was the only large structure in the vicinity and was young Samuel's childhood home. It stretched 258 feet to the banks of Boston Harbor, and featured the rooftop observatory that afforded a harbor view. The property was bounded by two wharves, Dawes's and Bull's. Adams planted trees and shrubs on the estate, and improved its landscape.

Shortly after acquiring the house, he proposed to Mary Fifield. She accepted and they agreed to wed the following year. They talked about their future in Boston. They wanted a large family and their children to be educated and devout, to rise to the leadership in the city.

Adams and Mary were married in 1713 and settled into the home on Purchase Street. True to their Puritan heritage, their life centered on the church. Samuel Adams Sr. quickly rose among the leaders of the congregation and became a deacon. In 1715, he led a petition drive of twenty laymen to make a formal request at the Boston town meeting for his church to buy land to build the Old South Congregational Church.

Mary soon became pregnant. Children are commonly called miracles, but any child who survived the high mortality rates of the times defied the odds. Mary lost her first child, but bore a daughter, Mary, in 1717, who became her likeness not only in name but also in the same religiously devout spirit.

While pregnant with Samuel, her next child, Mary stitched a delicate christening blanket, decorated with twill of cotton and wool yarn in colors of pink, blue, green, and yellow. She wove a delicate floral border along its edges with larger plants extending from each corner to its center and scattered depictions of smaller herbs throughout.

Samuel was born on Sunday, September 16, 1722, then placed on the blanket and baptized at the Old South Congregational Church the same day. He was the oldest son, and in him the family placed much of their hope for the future. Mary bore a total of twelve children between 1716 and 1740. Only three lived past their third birthdays: Mary (1717), Samuel (1722), and Joseph (1728).

Samuel's sister, Mary, became a strong influence in his young life. He felt fortunate for her attention. She kept a memorandum book and carefully transcribed in neat handwriting the sermons of the renowned religious speakers who passed through Boston, such as George Whitefield (the English evangelist who sparked a revival toward Puritan values in England and the American colonies that came to be known as the Great Awakening), the aged Cotton Mather, and the pastor of their church, the Reverend Samuel Checkley, as well as others such as Jonathan Edwards, who embodied the religious revival and moved audiences with his famous sermon "Sinners in the Hands of an Angry God." She studied the sermons, looking up verses of scripture cited. Samuel, an unusually obedient child, reflected the religious bent of his mother and sister. He also was afflicted with a congenital palsy that caused his hand to tremble when excited.

Deacon Adams, who believed that acquiring property was the surest way to secure his family's future, continued to build his holdings. He bought several dwelling houses, a wharf, and several parcels of land to develop. The deacon wanted his sons to receive the education he never had. Young Samuel was sent to Boston Latin School, a tradition-rich, prestigious academy that had opened its doors in 1635, a year before Harvard was founded, and that served as a feeder for the college. In one of his schoolbooks, he scrawled a note that learning was more important than riches. It is not known if this was merely the product of a school assignment or a heartfelt belief. The Greek and Latin authors were among his favorites, and he was fond of using classical allusions in his writings.[3]

Samuel marveled at the famous preachers he saw at church services. He was inspired by how their soaring words moved listeners' spirits, sometimes sparking a wellspring of heartfelt tears, vows to live better lives, and pledges to examine their beliefs. He too wanted to inspire people with his words and began to consider a career in the ministry. His parents were ecstatic; Boston's leaders were predominately ministers and merchants. He entered Harvard in 1736, at the age of fourteen, and began to study theology.

Samuel was also fascinated by his charismatic father, whom he thought of as "a wise man, a good man." The influence of Deacon Adams permeated Boston: he was justice of the peace, selectman and member of the colonial legislature, as well as a member in a host of politically active trade clubs. People in the city sought Deacon Adams' advice because of his skills as a political organizer, and he accepted invitations to join a variety of professional and trade clubs that were transforming the political landscape by creating a viable popular party to offset the loyalist leadership. The leading men in town were regulars at the Purchase Street home, including Elisha Cook, leader of the popular party. At dinner, young Samuel would sit in a lively classroom of debate and political discussion. Like many colonists, Deacon Adams opposed any extension of crown privileges. He believed these came at the expense of their rights, which were protected and laid out in the Massachusetts Charter of 1691, a document that served as the constitution for the province. This charter was a contract with the king that allowed inhabitants to pass their own laws and levy taxes. Royal governor William Burnet, however, and several officials, such as the chief justice of the court, were appointed by the king and acted as his representatives and were not under the colonists' authority. In 1739, the Boston town meeting selected Deacon Adams to help draft legislative instructions for the town's representatives in the elected general assembly to carry out during sessions. Samuel, intrigued by his father's political disputes, quickly grasped the issues. Deacon Adams instructed the Boston representatives to fight to retain their power under the Massachusetts Charter to grant a fixed salary to the governor and therefore keep his authority under their control. The British ministry wanted to pay the governor directly from the crown to maintain his allegiance to London.[4]

Watching his father, Samuel quickly learned how to push political causes through the Boston town meeting and even force action in the Massachusetts House of Representatives. Deacon Adams became a formidable political force thanks to tactics that were novel for the time. He formed clubs to further the agenda of his friends and supporters. Club members worked as a team, issuing slates of candidates and promoting opinions on local issues. In a port town like Boston, maritime financial interests dominated debates. The clubs gained a reputation for being able to turn ideas into action through well-orchestrated grassroots campaigns. Political adversaries derided these groups as "caulkers' clubs," after ship caulkers, denoting the way members acted in lockstep.[5] It is from this phrase that the word "caucus" evolved.

Beginning in the 1730s, political campaigns in Boston were increasingly run in smoke-filled caucuses, where candidates and agendas were decided on even before the official meetings convened. Club members carried out scripted parts at political meetings to win their goals.

Like his father, Samuel was keenly interested in civic affairs, especially the rights of colonists. During his teenage years, his family was caught up in a political battle over a land-bank scheme that pitted the Whig party, which represented the less affluent country folk, against the well-heeled Tory party. The controversy stemmed from his father's efforts to form a bank in which members put up the value of their land in exchange for bank notes. The American colonies, lacking a hard currency of their own, dealt in English coins. Parliament ordered the Massachusetts Bay Colony to call in all its government notes by 1741 because of its heavy debt. As the economy in New England grew, gold or silver coins became scarce, and many colonists, including Benjamin Franklin in Philadelphia, argued for a paper currency to boost local economies. But many British and colonial merchants opposed paper because they profited by advancing credit to customers in need of goods. Paper notes would allow inhabitants to avoid these interest rates.[6]

In 1739, Deacon Adams talked with farmers, mechanics, traders, shipyard workers, and shopkeepers about the hardships caused by the absence of ready cash; many were nearly impoverished and needed currency to invest in their businesses; farmers needed money to buy seed and livestock or to make improvements to their land; mechanics lacked tools and equipment; traders could not build their stock without going into hock to creditors. Without cash, bartering was the only way to obtain items they could not make themselves. The land bank promised to offer a solution by issuing notes for customers to trade.

Royal governor Jonathan Belcher, whose Tory party represented affluent merchants both in England and Boston, tried to put an end to the land bank. Several merchants and Tory officials formed a rival bank that issued notes based on silver deposits, which only the affluent possessed. No member of the land bank could also subscribe to the silver bank. To further discourage the land bank, Belcher vetoed appointments of its directors to his council, the upper house of the legislature. Justices of the peace and militia officers who served on its board were dismissed, and Deacon Adams, a justice and a soldier, was removed from both posts.

As events took place, he ruminated on political concepts, such as natural rights and freedom, and began to develop a deep understanding of political theory. In a college debate with several classmates, he chose "liberty" as his subject. He was convinced that many colonists took their freedom for granted. In conversations with friends, he warned about British intrusion into their self-government and tried to impress the need to defend their political power. He felt the persecution his family endured from the land bank could happen to others. By the time he graduated from Harvard in 1740, his interests had moved from theology to politics.

The crown party and English merchants also appealed to Parliament, which in 1741 issued an act that dissolved the land bank. Parliament applied a 1719 law that held directors personally liable for losses and cited another all-but-forgotten statute extending legislation in England to the colonies. Members of the land bank protested that this act was unconstitutional, to no avail.

Because directors could be held directly responsible for losses incurred from the bank enterprise, over the next two decades Samuel Adams Sr. and his son would wage repeated legal battles to prevent seizure of their home and personal holdings. Political enemies went to court to divest the family of all it owned, claiming losses from the shuttered venture. The suppression of the bank sparked a deep resentment toward Parliament in rural districts of Massachusetts. "The act to destroy the land-bank scheme," John Adams wrote years later, had "raised a greater ferment in the province than the Stamp Act did."/ Young Samuel felt bitter over the dispute and the injury to his family. The fight clearly demonstrated who held the power in Massachusetts and America. The lawsuits caused his father to lose much of his fortune, and Samuel's potential inheritance was sliced to a fraction of its former worth.

While a graduate student at Harvard, he spent much of his time thinking about politics and the rights of colonists. He believed that the royally appointed governor, Parliament, and merchants in Massachusetts and England had no right to meddle in his father's affairs. He began to believe that England viewed the colonies as different from the realm: not equals, but subordinates. British leaders looked on colonial businesses as rivals to their home market and wanted to keep America's economic growth in check, in his view. The more Samuel thought about the conflict, the more he became convinced that English and colonial interests would eventually lead to a showdown.

To protect his family in the future, he searched for a way to argue for limits to the royal government's intervention in colonial affairs. He pored over the works of the leading political writers of the day, authors of the Enlightenment, searching for answers. He was greatly influenced by the writings of John Locke, whose ideas buoyed his own thinking on civil rights. Locke's *Second Treatise on Government* had provided the English with the justification for forcing James II from the throne in 1688 and installing William of Orange. Parliament then instituted the English Declaration of Rights. Locke argued that all men were born with natural rights ordained by God. Men and women were given the capacity to live, make decisions, and work to better their lives by obtaining property and possessions. They were entitled to "life, liberty and property," Locke maintained. The role of government was to protect these rights, not limit them. Locke rejected the "divine right" of kings in which subjects blindly obeyed the government.

Samuel likely thought of the role the royal governor and Parliament played in the land-bank scheme when he read Locke's words: "It is a mistake to think this fault is proper only to monarchies; other forms of government are liable to it, as well as that: for wherever the power, that is put in any hands for the government of the people and the preservation of their properties, is applied to other ends, and made use of to impoverish, harass."[8]

At Harvard, Samuel continued to immerse himself in political thought. He staged debates with classmates and learned how to make persuasive arguments for his case. He developed an uncanny ability to understand his opponents' views and remain one step ahead, and to use their own arguments against them. Just how deeply he thought out the implications of political concepts and how they possessed his mind and passions became evident during his years at Harvard. For the commencement speech for his master's degree in 1743, the twenty-year-old Adams chose as his thesis: "Whether it be lawful to resist the Supreme Magistrate, if the Commonwealth cannot be otherwise preserved."[9] He argued that such resistance was both legal and morally justified. No one but Samuel Adams seemed to be thinking about breaking with the British Empire in 1743. An acquaintance remembered that such an idea "was scarcely contemplated in that day, unless in the retirement of a closet."[10]

Samuel lacked strong convictions about a career, however. His mother still wanted him to take up the calling. As the population of the colony grew, the number of church spires multiplied. But Samuel felt no inspiration to take to the pulpit. Respecting his wishes, his parents reluctantly relinquished their efforts to convince him to pursue a life in the ministry. His growing obsession with political thought pleased his activist father who urged him to study law, which would certainly prove helpful in politics.

But his mother still held sway in her son's heart, and she dissuaded him from legal studies. The family was entangled in acrimonious battles to protect their property, and she likely did not want her son to make these kinds of battles a way of life.

He was still devout, however, and attended church each Sunday, to hear sermons from the Reverend Checkley. Soon he developed a fondness for the reverend's daughter, Elizabeth Checkley, who was three years younger than himself, and they began to court. His mother was pleased that his romantic interests settled on the daughter of a clergyman.

Deacon Adams believed Samuel needed to learn to make a living. His education prepared him for the life of gentleman, but he still needed to learn a trade. His father suggested that Samuel learn the mercantile business. Rather than taking him directly into the family's malt-brewing business, he arranged for his son to take a job at the counting house of Thomas Cushing. Samuel went to work but found his duties uninteresting. While other young men bent over the ledgers in sharp, frugal focus, believing the seeds of prosperity lay in their work, Samuel had trouble focusing on business. Cushing thought him to be a dreamer. Despite his palsy, Samuel was energetic, muscular, and restless, with short but powerful arms. But he was given to contemplation about the world around him and the political forces that controlled their lives. Other young men dreamed of fortunes and large estates. Samuel, however, never gave a thought to laying aside savings or planning his financial future. He did not covet a mansion or property of his own. It soon became apparent to Cushing that Samuel was not cut out for business: He lacked the requisite zeal for making money. Cushing quietly advised the elder Adams to find another path for his son.

Deacon Adams was uncertain what to do with Samuel. He noticed his son's growing dislike for authority of any kind. He was very independent in thought, shaped more by his collegiate studies and political reading than by his father's example as a businessman or his family's hopes that he rise among the leaders in Boston. Despite the Deacon's interest in civic affairs, he knew that politics was only a part-time job that would not earn his son a living. Would Samuel become more engaged in a venture of his own choosing? He loaned his son the hefty sum of £1,000 sterling, but the younger Adams was characteristically indifferent with the money. He loaned half to a friend who needed to satisfy creditors, and never received repayment, and squandered the remaining £500. Finally, his exasperated father took him into a partnership at the family's malt house on Purchase Street. Samuel was soon seen lugging bags of malt up and down the street. Seeing him, people called him "Sam the maltster."[11]

Samuel continued to court Elizabeth Checkley, and would visit her at her home and talk with the Reverend Checkley about church matters. He appreciated Elizabeth for her piety and quiet demeanor; she was much like his mother and sister. The couple shared a mutual interest in theology and talked about plans of getting married someday. He was getting older, now in his mid-twenties, and had still not settled in a career. He was still financially dependent on his father. She was no longer a teen but seemed to be willing to wait on marriage until he found his life's calling.

In 1748, Samuel and his friends formed a club to stage debates and launch a publication to shape public opinion. They each agreed to furnish essays for a newspaper to be called *The Public Advertiser*.[12] Adams' father was pleased by his son's enthusiasm for this venture. Samuel was still in debt to his father, and likely relied on him to back his share.

The inaugural weekly issue of the newspaper appeared in January 1748. Across the masthead, a woodcut illustration of Britannia caught readers' attention. She was portrayed liberating a bird tied by a cord to the arms of France. The paper carried little news, its columns consisting mostly of editorials and commentary, its stance naturally Whig. The publication proclaimed itself open "to whatever may be adapted to state and defend the rights and liberties of mankind."[13]

Adams, then twenty-six, threw himself into this outlet for his political vision. The publication gave him the opportunity to convince his neighbors to be on guard against intrusions on their rights. He believed Parliament overstepped its bounds by applying legislative acts to America and that the greatest safeguards against British authority lay in the English Constitution and the Massachusetts Charter of 1691.

For his first article, he chose the subject of loyalty, arguing that allegiance should be given to laws rather than to government leaders. "[Loyalty] is founded in the love and possession of liberty," Adams wrote. "It includes in it a thorough knowledge of our constitution, its conveniences and defects as well as its real advantages; a becoming jealousy of our immunities, and a steadfast resolution to maintain them."[14]

Adams applied the same moral constraint he felt as a Puritan to political thought. He told readers that just as men should not be ruled by mercurial emotions, citizens should be wary of cries of sedition and revolution. "It is a weak, feverish, sickly thing, a boisterous and unnatural vigor, which cannot support itself long, and oftentimes destroys the unhappy patient."[15]

Adams warned readers not to get caught up in the respect for high office and the lavish praise that is often bestowed on leaders. "This has led millions into such a degree of dependence and submission." Citizens should place their loyalty with the constitution. "Whoever, therefore, insinuates notions of government contrary to the constitution, or in any degree winks at any measures to suppress or even to weaken it, is not a loyal man."

He believed that with the British Constitution and the Massachusetts Charter, his ancestors created a society that enjoyed more freedom than anywhere in England. "From this happy constitution of our mother country, ours in this is copied, or rather improved upon. Our invaluable charter secures to us all the English liberties, besides which we have some additional privileges which the common people there have not."

This expanded freedom was the reward of the Puritan pilgrimage to America, he told readers. "We, their posterity, are this day reaping the fruits of their toils," he wrote. "Happy beyond expression!—in the form of our government, in the liberty we enjoy—if we know our own happiness and how to improve it."[16]

Whatever satisfaction Adams may have taken from his first public literary efforts was soon overshadowed by the death of his father. A day before he died in March 1748, Deacon Adams took care to finalize his will. The cause of death is unknown. The *Boston Independent Advertiser* noted his contribution to Boston politics in an obituary: "He was one who well understood and rightly pursued the civil and religious interests of this people; a true New England man; an honest patriot."[17]

In his will, Samuel's father bequeathed him a third of his estate, which was shared with his sister, Mary, who had married James Allen, and his brother, Joseph, who was the clerk of the town market. The estate and property were left to his mother. His father also erased the debt of the £1,000 loan made years earlier to his son. Samuel must have been chagrined to hear some of his father's final words to him: "My son Samuel, being my eldest son, to receive his full third part, exclusive of and besides the sum of a thousand pounds, old tenor, he has already received, and for which he is made debtor in my books; it being my will that he be discharged from said debt at my decease."[18]

The loss of his father left Samuel without the guiding hand and financial protector who had sheltered his life. He had little sense of himself outside the influence of his father, who had been his role model, his advisor, his financial stability, his political mentor. His father's affairs, including the management of the malt house, fell to him. He must have felt a poor substitute.

Samuel's life was left with no clear direction. The responsibilities of running the brewery and tending to family affairs, including the fights to preserve their property from the land-bank suits, provided a routine of daily challenges. He spent his days at the brewery. At the age of twenty-six, he stepped into his father's shoes, keeping up relations with friends and joining political clubs in which his father had once held a membership.

Samuel proposed to Elizabeth Checkley, and she agreed to become his wife. They both wanted a large family. His mother was ecstatic over the union. Samuel's father-in-law would be the highly esteemed pastor at the Old South Congregational Church. They were married at the reverend's house on October 17, 1749. Samuel was then twenty-seven, Elizabeth, twenty-four.

They settled into the home on Purchase Street. Samuel adored Elizabeth, and they enjoyed a passionate marriage. But their love became mixed with deep grief. They were overjoyed when she became pregnant. A son, whom they named Samuel, was born at 2:15 A.M. on Friday, September 14, 1750, and baptized by Elizabeth's father on Sunday. Sixteen days after his Christening, the infant Samuel died, leaving them in anguish. A year later, a second child, whom they also named Samuel, was born at 10:15 A.M. on Wednesday, October 16, 1751, and baptized. He grew healthy and energetic. Two years later, a second son, Joseph, was born on June 23, and died the following day.

Their first daughter, Mary, was born exactly a year after Joseph, on Sunday, June 23, 1754. She lived just three months and nine days, dying on October 3. Eighteen months later, Hannah was born on January 21, 1756, and remained healthy.

Elizabeth had given birth to five children in six years; three did not live past infancy. The couple endured the repeated, wrenching emotional turmoil of pouring out love and hope on an offspring whom they would quickly bury.

Elizabeth became gravely weak after delivering a stillborn son on July 6, 1757. Samuel prayed for her as she struggled for life. But the toll of her pregnancies and the sorrow of losing successive children sapped her strength. She died on July 25, 1757, at the age of thirty-two. A heart-broken Samuel took out a quill and opened the family Bible. In memo-rial, he sat to write: "To her husband she was as sincere a friend as she was a faithful wife. Her exact economy in all her relative capacities, her kindred on his side as well as her own admire. She ran her Christian race with remarkable steadiness, and finished in triumph! She left two small children. God grant they may inherit her graces!"[19]

He was in need of grace himself. He was the single parent of two, still trying to find solid financial footing, running a brewery that failed to satisfy his interests. To compound matters, he was still hounded by the legacy of the land-bank scheme. Commissioners were assigned to weed out the morass, but efforts were bogged down in disputes over ac-counts. To cloud the issues, much of the bank's records had been de-stroyed by a fire.

After authorities tried to seize his property, Samuel's private convic-tions that Parliament had no constitutional authority to dissolve the land bank became public. He believed both were a breach of his rights under the Massachusetts Charter. In August 1758, a notice appeared in the *Boston Newsletter* announcing that the land-bank commissioners ordered a public auction the following day of Adams' father's estate, which in-cluded the house in which Samuel still lived, the malt brewery, the wharf dock, flats and other buildings, along with gardens and other adjacent property. The notice was signed by Sheriff Stephen Greenleaf. Adams fired back a letter to the sheriff, pointing out that his predecessor had also tried to divest the family of its property but was unable to do so be-cause the action was deemed "illegal and unwarrantable."

Adams cautioned with a thinly veiled threat: "How far your deter-mination may lead you, you know better than I. I would only beg leave, with freedom, to assure you, that I am advised and determined to pros-ecute to the law any person whomsoever who shall trespass upon that estate."[20]

The sheriff wavered. He postponed the auction until September 22, then wavered again and rescheduled it for September 29. Adams showed up at the auction and threatened prospective bidders. He vowed to sue anyone who set foot on his property and told the sheriff he would file a lawsuit against him if the auction proceeded. The buyers backed down and left. Adams prevented the sale and retained his property. "The debt to the land-bank company remained unsatisfied," wrote Thomas Hutchinson, the chief justice in the colony, in an account of the affair.

Over time, Adams began to realize that he could play a critical role in preventing royal authority from trampling on the rights of colonists. The lessons he had learned from his father and the insights he had gained in saving his property convinced him to prepare for the Anglo-American struggle for power that he believed was coming. He continued to write a stream of articles about colonial rights, gaining a reputation for witty pieces and arguments, and soon became known as a tireless advocate of civil rights. In 1756, he wrote in protest of Massachusetts governor William Shirley's dual role as chief of the royal military forces and head of the civil government, arguing that too much power should not reside with a single individual.

By 1761, Adams was deeply involved in civic affairs. He served on a committee that oversaw the local school and on another that ensured that chimneys were properly inspected. He also served as a fire warden and worked to take precautions to prevent the spread of smallpox. In addition, he served on a committee from the Boston town meeting to draw up instructions for its representatives in the assembly.

Adams sparked up a conversation one day with John Adams, his second cousin from nearby Braintree, and stoked his feelings for their homeland. Samuel impressed upon him that they were fortunate in the freedom they enjoyed, and said he hoped it would continue. He said he was suspicious of British power in the colonies and believed that leaders in London had "hostile designs" to rule over them. For more than a century, Britain had a "hands-off" policy concerning the colonies, but that attitude seemed be changing. If British officials exerted control over colonial affairs, this would reduce the colonists' civil rights, rendering their legislature powerless and their votes meaningless. The town meetings would lose their authority, and they could end up without any political power. In fact, they could easily become slaves. John, uncertain about England's attitude toward the colonies, was somewhat skeptical. Samuel told him to be on guard for signs of growing power by royal officials. He urged his cousin to become involved in civic affairs and to attend his town meeting. It was critical that men be in a position to stand up when Britain passed laws concerning America.[21]

Samuel had similar conversations with the physicians Joseph Warren and Benjamin Church, the attorneys James Otis and Josiah Quincy, merchants John Hancock and Thomas Cushing, Jr. He talked to each about the fresh air of freedom, and warned that their liberty was in danger. He told them that they could not ever allow British interference in their affairs. They were not represented in Parliament, he told them, and urged them to get involved in local issues.

Samuel was elected as a tax collector in 1756, a position that put him in contact with a wide array of inhabitants, from wealthy merchants to tradesmen and farmers. He knew many from his participation in clubs. It was soon said that Samuel Adams recognized everyone he encountered as he walked the streets of Boston. He developed a feel for the pulse of public opinion that no other local leader could match.

Although he earned 5 percent of what he collected, Adams often sympathized with taxpayers who had trouble paying their obligations. In March 1763, it was revealed that Boston's tax collection was short by £4,000 for 1761. Adams was responsible for £2,200 of this shortfall, with the other two collectors each responsible for less than £1,000. This shortfall caused a financial crisis in the town, and leaders had to scramble to find ways to erase the deficit.

Adams' personal finances were in no better shape. Since the death of his father, his holdings had gradually dwindled. His property had been reduced to just his Purchase Street house. People whispered that he got by with financial help from friends. The malt business went bankrupt, in part for the same reasons his tax receipts were delinquent: he failed to put pressure on those who owed him money.[22]

2

CIVIL DISOBEDIENCE

Royal customs agents in Boston knocked on the door of attorney James Otis in the winter of 1761, hoping he would order a military escort to help them carry out their duties to put an end to smuggling in Boston.

Otis, the colony's advocate general, listened carefully as the agents explained their problem. Merchants suspected of smuggling had barred them from carrying out searches for contraband and had failed to heed "writs of assistance," or search warrants. Otis, a thirty-six-year-old portly gentleman with slightly offset, bulging eyes and a round chin, read over the writs. The British Exchequer had empowered the agents with warrants to search anyone's property without warning or even a probable cause.

Otis knew that his duty as the colony's chief attorney would be to enforce any writ ordered by the British ministry. Instead, he resigned his post immediately and became the attorney on behalf of the smugglers. He believed the writs were unconstitutional, and declared that he would take no fee for the case.

Otis had a reputation as a fiery, flamboyant attorney. Since childhood he had suffered from an excitable temperament and would burst into fits when overstimulated by games or debate. Once when, as a young man, friends asked him to play his violin, he obliged, and the audience began to dance. He abruptly broke off the impromptu recital and exclaimed in anger: "So fiddled Orpheus, and so danced the brutes!"[1]

Otis was born in 1725 in Barnstable, Massachusetts, to an exceptional family. His father had been an attorney, and his grandfather a lawyer before that. His father served as speaker of the Massachusetts assembly and spent time as a judge as well as a colonel in the militia.

Otis presented his case for the smugglers on a cold February day in 1761 in the council chamber of the state House, before a large, fervent crowd gathered around a roaring fire. Thomas Hutchinson, as chief justice, presided over a panel of five judges, each dressed in bright scarlet robes and crowned with powdered wigs. Seated in the audience was twenty-six-year-old John Adams, then in the fourth year of his legal practice. He took notes of Otis' four-hour speech, which he described as a "flame of fire."

Proper warrants required specific locations for searches along with sworn complaints that smuggled goods were suspected of being stored, Otis argued. Writs of assistance that allowed officials to search any dwelling without safeguards against government abuse were illegal, he told the court. "It is a power that places the liberty of every man in the hands of every petty officer. If this commission be legal, a tyrant in a legal manner, also, may control, imprison or murder anyone within the realm."[2]

Otis declared that "taxation without representation" was unconstitutional. The principle dated back to the Magna Carta but had fallen out of the popular consciousness. Otis' words electrified the courtroom. As John Adams put it, "Every man of an immense crowded audience appeared to me to go away as I did, ready to take up arms against writs of assistance."

Otis' performance made him an instant political star, a champion to the popular party, who elected him as one of the four Boston representatives to the assembly, where his father had once sat. This brought him in regular contact with Samuel Adams, who as a leading member of the Boston town meeting usually helped draft instructions for the assembly members to carry out during legislative sessions. Adams and Otis developed an instant rapport: Each possessed a strong personality, and each enjoyed debate, storytelling, speaking, and political writing. Both deeply believed in individual civil rights.

About this time, Samuel met Elizabeth Wells, the daughter of a family friend, and began to show interest in her. Then entering his forties, he was eighteen years her senior. She was the fifth in a line of sisters and possessed a lively, warm, friendly demeanor. He was considered suave and articulate. He called her Betsy and appreciated that he could confide in her. She enjoyed his stories about politics and felt convictions similar to his own. She enjoyed time spent with Samuel and was also fond of his two children, young Samuel and Hannah. They began a courtship.

She did not seem to mind that he did not dream of building a large estate or improving his meager income. He told her that he never thought about such things. They soon talked about marriage. Friends wondered aloud if Adams was a good match for her; his prospects did not seem very promising. Yet Elizabeth believed in him, and their courtship grew serious.

In the spring of 1764, many residents in the Boston area began to suffer from smallpox. Adams took his children in March to the office of his friend Dr. Joseph Warren for an inoculation. Warren was friendly as the children prepared themselves for the sting of the needle. At age thirteen, young Samuel showed an interest in medicine. Warren, a twenty-three-year-old class-of-1759 graduate of Harvard, was tall, energetic and graceful with a warm smile and curious eyes. His father had died a decade earlier when Warren was young Samuel's age after falling off a ladder while picking apples. Warren had watched workmen carry his father's broken body from the field in need of a physician. Adams took on a paternal role in Warren's life, and advised him to become involved with politics. Warren began to attend town meetings and write pieces in the Boston newspapers in protest of royal authority. Warren also inoculated the family of John Adams, and formed a similar friendship. The doctor's engaging personality and skills as a physician quickly attracted people from all over Boston, and his practice continued to grow.

Samuel continued to recruit friends into politics out of concern about the growing English authority in Massachusetts, and wondered how the British would treat the colonies after the end of the Seven Years War in 1763. France was defeated, and England stood as the most powerful empire Europe had seen since the fall of Rome. The war greatly enlarged its territory, which suddenly included the expanse of India. England, in debt by £140 million, needed to raise revenue to administer its vast holdings.

Talking the helm as First Lord of the Treasury, George Grenville looked across the Atlantic toward America as a source of income, noting that the war removed the threat of a French invasion in the colonies and provided inhabitants a vista for unimpeded prosperity.

On April 5, 1764, Grenville passed the first of his revenue measures concerning the colonies, the Sugar Act. It revived unenforced duties on wool, hats, and iron and increased customs on a variety of imported goods, including textiles, coffee, indigo, wines, and foreign-refined sugar. A court of admiralty to try smuggling cases was established in Nova Scotia.

Boston was the first town in America to receive news of the Sugar Act when a cargo ship arrived from London. Bostonians did not protest or complain about the prospect of the tax and a crackdown on smuggling plus the establishment of distant courts of admiralty. Most were unaware of the tax or unconcerned because the costs would be buried in the price of the products.

Samuel Adams was shocked to find himself alone in speaking out at the Boston town meeting and at political clubs and the caucus. He met with members of the elected general assembly and asked what protests were being lodged over the Sugar Act. No one had voiced any opposition. He learned that the agent hired to represent the colony in London had no instructions from the Colonial House, or general assembly. Adams told James Otis and Oxenbridge Thacher, another Boston delegate, that the Sugar Act was a violation of self-government and that colonists could not allow Britain to tax Americans. In his view, this would lead to more taxes, more royal officials, and dependence on Britain, and eventually would render the self-governing legislatures powerless.[3]

Many of his fellow townsmen felt that opposing the tax measures would be futile, but Adams, was determined to make a stand. He realized that he needed to rouse indignation over the taxes and turn theoretical arguments about government and liberty into battle cries.

Even if he could spark a fire in his townsmen, however, they had little influence in London. Complaints about taxes invariably fell on deaf ears. Getting the attention of British authorities three thousand miles away and convincing them to reverse course on taxes seemed highly unlikely.

Adams was seen publicly as a background figure in a quiet port town on the outer reaches of the civilized world; he had no access to the chan-

nels of power that flowed in London, no material wealth to launch a
lobby effort, no political connections among the courtiers or Parliament.

Yet Adams' experience with the land-bank controversy made him
acutely aware of the men who whispered in the ear of the king and Parliament: the English merchants.

As a low-level political activist, he would have to accomplish what
Benjamin Franklin had failed to do with his Albany Plan of 1754: unite
the disparate colonies. On the eve of the Seven Years War with France,
Franklin, along with Thomas Hutchinson, had offered a proposal to
unify the thirteen colonies in North America to coordinate trade and
military operations in case a war with France erupted. No assembly was
willing to give up any local autonomy, however.[4]

In the spring months of 1764, Adams began to plot a strategy he
hoped would transform the same group of English merchants into lobbyists on behalf of the colonial cause by orchestrating a boycott of English goods. It was a novel tactic of his invention. A boycott would be
ineffective without support from the other twelve colonies—that is, a
united America. Bringing the colonies together seemed impossible, especially for Adams, who did not even hold an elected post in his own
colonial assembly.[5]

But he knew he could control issues in the assembly by writing instructions to Boston's representatives and winning their approval at the
town meeting. Delegates like Otis and Thacher would be forced to carry
out instructions approved by Boston residents in the assembly. Boston
was then the third largest town in America and dominated Massachusetts' politics. The assembly met in Boston.

During the spring 1764 elections for representatives to the assembly,
Adams proceeded undaunted. He addressed the town meeting against
the tax measures, arguing that the Grenville taxes must be resisted to preserve the colony's autonomy. Adams spoke like a fire-and-brimstone
evangelist, in a deadly serious tone that stirred listeners. He explained
that the Grenville Acts were not like taxes levied by the Massachusetts assembly, in which townspeople voted for the representatives. Their freedom rested on their power to self-govern and self-tax, he thundered. If
an outside body such as Great Britain was allowed to tax them, their liberty was gone. This was the first step toward servitude. Adams' words

found their way into the hearts and minds of townspeople. Many realized for the first time that although they were British citizens, they had to protect themselves from England. Self-taxation was a pillar of their freedom.[6]

Adams asked residents if they wanted their lands taxed by the British, and all of their labor. He sparked indignation over the Sugar Act. At the town meeting, he was appointed to prepare instructions for the city's four representatives to protest the tax in the Massachusetts general assembly.

In Boston politics, the town meeting voted on instructions for their delegates in the assembly to follow strictly. These instructions, viewed as a mandate from the constituents, were printed in newspapers across the continent and in England as news of affairs in Boston. Adams laid out specific measures directing Otis and Thacher and the town's other delegates. In drafting these mandates, Adams framed the issue on his terms. From his home study, he penned arguments that would convince leaders in other colonies to take up the cause of resisting the Sugar Act. He scolded the general assembly's slow response to news of the tax measures and noted that the colony's London agent had asked for a public statement of Boston's position but had received little input from the House. "We cannot help expressing our surprise that when so early notice was given by the agent of the intentions of the ministry to burthen us with new taxes, so little regard was had to this most interesting matter, that the court was not even called together to consult about it till the latter end of ye year." As a result, instructions were not sent to their agent "till the evil had got beyond an easy remedy," Adams lamented.[7]

He instructed the representatives to demand that the duties be repealed on grounds that would appeal to British financial self-interest. Adams suggested that the assembly lay out the case that the acts would "prove detrimental to Great Britain itself; upon which account we have reason to hope that an application, even for a repeal of the act, should it be already passed, will be successful."[8]

Adams then proceeded with an economic argument. He believed that trade helped both economies to expand. Taxes slowed this growth and could threaten to choke it off. Americans spent millions on British goods, which outweighed any tax in terms of providing revenue for government coffers. At the time, the view that duties and taxes could reduce government revenues in the long run was rare even among European intellectuals. Adams was writing thirteen years before Britain's Adam Smith, the father of modern economics, published his seminal work, *The Wealth of Nations.* Later, Smith would make the same revolutionary case: Europe was cordoned off by trade restrictions, duties, and counterduties.

"It is the trade of the colonies that renders them beneficial to the mother country," Adams wrote in the instructions. "Our trade, as it is now, and always has been conducted, centers in Great Britain, and in return for her manufactures affords her more ready cash, beyond any comparison, than can possibly be expected by the most sanguine promoters of these extraordinary methods."[9]

Adams then turned his pen toward his domestic readers, aiming his words straight at their sense of independence and liberty. He, like Locke, believed economic and political freedoms were inextricably linked. "For if our trade may be taxed, why not our lands? Why not the produce of our lands and everything we possess or make use of? This we apprehend annihilates our charter right to govern and tax ourselves. It strikes at our British privileges, which as we have never forfeited them."[10]

Adams argued that the vice admiralty courts violated self-government and hinted that colonists could retaliate by boycotting English goods. Yet he was tactful. He acknowledged the colony's dependence on and subordination to the king and Great Britain and that colonists were duty-bound to submit to all just trade regulations. They sought no more than their chartered rights.

Samuel Adams' Boston instructions also made the first public call in America for the colonies to unite in opposition to Britain through a congress. Adams wrote "that by the united applications of all who are aggrieved, all may happily obtain redress."[11]

In roughly fifteen hundred words, this was the first public document to question Parliament's right to tax the colonies or its authority in America, the first call for the colonies to unite in protest in a congress, the first denunciation of non-American juries to try Americans, and the first threat of a boycott.

Adams attended the town meeting at Faneuil Hall on May 24, 1764, and urged residents to approve the instructions he had drafted. Voters gave their approbation and his instructions were printed in the *Boston Gazette* and reprinted elsewhere. Otis published a pamphlet arguing colonial rights that included Adams' instructions.

Otis won reelection as a delegate to Massachusetts' legislature and brought Adams' instructions before the House, including the call for a colonial congress. On June 14, the House approved the idea and sent the proposal for a congress to a committee. But Massachusetts' royally appointed governor, Francis Bernard, quickly shut down the assembly to prevent the measure from proceeding. As a representative of King George III and the British ministry, the governor wanted to prevent united protests over the Sugar Act. Under the Massachusetts Charter, the governor had the authority to shut down the legislature at any time. He suspended sessions until October, when it would be too late to call for a congress that year.

The Adams-authored instructions became a widely read manifesto on colonial rights. His instructions lit a slowly smoldering fire in the hearts of many readers across the continent, including Patrick Henry in Virginia, who decided to run for a seat in the House of Burgesses the following year to fight British taxes. Through his instructions, Adams had demonstrated his ability to define the issues in Massachusetts and in other colonies. He framed the debate over the Sugar Act as a civil rights matter. Many colonists agreed, and began to view the tax in the same light. For royal officials, however, the revenue acts did not involve constitutional principles but English debt from defending America. Forcing the French from the continent cost the British £60 million, and the empire was reeling. The British were asking for the colonies to pay for a third, or £100,000 of the cost of administering their land. All the taxes collected in America were stipulated to stay in America. Yet British leaders were unable to match Adams' arguments against the tax in the minds of many colonists.[12]

Adams began to formulate novel strategies of civil disobedience. His maxim was to "put and keep the enemy in the wrong."[13] He decided to try to push for a regional boycott. His idea for the tactic was so new that a word for it did not exist—the word "boycott" was coined in 1880 after Irish tenants used the tactic against an estate agent, Charles C. Boycott, in an attempt to reduce rents. He introduced his plan under the awkward term "non-importation agreement."

In August 1764, Adams met with several professional clubs. He told them that if British taxes were unopposed, more taxes would follow. Their land and shops could be taxed. They would begin to see their hard-earned profits sent overseas, and they would get no benefits in return. Yet they had the power to get the attention of the British government, they had means to retaliate. If they stopped buying English imported goods and cancelled orders, British merchants would complain to their government and call for a repeal of the Sugar Act. Boston shop owners agreed to try and pledged to stop ordering luxury items, including fashionable lace and ruffles, from England.[14] In September, Adams met with Boston silversmiths and blacksmiths and convinced them to boycott leather work clothes. Soon the non-importation policy began to spread to surrounding colonies in New England.

3

A BUNDLE OF STICKS

While Samuel's public status rose, his family got by on meager means. His concern with civic affairs seemed to come at the expense of his family. He was a single father who spent most of his time tending to public business. The time he spent with his children was devoted to their education. It was as if the words he wrote as a child were still engraved on his heart—that learning was more important than riches. His children were not well clothed and enjoyed no luxuries. He spent hours, however, overseeing their lessons and trying to instill strong moral principles.

His courtship with Elizabeth Wells turned to devotion. He proposed to her and they agreed to wed, exchanging vows in a small ceremony on December 6, 1764. He was forty-two years old; she was twenty-four. In a letter to a friend who was about to be betrothed, Adams gave a glimpse of his wedded bliss: "Believe me, my friend—I wish could persuade all the agreeable bachelors to think so—there are social joys in honest wedlock which single life is a stranger to."[1]

In 1765, Adams enrolled his son, aged fourteen, in Harvard College. The family hoped he would pursue a career as a doctor. Since Adams had little money, it is likely that his son's tuition was paid for by donations from friends.

Despite the joy he felt at home, he believed public events demanded his attention. Samuel Adams realized in early 1765 that he had failed to defeat the Sugar Act. Bernard had shut down the legislature the previous summer to prevent his call for a congress from being extended across

America. He also felt that Jasper Mauduit, Massachusetts' agent in London (colonies hired agents to go to London and represent their interests with the British government), was too cozy with British officials. Jasper was the brother of Israel Mauduit, a close ally of Prime Minister John Stuart Bute as well as the King. Jasper was praised in London for his submissive cooperation, and other colonial agents were equally obliging. In a meeting with Grenville in February 1765, several agents, including Pennsylvania's Benjamin Franklin, not only dismissed protests over the Sugar Act but extended consent for a more extensive tax plan, a Stamp Act.

The Stamp Act required government-issued seals on legal documents, newspapers, and all printed materials sold within the colonies except books; the act included almanacs, broadsides, pamphlets, insurance policies, ship's papers, and many other articles—even playing cards and dice. The act would also mean that a British stamp of approval was required for colonial governments to operate, court proceedings to convene, and marriages to be officially sanctioned. The stamps would be required to validate deeds and wills. Ships could not sail without them. Newspapers could not be published unless a government-controlled stamp was attached to the masthead. Proceeds from the tax were earmarked, along with those from the Sugar Act, to pay a third of the cost of putting ten thousand British troops, designated to protect the colonies from invasion by another power (such as France), in America.

Franklin worked to get a friend, John Hughes, appointed stamp master. Franklin believed protesting the Stamp Act would be senseless. "We might as well have hindered the sun's setting," he remarked.[2]

The only concerns in London over the proposed Stamp Act came from merchants, who worried about the threats of boycotts. They held millions of pounds of orders to American importers that stood to be cancelled if the tax plan was approved. When the debate over the act came before Parliament in early 1765, it barely drew comment.

Yet when news of the latest tax measure arrived in the colonies in April, a firestorm erupted. Ministers railed against it from pulpits, residents rose up to complain in town meetings, legislators began drafting resolutions denouncing the tax. Stamp agents were threatened. The change in public temper from the previous year was due in part to the protest campaign launched by Adams over the Sugar Act. Before he alarmed colonists over the previous tax measure, few people in America complained about duties to England. A year later, after his arguments were published across the continent, residents was no longer indifferent. Leaders in other colonies, such as Patrick Henry, began to launch campaigns to fight the Stamp Act.

Adams worked nonstop to develop a strategy to oppose the measure. If opposing the act was akin to "hindering the sun's setting," as Franklin believed, Adams was prepared to try for a miracle. He called together a meeting of local merchants and tradesmen and explained that Britain would be able to control the American economy if the tax measures were successful. London viewed them as trade rivals, not trade partners, and wanted to check their growth to protect British merchants and tradesmen. They agreed to continue the boycott.

Adams rose at the Boston town meeting and stirred crowds with warnings that the act amounted to servitude. "A man's property is the fruit of his industry, and if it may be taken from him under any pretence whatever, at the will of another, he cannot be said to be free, for he labors like a bond slave, not for himself, but for another," he later wrote in recalling the debate. He told his audience that the colonies did not ring up a farthing of Britain's £140 million debt. America received no help from the British that was advantageous to them, he said. The Seven Years War with France was fought for the benefit of England, not America.[3]

"Did England alone run deeply in debt in conquering the French in America? Did not the colonies bear a great share in the expense of it?" Adams asked.[4] He urged colonists to realize that if the British were successful in stationing ten thousand troops in the colonies, their self-government would be over. The military would function under its own set of rules, obedient to the crown, not to local voters. He admonished them to refrain from buying British goods, to find alternatives or make their own, and he asked them to resist any attempts by crown officials to allow the tax act to be implemented.

Adams wanted to renew his call for a congress. If the Massachusetts House extended an invitation to unite, he realized that each colonial assembly would be forced to take up the debate over the tax, even if they turned down the invitation to attend the congress. The idea of colonial legislatures debating an act of Parliament was unheard of. Yet Adams knew that a Massachusetts summons would trigger discussion up and down the seaboard and through the country regions of each province. Elected representatives throughout America would be obligated to introduce the issue to voters, and to discuss the ramifications of Parliament's authority. The questions would be discussed at hundreds of town meetings, in taverns and working guilds, in daily conversations on street corners. Countless publishers and pamphleteers would write editorials. His instructions from the previous year would spell out the position of the Massachusetts House on Parliament's authority to tax. Other legislatures would be compelled to examine each of his arguments in formulating their own position and in deciding whether to attend the congress.

Adams decided that another public call for a congress at the town meeting would likely cause Governor Bernard to shut down the assembly again. The measure had to be approved by the House before the governor could react. Thus, Adams urged James Otis to use the authorization from the former instructions as a mandate from Boston to again propose the congress in the House. Otis was having second thoughts, however. He wondered where the protests would lead and whether the king would revoke the Massachusetts Charter if colonists resisted the Stamp Act. "It is the duty of all," Otis told friends, "to humbly and silently to acquiesce in all the decisions of the supreme legislature. [They] undoubtedly have the right to levy internal taxes on the colonies. He was a damned fool who denied it; that this people never would be quiet till we had a council from home, till our charter was taken away, and till we had regular troops quartered upon us."[5] Otis was beginning to show signs of mental illness. He praised royal officials one minute, and cursed them the next. Adams pressed upon him to carry out the will of Boston and make the call for a Stamp Act congress in the Massachusetts House when session began. Otis agreed.

Governor Bernard opened the general assembly at the House in Boston in May. He urged compliance with the Stamp Act and stated that Parliament had the right to legislate for the colonies as the "conservators of liberty." In his view, the settlement of the American provinces by Britain was a foregone conclusion and would proceed quickly with the French removed. "Submission to the decrees of the supreme legislature, to which all other powers in the British Empire were subordinate, was the duty and the interest of the colonies."[6]

As Samuel Adams listened to the governor's words, he felt that his greatest fears were materializing. The English planned to encourage immigration to the interior regions of the continent, westward to the Mississippi. Royal governors would be endowed with titles of nobility. Colonial democracy would vanish. He began to weigh alternatives, and wondered if America's only hope lay in independence—a new nation.

In June, Otis launched Adams' call for the colonies to unite in opposition to Britain in a Stamp Act congress. Otis cited the Adams-authored Boston instructions from the previous year that demanded a congress and proposed that Massachusetts' House reach out to other colonies with invitations. The measure passed, and letters were immediately sent to speakers of each colonial legislature.[7]

Governor Bernard then shut down the assembly again. But this time he was too late to stop the call for a colonial congress. He told leaders in London not to be concerned that the colonies might unite. "Nothing will be done in consequence of this intended congress," he wrote in July.[8] He recommended, however, that Britain increase the number of royal appointments of civil officers in Massachusetts to strengthen his hand and to offset the growing power of popular leaders such as Adams.

Lieutenant Governor Hutchinson scoffed at the idea of a congress: "No two colonies think alike; there is no uniformity of measures; the bundle of sticks thus separated will be easily broken." Hutchinson recalled the lack of success he and Franklin had in uniting the colonies under the Albany Plan of 1754 and believed the people would accept the tax. "The Stamp Act," he reported to London, "is received among us with as much decency as could be expected; it leaves no room for evasion, and will execute itself."[9]

The initial reactions to the invitations to the Stamp Act congress were not encouraging for Adams. New Jersey and New Hampshire declined. The governor of Virginia refused to call the House of Burgesses together to consider the proposal. The governor of Maryland reported that "the resentment of the colonists would probably die out; and that, in spite of the violent outcries of the lawyers, the Stamp Act would be carried into execution."[10]

But the tide turned on a steamy summer day in July at the South Carolina legislature. During deliberations over the matter, many objected to the legality of a colonial congress. Others felt it was ill-advised. Representative John Rutledge made an impassioned speech to his fellow legislators that every colony faced the same danger of British domination. The colonies were powerless against Great Britain unless they stood united. Representative Christopher Gadsden guided the measure through committee and won its support in the legislature on August 2. He later recalled with pride that South Carolina was the first "to listen to the call of our northern brethren in their distresses. Massachusetts sounded the trumpet, but to Carolina is it owing that it was attended to."[11]

Within weeks, nine other states accepted the invitation to attend: Connecticut, Delaware, Maryland, Massachusetts, New Jersey, New York, Pennsylvania, Rhode Island, and South Carolina. As summer wore on, the debate in churches, in meeting halls, and at dinner tables continued despite predictions to the contrary by royal governors. "Power is a sad thing," wrote the Presbyterians of Philadelphia. "Our mother should remember we are children and not slaves." In Georgia, merchant James Habersham considered it an insult "to talk of our being virtually represented in Parliament."[12]

Governor Bernard announced that the Massachusetts House could reconvene in September. Adams was appointed by the town to write up a list of instructions for Otis and its other legislators. Sitting in his second-story study, Adams took out his pen to prepare the draft. He did not forget Bernard's prediction that England would settle the rest of the continent. If independence was the only alternative, Adams wondered what he could do to prepare Boston, Massachusetts, perhaps the entire continent.

Hutchinson later claimed that it was at this time that Adams began privately advocating independence. Adams did not take the idea public, however. In 1765, most colonists were far from considering life without Britain.

Even Adams had to wonder if his imagination was deluding him. The hope of prodding the colonies into a break with England seemed absurd. Could he split an empire? He invited John Adams to his study to discuss the issues surrounding the Stamp Act. John, who had been assigned to write the instructions for the assemblymen representing his hometown of Braintree, found his older cousin mysteriously weighing future prospects that he was not willing to disclose completely. "He felt an ambition, which was very apt to mislead a man, that of doing something extraordinary, and he wanted to consult a friend who might suggest some thoughts to his mind," John recalled. "I read him my instructions and showed him a copy of mine."[13]

In writing Boston's instructions, Samuel needed to consider not only his hometown and his fellow inhabitants of Massachusetts, but also aim his message at each of the thirteen colonies as well as officials in London. His message was also meant for the Stamp Act congress. He criticized the House of Commons for not even acknowledging the Massachusetts colonists' petitions to repeal the previous tax measures. He reiterated his case for colonial rights, and, in a not-so-subtle warning to London, he touted the upcoming Stamp Act congress: "It affords us the greatest Satisfaction to hear, that the Congress proposed by the House of Representatives of this Province, is consented to by the representatives of most of the other colonies on the continent."[14] His instructions directed James Otis in the Stamp Act congress to get approval of a statement of colonial rights and a petition to King George III to address their grievances.

The debate over the Stamp Act, which was slated to go into effect on November 1, grew heated in the streets of Boston, where protests of angry workers, merchants, and sailors turned violent. The Sons of Liberty, a secret Whig society, formed to pressure stamp masters into resigning. As Bostonians gathered on August 12 to commemorate the birthday of the Prince of Wales, the future King George IV, small groups began to shout "Pitt and Liberty," invoking the name of William Pitt, the popular member of Parliament known as the Great Commoner who opposed the Stamp Act there.

The demonstrators agreed to return later in the week and hang the colony's appointed stamp master in effigy. Two days later, on the morning of August 14, they gathered at an elm tree near the Boston Common, which soon after became known as the Liberty Tree. Adams is not believed to have been part of the protest. The crowd was boisterous. A stuffed effigy of the stamp master, Andrew Oliver, was tied to a rope, slung over a branch of the tree, hoisted in the air, and swung in a mock public hanging, to jeering laughter. A large boot was dangled from a branch to mock Lord John Stuart Bute, King George's prime minister. Peering from the leg of the boot was the fashioned head of a devil adorned with horns.

A sign was posted: "A goodlier sight whoe'er did see? A Stamp man hanging on a tree."[15]

Lieutenant Governor Hutchinson immediately ordered the colonel of the militia to beat an alarm. "My drummers are in the mob," the colonel exclaimed to Hutchinson, who then ordered the sheriff to disperse the crowd. "Stand by, my boys," cried one of protesters. "Let no man give way."[16]

By evening, the figures were cut down and carried through town on a plank. The procession swelled as it paraded by torchlight through the streets, past the council chamber where Governor Bernard and his officers were in session. "Liberty, property and no stamps!" the agitators yelled for Bernard's benefit.[17]

That night, the Sons of Liberty were joined by about fifty tradesmen and a crowd of more than two thousand. They marched up King Street, where they came upon the unfinished frame of a building that was said to be the stamp master's future office. In minutes, the frame was demolished. Not yet satiated, the crowd moved to Fort Hill, still carrying pieces of timber from the demolished office. A bonfire was built, and the effigies were beheaded and burned at the stake.

Many in the crowd headed for their homes, but a small group decided to visit the home of the stamp master. They laid torches to his coach and set it on fire, trampled his garden, destroyed the outdoor furniture, smashed windows, and got drunk on wine from his cellar.

Andrew Oliver resigned as stamp master the next day.

The demonstration in Boston was widely hailed throughout the colonies. Samuel Adams wrote: "The people shouted and their shout was heard to the distant end of the continent."[18]

Twelve days later, Hutchinson heard rumors in town that a crowd planned to attack the customs house and the admiralty office later that night. Friends assured him that he was not a target and that he remained popular with Boston residents. As night descended, a mob formed at the office of the admiralty, setting fire to its records. It proceeded to ravage the customs office, then turned toward the Hutchinson mansion.

This mob was not called by the Sons, which had been satisfied with Oliver's resignation. The horde included criminals and debtors, along with rowdy seafarers and dockworkers, men who felt powerless and wanted to unleash their festering anger on the authorities. Boston had suffered through hard times the previous year. Smallpox decimated the population, followed by a dour economy that left many without work. The Sugar Act had drained much of the coinage from the colonies, and many gangs along the docks hated the British, who were cruelly pressing men into service in the royal navy in a kind of conscription slavery.

As the lieutenant governor dined quietly with his family, a messenger burst into the elegant home, crying that a mob was on its way. "I directed my children to fly to a secure place, and [I] shut up my house as I had done before," Hutchinson recalled. His daughter refused to leave without him. He did not deny her, and they fled to a neighbor's house, eluding the angry throng by just seconds. "The hellish crew fell upon my house with the rage of devils, and in a moment with axes split down the doors and entered."[19]

His son was still in the house and heard the invaders yell, "Damn him; he is upstairs. We'll have him." As the attackers searched the house from the top floors to the cellar, the son escaped. Another friendly messenger tracked down Hutchinson and told him the mob was frantically looking for him. "I was obliged to retire through the yards and gardens to a house more remote," Hutchinson said. "I remained until four o'-clock, by which time one of the best finished houses in the province had nothing remaining but the bare walls and floors.

"Not contented with tearing off all the wainscot and hangings, and splitting the doors to pieces, they beat down the partition walls; and although that alone cost them two hours, they cut down the cupola, and they began to take the slate and boards from the roof, and were prevented only by the approaching daylight from a total demolition of the building. The garden-house was laid flat, and all my trees, etc., broke down to the ground. Such ruin was never seen in America."[20]

The vandals destroyed expensive china, family portraits, household furniture, and all his family's clothing. Thieves carried off £900 and left the house completely bare.

Whatever moral high ground Samuel Adams was trying to maintain in the protests over the Stamp Act suddenly vanished; claims of "natural rights" of life, liberty, and property rang hollow after a mob destroyed property and threatened the lives of others. Adams believed in the rule of law, that freedom entailed an obligation of moral and rational behavior. He sought not to overturn colonial society but to preserve it from British intrusion.

The destruction of Hutchinson's home seemed to vindicate British claims that American resistance was not born of high ideals but of base motives. It confirmed the notion that the colonies could not govern themselves without lawlessness breaking out. It also fed suspicions that a lack of respect for royal authority would unleash latent passions resulting in upheaval.

Samuel Adams realized that future protests must be carefully orchestrated and that a nonviolent form of passive resistance was preferable. He needed to keep moral opinion on the colonial side, which meant keeping demonstrations within the law and portraying British interference as unconstitutional. Adams decided that petitions, boycotts, and well-designed campaigns would be the chief components of popular protests in Boston. Soon Sons of Liberty chapters were established in several colonies, gathering thousands of members.

At a town meeting the day after the riot, the acts of destruction were condemned and a series of resolutions was drawn up asking for the help of the town's selectmen to prevent future vandalism. Townspeople pledged their assistance in keeping the peace, and Samuel Adams denounced the misguided demonstration as "high-handed outrages."[21]

However, in writing to the colonial agent in London, Richard Jackson, Adams blamed the Stamp Act for the violent passions. "All was done the day following that could be expected from an orderly town, by whose influence a spirit was raised to oppose and suppress it. It is possible these matters may be represented to our disadvantage, and therefore we desire you will take all possible opportunities to set them in a proper light."[22]

By September 5, Governor Bernard openly acknowledged that the Stamp Act was unenforceable in Massachusetts. The seals were expected to arrive by ship any day. With Oliver's resignation, the governor became the de facto stamp master. An unwilling target, Bernard told the council that "he had no warrant whatsoever to unpack a bale of them or to order anyone else to do so; and it could not be conceived that he should be so imprudent as to undertake the business."[23]

The ship carrying the stamps entered Boston Harbor four days later, bringing news that the Grenville ministry had been dismissed by King George III in July and replaced by the Marquis of Rockingham, who was sympathetic with the colonists' protests. This raised hopes that the act might be repealed. Also aboard the ship was George Meserve, the stamp distributor for New Hampshire, who resigned his post before stepping foot on land. The stamps were unloaded at the barracks on Castle William Island, and a guard was placed around them.

The Massachusetts House was scheduled to reconvene in mid-September after three months of inactivity. Oxenbridge Thacher, one of Boston's four representatives in the assembly, had died during the summer. Adams decided to run for election to fill Thacher's seat. His days as a tax collector had introduced him to almost everyone in town, and he could count on the support from a variety of political clubs. His prominence at the town meeting won him many supporters. But he was opposed by a large body of Tories, who were unhappy with his protests over British tax policies, and desperately wanted to keep him out of the House. The election drew an unusually large turnout. No candidate won a clear majority on the first ballot. Adams was elected on the second ballot by a vote of 265 to 183.[24]

Governor Bernard addressed the legislature to reopen sessions in September, arguing that Parliament would be unwilling to repeal the tax while colonists denied its authority over America. He warned that lawless chaos would result if the courts and custom houses were closed because of a refusal to use stamped paper. Bernard lost his patience the next day when the assembly introduced a bill expressing the need to carry on business without the stamps. He retaliated by sending orders to close the assembly, ostensibly because representatives from outlying towns needed more time to make the trip to Boston.

But before the orders arrived, Samuel Adams took a seat among the
delegates in the assembly. He had no time to settle in before proceedings
were shut down.

Adams showed his penchant for wit in writing the House's response
to the governor's speech, which was presented when session resumed in
October. Members were perplexed by Bernard's request for more authority to avert a crisis, Adams wrote. "We indeed could not have
thought that a weakness in the executive power of the province had been
any part of our danger, had not your Excellency made such a declaration
in your speech."[25] Bernard pointed to no defect in the laws yet seemed
to feel helpless, Adams continued. "Yet you are pleased to say that the
executive authority is much too weak." The assembly did not find "anything criminal" in the vows by some citizens to refrain from paying the
stamp tax. The assembly could not force their opinions. "Your Excellency tells us that the right of the Parliament to make laws for the American colonies remains indisputable in Westminster," his response
continued. "Without contending this point, we beg leave just to observe
that the charter of the province invests the general assembly with the
power of making laws for its internal government and taxation; and that
this charter has never yet been forfeited." He dismissed the idea that Parliament did, or ever could, represent the colonies. "Indeed we think it
impracticable."[26]

Adams scolded the governor for apparently condemning everyone
in the colony over the destruction of Hutchinson's home. "We are sure
your Excellency will not expressly charge us with encouraging the late
disturbances; and yet to our unspeakable surprise and astonishment, we
cannot but see, that by fair implication it may be argued from the manner of expression, that an odium was intended to be thrown on the
province."[27]

A day after his House response was presented in Boston, the Stamp
Act congress wrapped up its efforts in New York. James Otis attended on
behalf of Massachusetts. Nine states participated: Connecticut,
Delaware, Maryland, Massachusetts, New Jersey, New York, Pennsylvania, Rhode Island, and South Carolina. New Hampshire was absent but
sent word that it would abide by the group's actions. Georgia sent representatives from a thousand miles away to transcribe the proceedings.

James Otis rediscovered his brilliance and quickly distinguished himself in these debates. As a fellow delegate put it, "not one appeared to be so complete a master of every subject, or threw so much light on every question, as James Otis."[28]

The Stamp Act congress hammered out a series of resolutions and the first-ever united petition to the King of England and Parliament. Congress members stated that taxation without representation violated basic civil rights of all British subjects, and they maintained that only colonial legislatures could levy taxes in America. The jurisdiction of the vice-admiralty courts over the enforcement of the Stamp Act was protested as unconstitutional.

In Boston, Samuel Adams was pleased with the results. He believed the Stamp Act provided a crisis to bring the colonies together. "Happy was it for us that a union was then formed upon which, in my humble opinion, the fate of the colonies turned," he later wrote. "What a blessing to us has the Stamp Act eventually or, to use a trifling word, virtually proved, which was calculated to enslave and ruin us. When the colonies saw the common danger, they at the same time saw their mutual dependence, and mutually called in the assistance of each other; and I dare say such friendships and connections are established between them as shall for the future deter the most virulent enemy from making another open attack upon their rights as men and subjects."[29]

Adams learned that he needed to find a more universal foundation than colonial charters to unite America in a plea for civil rights. During the Stamp Act congress, delegates struggled to find a common legal ground. Only three of the colonies were chartered, and each had its own government framework. Some were unchartered and had been granted to nobles, such as Lord Baltimore and William Penn, while others were under the direct control of King George III. In drafting Massachusetts' opposition to the Stamp Act, Adams sounded the theme of natural rights common to all men. Americans were "unalienably entitled to those essential rights in common with all men: and that no law of society can, consistent with the law of God and nature, divest them of those rights," he wrote, anticipating the language of the Declaration of Independence.[30]

For the first time, he expressly denied Parliament's authority over Massachusetts: "All acts made by any power whatever, other than the general assembly of this province, imposing taxes on the inhabitants, are infringements of our inherent and unalienable rights as men and British subjects, and render void the most valuable declarations of our charter."[31]

When Adams wrote these resolutions, most colonists still thought of their land as an extension of the British Empire. They thought of Parliament as their government, despite complaints about taxation. In a letter to London, Thomas Hutchinson reminded the British ministry that the colonists supported the empire during the recent war. "It is not more than two years since it was the general principle of the colonists that, in all matters of privilege or rights, the determination of the Parliament of Great Britain must be decisive."[32]

The assembly voted in approval of the statement by Adams, which became known as the Massachusetts Resolves. When Hutchinson read them, he sensed that the assembly had fallen under the control of Adams, and called them a colonial Magna Carta. "They are agreeable to his [Samuel Adams'] professed principles, which he owned without reserve in private discourse to be independency; and from time to time he made advances towards it in public as far as would serve the great purpose of attaining to it," Hutchinson wrote in a letter to leaders in London.[33]

The Adams-authored resolves were published extensively. The reaction was less than positive in London, where they were dismissed as "ravings of a parcel of wild enthusiasts."[34]

The Stamp Act was scheduled to become law the first day of November. Bostonians demonstrated their defiance, commemorating it like a wake. Bells tolled and guns were fired into the air. In Boston Harbor, ships' flags flew at half-mast to signal a day of mourning. Shops were shuttered. People carried copies of the Stamp Act with the inscription "The folly of England and the ruin of America."[35] Newspapers published with a skull and bones in the spot where the stamp was required. The government found it impossible to distribute the stamps. Throughout the colonies, supplies of stamps were seized and burned. Crowds gathered around the Liberty Tree and hung effigies of Grenville and other British officials. By midafternoon, the figures were cut down and a solemn crowd then marched to the town gallows at Boston Neck, where the effigies underwent another ceremonial hanging, then were torn to pieces and thrown to the wind. Violence and destruction was carefully avoided. At the end of the demonstration, leaders told participants to return peacefully to their homes. Governor Bernard had no idea how to handle the situation. The Massachusetts stamps were still on Castle William Island in the middle of Boston Harbor.

Adams became a ubiquitous presence in the assembly. He chaired one committee to come up with ways to allow businesses to continue without the stamps, and he led another to protest the cost of the troops guarding the stamps. As chair of yet another committee, Adams was responsible for forming a legal team to appeal to Governor Bernard to open the judicial courts. He hired John Adams to appear before the governor, along with James Otis and Jeremiah Gridley, to make the plea. John stood before Bernard with his shoulders erect, proud to be arguing a case with two of his legal mentors. While studying law in 1759, he called them "the greatest lawyers, orators, in short, the greatest men, in America."[36] Gridley had conducted John's requisite interview to be admitted to the bar. The men argued that the courts must reconvene, regardless of the absence of stamps. Bernard denied their request.

Between Samuel Adams' assorted duties, he still found time, however, to direct the lobbying effort in London. He drafted letters to supporters of colonial rights. Massachusetts hired Dennys DeBerdt, a successful English merchant, to represent the colony in England. Adams urged him to warn British merchants of America's vow to continue the boycott: "There will be a necessity of stopping in a great measure the importation of English goods. And indeed the people of the colonies seem more and more determined to do without them as far as possible."[37]

English merchants needed no reminder. They held cancelled orders from American customers. Many became panic-stricken with worries of bankruptcy, according to the economist Adam Smith: "The expectation of a rupture with the colonies . . . has struck the people of Great Britain with more terror than they ever felt for a Spanish armada or a French invasion. It was this terror, whether well- or ill-grounded, which rendered the repeal of the Stamp Act, among the merchants at least, a popular measure."[38]

As Samuel Adams had foreseen, the non-importation agreements successfully turned British merchants into his most energetic lobbyists. They called on the British ministry to repeal the Stamp Act. As Smith reported: "If the total exclusion from the colony market, was it to last only for a few years, the greater part of our merchants used to fancy that they foresaw an entire stop to their trade; the greater part of our master manufacturers, the entire ruin of their business; and the greater part of our workmen, an end of their employment."[39]

Throughout America, stamp officers were compelled to resign. With American opinion solidified, Adams launched a letter-writing campaign to stir support in England, supplying arguments to colonial agents, including DeBerdt. Adams pointed out that Americans already paid extra fees to boost the English economy; this was the entire purpose of regulating colonial trade.

To a friend in London, he wrote: "This is an indirect tax. The nation constantly regulates their trade, and lays it under what restrictions she pleases; and the duties on the goods imported from her and consumed here, together with those which are laid on almost every branch of our trade, all of which centers in cash in her coffers, amount to a very great sum."[40]

Adams believed that if Americans were overburdened with taxes, their economy would collapse. "By restrictions and duties she is even now in danger of putting an end to their usefulness to her; whereas, by abolishing those duties and giving them indulgences, they would be enabled to repay her a hundredfold."[41]

Yet while Adams seemed to be pushing the colonists in the direction of independence, as Hutchinson believed, he remained careful to avoid calling for independence prematurely. His letters dismissed the idea, despite his private conversations. In a letter to a colonial supporter in England, he feigned to take exception to a London newspaper editorial alleging this motive. "Where did he learn that ye colonies were struggling for independence? The contrary is most certainly true. . . . There is at present no appearance of such disposition as this writer would insinuate, much less a struggle for independence; and I dare say there never will be unless Great Britain shall exert her power to destroy their liberties. This we hope will never be done."[42]

Adams furnished agents in London with several more arguments to state the case for repeal. He wrote that the tax would drain the limited amount of coin in the provinces. He reminded readers that the colonists bore much of the expense of the recently concluded war with France. He also repeated threats of a continued boycott and warned that the colonists could erect their own manufacturing plants to compete directly with those in Britain. His arguments were disseminated among agents for the colonies, which included Benjamin Franklin on behalf of Philadelphia.

As the clamor of British businessmen increased for repeal, Parliament reconsidered the Stamp Act in early 1766. The Tory government of Grenville was replaced by the Whig prime minister Charles Watson-Wentworth, Marquis of Rockingham. Edmund Burke served as Rockingham's chief advisor and private secretary.

In February at a secret meeting of Parliament, Benjamin Franklin was summoned as an agent for the colonists and questioned as to whether the colonists could afford to pay the tax. "In my opinion there is not gold and silver enough in the colonies to pay the stamp duty for one year," Franklin answered. Did America not have an obligation to pay for the cost of protection? "That is not the case," Franklin said. "The colonies raised, clothed and paid, during the last war, near twenty-five thousand men, and spent many millions." Would America pay a modified stamp tax? "No, never, unless compelled by force of arms."[43]

During the parliamentary debate, Franklin and other colonial supporters watched from the gallery. William Pitt rose from a sickbed to make a rare appearance in defense of the provinces. "I have been charged with giving birth to sedition in America," Pitt began. "They have spoken their sentiments with freedom against this unhappy act, and that freedom has become their crime." Like Adams, he argued that America did not owe Britain. "The gentleman asks, when were the colonies emancipated? But I desire to know, when they were made slaves?" Pitt bellowed.[44]

When the issue advanced to the House of Lords, Lord Mansfield reaffirmed the doctrine of "virtual representation." He said: "There are 12,000,000 people in England and Ireland who are not represented; the notion now taken up, that every subject must be represented by deputy, is purely ideal. [45]

Just as Samuel Adams had foreseen in orchestrating the boycott, English businessmen became powerful lobbyists for the repeal of the Stamp Act. On the morning of March 17, the leading British merchants who exported goods to America met at King's Tavern in Cornhill, England to draft a petition to the king asking that he rescind the tax. At 11 A.M. they boarded fifty coaches and rode in a procession to the House of Lords to meet with his majesty.

The following day when King George III, attired in resplendent royal robes, arrived at Parliament to give his assent to the repeal, he was met with "a vast concourse of people, huzzaing, clapping hands, etc., that it was several hours before His Majesty reached the House." Church bells in London rang out. Ships were immediately dispatched to America with the news.[46]

Burke described the repeal as "an event that caused more universal joy throughout the British dominions than perhaps any other that can be remembered."[47]

News of the victory came with the arrival of the brigantine *Harrison,* which reached Boston Harbor on May 16. In the invigorating spring air, against the backdrop of trees just sprouting lush leaves, Adams watched townspeople celebrate the end of a long, cold season of political turmoil. Residents rushed into the streets and shouted their joy. Music rang out. Salutes were fired from the batteries around the city. Ships were dressed with flags. People declared a day of celebration, forsaking work to hold picnics in the fresh air. Adams thought them "mad with loyalty."[48] James Otis threw open his home to guests. Even Governor Bernard was caught up in the excitement and voiced his approval. The celebration continued into the night. Crowds again gathered at the Liberty Tree, this time to hang from its branches lanterns, not effigies. Fireworks were presented at Boston Common, and John Hancock gave out Madeira wine from his house opposite the common.

On behalf of the Massachusetts assembly, Adams publicly expressed gratitude toward the British merchants who helped win a repeal of the Stamp Act in a statement that was printed in newspapers in America and

London. "The House is very sensible of the kindness of the merchants of London in warmly espousing their cause," he wrote.[49]

But news of the repeal came with the revelation that Parliament also passed the Declaratory Act, which mandated that the colonies were completely under the authority of Parliament. It was clear that Parliament and the king were not persuaded by arguments about colonial rights.

When Adams first decided to protest the Sugar Act two years earlier, the idea that he could make the slightest impression on the policies of the king and the British government seemed sanguine. He was a back-street political manager, a failed tax collector on the lowest rung of civil officials, and few people in the colonies were inclined to publicly defy a levy by the parental government.

Yet Samuel Adams possessed a rare political genius that was only beginning to show itself at the age of forty-four. His achievements so far were stunning. During the previous two years, he had roused the continent, engineered the first boycotts, helped unite the colonies for the first time, implanted a reverence and stoked the love of liberty based on individual rights. He supplied colonists not only with the reasons to fight for their rights but with the political weapons to do battle.

4

THE TRUE SENTIMENTS
OF AMERICA

Samuel Adams wanted to recruit his second cousin into Boston politics. In John Adams, who was thirteen years younger, he saw a curious intellect, a growing legal scholar, an able pen, and a stubborn streak reminiscent of his own. In Samuel Adams, John saw a savvy politician and a potential mentor. John, a restless lawyer, was thirty years old, small in stature, stout, with a round face and piercing eyes, who walked with his shoulders upright and square. He was still uncertain about his future and questioned whether he yearned for power, wealth, or the chance to do something memorable. He was certain, however, that the time he spent running from court to court in the local legal circuit, arguing cases one day in Barnstable and then off to Salem or Concord or Martha's Vineyard, Worcester or Cambridge, Boston, and elsewhere, was leading nowhere.[1] Following the example of his elder cousin, John began to make a name for himself with his pen, writing several political articles for the Boston newspapers. His neighbors in Braintree noticed his promise and recruited him to write the town's instructions for its representatives in the House.

Two days before Christmas in 1765, Samuel invited John to a caucus meeting attended by some of the leading popular-party figures in Boston. The club initially met at members' homes, where they carefully planned strategies before elections, hammered out arguments to take before voters, and chose subjects to write opinion pieces about for the newspapers. As membership grew, the club moved to a small wooden building on Milk Street owned by a local grocer. The club included assembly delegates, such as Thomas Cushing and James Otis, along with other Boston leaders. The group was friendly and welcomed John. He knew many of the members from his legal work. Cushing, a successful merchant and the son of the man Samuel once worked for, had a reputation for secrecy and a talent for procuring intelligence concerning royal officials. At the meeting, Otis seemed temperamental and fiery, often sounding angry and despondent; he was showing signs that his mental illness was becoming more severe, perhaps causing his uneven moods. John watched Samuel's tactful touch with other members: "[He is always for softness and prudence, where they will do; but is stanch, and stiff, and strict, and rigid, and inflexible in the cause."[2]

When the political campaigns for election to the House began in spring, Samuel rounded up support for friend and political protégé John Hancock, who at twenty-nine was already perhaps the richest man in Massachusetts, more affluent than even Thomas Hutchinson. Orphaned as a youngster, John had been adopted by his uncle, Thomas Hancock, Boston's wealthiest merchant. Upon his uncle's death, John inherited in 1764 an estate worth £400,000, which included shipping and real estate interests. He loved attention and craved popularity even more than money. His generous gesture of passing out Madeira wine during the celebration of the repeal of the Stamp Act was characteristic.

In the May 1766 election for the annual assembly, Adams was reelected along with Otis and Cushing. Hancock won a seat for the first time. Governor Bernard, concerned that Adams was cementing control of the House, wanted help from England. He sent Charles Paxton, a mutual friend of Charles Townshend, Chancellor of the Exchequer, as his agent to London. He advised the ministry to appoint the governor's council (the upper house of the legislature), rather than leaving it open to elections. A handpicked council could be stacked with Tories to offset the influence of the lower House and Samuel Adams: "The making the king's council annually elective is the fatal ingredient in the constitution," Bernard wrote. "The only anchor of hope is the sovereign power, which would secure obedience to its decrees, if they were properly introduced and effectually supported."[3] He warned London that the radicals wanted independence from England.

Adams accurately divined the political winds. He closely read reports coming out of London for indications of an emerging, hostile British policy toward America. He correctly deduced that the British strategy was to beef up civil offices funded directly by Britain to offset popular leadership and to send a military force to back up royal authority.

He wrote Christopher Gadsden, a South Carolina legislator: "I have heard that George Grenville was told to his face that he missed it in his politics, for he should have stationed a sufficient number of troops in America before he sent the Stamp Act among them. Surely, we cannot consent to their quartering among us; and how hard is it for us to be obliged to pay our money to subsist them!"[4] Adams urged DeBerdt in London to oppose any military presence in America.[5]

British soldiers were already stationed in New York, to the dismay of colonists. The soldiers, often unruly teenagers and young men who did not want to be there, were not answerable to the city. They cursed the populace and cut down their flagstaff.

The storm signs became more ominous when in August 1766 King George replaced the Rockingham government—champion of the repeal of the Stamp Act—with William Pitt as prime minister. Pitt was in poor health and unable to provide much leadership. The leading figure in the new government was Charles Townshend, Chancellor of the Exchequer, who planned to succeed where Grenville had failed. He set a goal of raising revenues from America regardless of the political squabble.

King George III felt the repeal of the Stamp Act had been a "fatal compliance."[6] Townshend declared himself a "firm advocate of the Stamp Act—for its principal and duty." Standing on the floor of the House of Commons, he proclaimed, "So long as I am in office, the authority of the laws shall not be trampled upon."[7]

Townshend valued the input of Charles Paxton, Bernard's agent, and took his advice to target the colonial charters and bolster the power of royal officers. He told Parliament that "America should be deprived of its militating and contradictory charters, and its royal governors, judges and attorneys be rendered independent of the people."[8]

During the debate in Parliament, Townshend paused dramatically in midspeech. Looking sternly in the direction of colonial agents watching the deliberations, he intoned: "I speak this aloud, that all you who are in the galleries may hear me; and, after this, I do not expect to have my statue erected in America. England is undone if this taxation of America is given up."[9]

The Townshend Acts became law in June 1767 and were scheduled to take effect by November 20. The measures increased the number of customs officials for the colonies and laid duties on glass, paint, paper, and tea to stop smuggling in ports such as Boston, and to enforce duties on English goods. Townshend expected to raise £40,000 pounds a year from the tax, earmarked to pay for royally appointed agents in America as well as military troops to bypass the authority of elected legislatures. The laws concerning the writs-of-assistance search warrants were strengthened to allow officials to search the property of colonists suspected of dealing in smuggled goods. Royal customs officials, judges, and governors were to be paid directly from England and thus freed from the control of colonial assemblies. When news of the measures reached America, reaction was mixed. Some became outraged while others urged caution.

Adams believed that a puppet government was being installed to rule over America. In Boston, twenty-three-year-old Josiah Quincy, a protégé of Adams, wrote newspaper pieces urging armed resistance to the Townshend Acts. Adams thought this rash and unwise. He supported a more peaceful form of resistance, economic warfare through wider boycotts of British products, and helped pass a petition at the Boston town meeting requesting Bernard to convene the legislature. The governor refused.

Adams chaired another town meeting in Boston on October 28 to draw up strategies and send out commissioners to encourage nonimportation agreements in other colonies. A long list of English luxuries was created so that colonists could cross them off their shopping lists. But this strategy would take time to produce results.

Many people in Massachusetts and the other colonies were wary of the friction caused by defying England and wanted to maintain harmony. While Adams and others worked behind the scenes on non-importation and non-consumption agreements, the mood in Boston seemed tranquil. Tories believed that Adams and the radical faction were too discouraged to protest.

In October 1767, news arrived from England that Charles Townshend had died in September from complications of a fever, leaving uncertainty over how the laws would be implemented. King George III named Lord Frederick North, a former head of the treasury, as his prime minister. He was a favorite of the king, intelligent but not brilliant, good-humored and competent. He was opposed to republicanism and reform and suspicious of popular measures, had voted for the Stamp Act and against its repeal, and adopted the policies of Townshend with the blessings of the king.

In Boston, James Otis buffeted conciliatory hopes in a speech at a town meeting on November 20, the day the Townshend Acts went into effect. Unlike Adams, he believed that the king had the right to appoint as many customs agents as he desired. Five customs commissions had been assigned to Boston. Three had arrived in the first week of November, including Charles Paxton, the man who had lobbied to establish the law.

The Townshend Acts were not easy targets to challenge. Britain had a long-established practice of regulating colonial trade. Fighting this regulation implied tacit approval of smuggling. Many colonists viewed the duties as the price of doing business and were for the most part unaware or unconcerned about the buried costs.

As his first act, he authorized a £200 pension to Massachusetts' Thomas Hutchinson, chief justice of the court and lieutenant governor, to be paid from proceeds from customs duties. This made Hutchison free from the will of the electorate and a salaried employee of the king. Any pretense of judicial independence was gone, Adams believed. In his rulings, Hutchinson answered only to Britain.

Adams remained uncharacteristically quiet as alarm in Boston began to mount, despite accusations from Bernard that Adams' faction "dared not show its face."[10] Hutchinson wrote: "Our incendiaries seem discouraged."[11] Adams spent much of his time holed up in his study, laying out strategy. He began work on a document that could be used to rally the colonies into a single chorus of protest. His first step was to draft a petition to the king. He planned to gain continental agreement on the issues and make his arguments the policy statement for America.

As his eleven-year-old daughter, Hannah, watched him work, she became captivated by the idea that the paper on her father's desk would be presented to the King of England. She asked if it would be touched by the royal hand. Her father answered with amusement, "It will, my dear, more likely be spurned by the royal foot."[12]

In preparing his thoughts, Adams had to consider not only the king's eyes but the colonists' hearts and to appeal to both audiences at once. In previous statements, he had warned that British measures could eventually lead to servitude. The situation was no longer hypothetical, he believed; servitude was the stark reality before them.

The Townshend measures undercut the colonies' democratic institutions and rendered them impotent, he believed. In England, the economist Adam Smith drew the same conclusion: "Should the Parliament of Great Britain, at the same time, be ever fully established in the right of taxing the colonies, even independent of the consent of their own assemblies, the importance of those assemblies would from that moment be at an end, and with it, that of all the leading men of British America."[13]

Samuel Adams was desperate to prevent the loss of home rule. By raising taxes and paying royal officials, judges, and governors, the votes of the colonists became meaningless. A puppet government controlled by England was being put in place and self-government was being destroyed. The experiment their ancestors had started could be over. Adams needed to make this clear to all colonists in America. The New York assembly had been dissolved by Parliament in July 1767 after it refused to comply with the Quartering Act, which required it to buy provisions for British soldiers in New York City. The Massachusetts charter was in danger of being revoked. The chief justice in the Bay Colony was on the king's payroll.

But Adams also needed to win advocates in Britain, so he took a subtle path in writing his petition to the king, treading a line that firmly stated the colonial case while encouraging empathy abroad. Avoiding inflammatory language, he began by stressing that the colonists were not represented in Parliament and therefore could not be taxed by it.

In arguing that a right of property was universal to all cultures, Adams used imagery that the colonists could relate to. He pointed out that Native Indian cultures recognized individual property rights in "the bow, the arrow and the tomahawk, the hunting and fishing grounds," which were to them as important as "rubies and diamonds to the Mogul, or a nabob in the East" or "gold or silver to the Europeans."[14]

He rejected visions of societies without property rights, where everything was publicly commandeered: "The utopian schemes of leveling, and a community of goods, are as visionary and impracticable as those which vest all property in the crown are arbitrary, despotic and, in our government, unconstitutional."

Property rights and democratic self-government were inextricably linked. "The security of right and property is the great end of government," Adams continued. "Surely, then, such measures as tend to render right and property precarious tend to destroy both property and government; for these must stand and fall together."

Anglo-American relations were at an all-time low, he warned, worse than when the first settlers had fled to America. After that time, it was readily acknowledged that wherever an Englishman set foot, the British Constitution went with him to protect his rights, whether on the deck of a ship on the high seas or on the soil of a foreign land. Parliament protected their rights. But during the present season, Parliament not only sought taxation without representation but a whole apparatus of government without consent, he pointed out. Royal governors, judges, custom officials, soldiers were being sent to the colonies to rule and subjugate.

Adams was careful with his words. "Such a power under a corrupt administration, it is to be feared, would introduce an absolute government in America; at best, it would leave the people in a state of utter uncertainty of their security, which is far from being a state of civil liberty." He objected to the use of an unlimited number of customs agents, empowered with blank-check search warrants that required no probable cause, as equally dangerous to liberty.

Yet as he ran down the litany of complaints, he continued to intersperse the recurring theme of harmony, placing the burden of rupture on Britain: "We are happy and safe under his present Majesty's mild and gracious administration, but the time may come when the united body of pensioners and soldiers may ruin the liberties of America." He raised the issue of the suspension of the legislature of New York as a blatant violation of self-government: "There can be no material difference between such a legislature and none at all."

Adams was particularly concerned by reports from England that some favored subduing America through the clergy by setting up an episcopate of the Anglican Church. Adams lamented that it had become fashionable in London conversation and newspapers to mention "charter rights" with contempt.

The boldness of his essay, which he intended as the official policy statement from the Massachusetts assembly, made that body pause before adopting it. The paper, presented on January 6, 1768, was examined and reexamined by the House. Seven times it was revised. Every sentence, every word was carefully weighed for the implications it would convey at home and abroad. On January 12, the statement was approved to be sent to the London agent for presentation to the British ministry and King George III.

Adams had little faith that England would be sympathetic to Massachusetts' petition. The paramount goal was for it to be embraced by the other colonies and crystallize a united front of resistance. In one stroke, he planned to author a continent-wide "American" policy statement toward the Townshend Acts through a "circular letter" to each provincial legislature. Letters would be sent to speakers of assemblies or houses of burgesses detailing Adams' case against the Townshend measures as Massachusetts' position. The letters would invite other colonies to discuss the tax and coordinate efforts between assemblies.

Adams needed first to get official approval of the circular letter from his own assembly. On January 21, he made a motion in the Massachusetts House to proceed with the plan to contact other colonies. But many representatives were uneasy, believing London would view a circular letter coordinating colonial resistance as a second Stamp Act congress that would only fuel fears about American independence.[15]

Of the House's 110 members, 82 were present for the debate, mostly representatives from the cities. Many of the country members were absent due to the winter weather and impassable roads. As a result, the motion to send out the circular letter failed by a two-to-one margin, a stunning defeat for Adams. Bernard expressed "great hopes" that a mood of obedience had returned to the Bay Colony.[16]

Adams was not ready to concede in a matter critical to his cause. A master of backroom politics, he worked behind the scenes, rounding up votes, applying pressure, and turning the prevailing attitude in his favor. On February 4, another vote was taken on the circular letter. This time, the question was carried by a large majority of the 83 members present. The previous vote was erased from the journals.

In drafting the circular, Adams wanted to cause each colonial legislature to carefully deliberate each of the arguments laid out in his petition to the king and the British government. The circular would also encourage each to offer input, thus promoting unity. To speakers of colonial legislatures, Adams wrote: "It seems to be necessary that all possible care should be taken, that the representations of the several assemblies, upon so delicate a point, should harmonize with each other. The House, therefore, hope that this letter will be candidly considered in no other light than as expressing a disposition freely to communicate their mind to a sister colony upon a common concern, in the same manner as they would be glad to receive the sentiments of your or any other house of assembly on the continent."[17]

Adams denied that Massachusetts was vying to break from England. He remained careful not to provoke provincial jealousy or raise fears that Massachusetts wanted to take the helm of an independent America. "The House," he concluded, "is fully satisfied that your assembly is too generous and enlarged in sentiment to believe that this letter proceeds from an ambition of taking the lead or dictating to the other assemblies. They freely submit their opinion to the judgment of others, and shall take it kind in your house to point out to them anything further that may be thought necessary."

The colonies' reception to the circular letter was enthusiastic. In England, the Massachusetts petition and the Adams-authored circular letter were published in London by Thomas Hollis, an American advocate, under the title "The True Sentiments of America."[18]

The publication made a deep impression on readers in Britain and America and attracted more attention than any other colony paper at the

time. British leaders were alarmed at the impact, especially at the threat
of a united America. Lord Hillsborough, the American secretary for
Britain, refused to forward the petition to the king. The ministry viewed
the circular letter as the colonies' most defiant act yet toward the British
government. The cry from London was to "send over an army and a fleet
to reduce them to reason."[19]

Hillsborough responded to the circular letter with his own letter to
each of the colonial governors. He branded the circular letter as being "of
the most dangerous and factious tendency," written to "inflame the
minds" of the people "to promote an unwarrantable combination, and
to excite open opposition to the authority of Parliament." He ordered
the governors to suppress it—even if assemblies had to be suspended.
"You will therefore," Hillsborough commanded, "exert your utmost influence to prevail upon the assembly of your province to take no notice
of it, which will be treating it with the contempt it deserves."[20]

Royal leaders in Massachusetts were, however, in a state of panic.
Bernard and the customs agents sent a secret letter to London asking for
a fleet and regiments to quell the growing agitation. "We have every reason," they added, "to expect that we shall find it impracticable to enforce
the execution of the revenue laws until the hand of government is properly strengthened. At present, there is not a ship-of-war in the province,
nor a company of soldiers nearer than New York."[21]

London began to view the Bay Colony as a hotbed of radicals.
Bernard was ordered to demand that the House rescind the circular letter under the threat of a permanent suspension. "If the new assembly
should refuse to comply, it is the king's pleasure that you should immediately dissolve them," Hillsborough ordered the Massachusetts governor.[22] To add muscle to the threat, General Thomas Gage, commander
of British forces in America with headquarters in New York, was directed
to "maintain the public tranquility."[23]

But the orders from the king and Hillsborough were to no avail. By
the end of April 1768, the legislatures of Connecticut, New Hampshire,
and New Jersey passed resolutions in support of Adams' Massachusetts
circular letter. Virginia, the largest southern colony, proclaimed its endorsement in another circular letter urging each of the other colonies to

do the same. Hearing the news of support from the Old Dominion, Adams said, "It is a glorious day."[24]

Adams reflected on Hillsborough's unsuccessful attempt to censure the invitation: "As the sentiments contained in the letter of the House were so exactly similar to those of the other colonies, and the subject of it was of equal importance to them all, it was not in the power of his Lordship to efface the impressions it made, or to disturb that harmony which was the happy effect of it. That union of the colonies in their common danger, by which they became powerful, was the occasion of the greatest perplexity to their enemies on both sides the Atlantic; and it has been, ever since, their constant endeavor by all manner of arts to destroy it."[25]

In executing his plan, Adams not only authored a paper, *The True Sentiments of America,* which colonists would view as a treatise on their rights, but displayed a mastery of House politics in getting its approval. Once again, he framed the issues on his own terms. America accepted his arguments.

This fact was not lost on London. A battleship was on its way to Boston.

5

ALL THE KING'S MEN

On a spring day in May 1768, the men working along the wharves could see an imposing British battleship entering Boston Harbor. The square-rigged frigate with the Union Jack atop its mast was the fifty-gun *Romney*, the most powerful British ship in North American waters. Word of the warship's arrival quickly spread alarm through the streets. Hundreds of townspeople poured from their homes, workshops, and the shipyards. Samuel Adams saw "awe" in the faces of his neighborhoods as they lined the docks.[1]

After anchoring the vessel, Captain John Corner disembarked, surrounded by a host of military officers and seamen in resplendent uniforms. Corner, grim-faced and iron-willed, announced sternly to town leaders that sailors from merchant vessels could be pressed into service of the British navy to fill his crew. This sent a chill through the wives and families of seamen, who worried that their loved ones could suddenly vanish to conscription, never to be seen again. Corner planned to target crews aboard ships suspected of smuggling.[2]

The captain's mission was to strike fear into Boston residents, to extinguish any hopes for rebellion. He ordered his men to position the *Romney* and its heavy iron guns where she would be the most useful to the governor and customs agents in enforcing the revenue laws. Corner's report on his arrival in Boston to Commodore Samuel Hood, admiral of the North American fleet, said the sight of the *Romney* silenced Boston.

Prior to the ship's arrival, dutiable articles were being landed in Boston in open defiance of customs law. Customs officials complained about the landing of John Hancock's ship *Lydia* in early April. The customs board wanted to prosecute Hancock, but Attorney General Jonathan Sewall had little faith in the case, and decided against it. Another Hancock sloop, the *Liberty*, arrived in early May, and a cargo of Madeira wine was unloaded without duties being paid.[3]

At the town meeting in Boston, Samuel Adams expressed his dismay at the presence of a vessel of war hovering in command of the town "with the design to over awe and terrify the inhabitants of this town."[4]

The customs commissioners mistrusted the air of restraint, writing London: "It does not appear that it is their plan to molest us immediately."[5]

For Adams, the appearance of a battleship, coupled with rumors that more troops were on the way, erased any doubts that America was on a collision course with England. He believed that the colonies must eventually submit or become independent. He told his closest political allies, including John Adams and Joseph Warren, a leading Whig, that his mind was decided: "The country shall be independent, and we will be satisfied with nothing short of it."[6] He planned to make it his life's mission to split the empire and preserve home rule. No conciliatory solution existed. Britain's decision to use military force was proof of this.[7]

Intellectuals in Britain were coming to the same conclusion. Adam Smith believed the only remedy to the Anglo-American conflict was for Britain to allow the colonies to govern their own affairs and capitalize on America's growing economy through open trade. But in the same breath, the economist admitted this solution was politically unthinkable. "Under the present system of management . . . Great Britain derives nothing but loss from the dominion which she assumes over her colonies," Smith wrote. "To propose that Great Britain should voluntarily give up all authority over her colonies and leave them to elect their own magistrates, to enact their own laws, and to make peace and war as they might think proper, would be to propose such a measure as never was, and never will be adopted, by any nation in the world. Such sacrifices, though they might frequently be agreeable to the interest, are always mortifying to the pride of every nation."[8]

The issue of impressing sailors quickly sparked open conflict. A Boston resident was cornered by British officials who were rounding up prospective sailors. His neighbors came to his rescue and pulled him from his captors. They appealed to Corner for the man's freedom and offered to find a substitute to serve in his place. Captain Corner exploded in anger to residents, exclaiming "The town is a blackguard town, ruled by mobs."[9]

Corner's roundup of local men to serve aboard the *Romney* inflamed residents, who were ready to strike back. An opportunity arose when Hancock's sloop *Liberty* was seized for suspected smuggling on June 9. By the next evening, shopkeepers and importers marched into the streets. They were soon joined by workers from the docks and shipyards. Many feared loss of business, work, and revenues if smuggling was shut down.

The crowed followed the customs collector and the comptroller as they headed to Hancock's wharf, where the *Liberty* was docked. There the customs commissioners ordered that the ship's moorings be cut so the vessel could be towed alongside the *Romney* for protection.[10]

The angry townspeople demanded that the *Liberty* remain at the wharf. Sailors from the *Romney* quickly cut the *Liberty*'s ties to the dock and navy seamen in lifeboats ran abreast of the vessel, latched on, and towed it alongside the frigate.

The incensed crowd chased the customs officials, throwing rocks, bricks, and anything handy. Some went to the customs office and shattered the windows. Others searched for a customs boat to seize in retaliation for the taking of the *Liberty*. A craft owned by one of the agents was found and hauled to Boston Common, where it was burned in a bonfire.

The customs officials, fearing for their safety, fled to the *Romney*, pleading to Captain Corner to "shelter us from insult."[11] The agents were rowed to Castle William Island, where they remained for the time being, and the *Romney* was positioned to prevent an attack to the island.

Bernard and the royal officers sent pleas to London, calling the incidents a mob riot and requesting that troops be sent to Boston immediately. To Adams, the incident amounted to little more than a few broken windows and a vandalized boat. Similar incidents were common in London, where there was a huge population of poor people. The crown officers, however, painted a picture of a large crowd of ruffians and rebels bent on social upheaval.

A public meeting was held June 14, 1768, at the Old South meetinghouse. Adams attended, as did hundreds of other residents. Clouds
filled the sky, and clattering rain fell to add to the feeling of turmoil.
James Otis, still as popular as ever with his fellow citizens, was chosen as
moderator and took the podium to thunderous applause. He urged restraint and told residents to maintain order and preserve the town's reputation. He believed their complaints would be addressed in time. But
characteristic of his blazing rhetoric, he added: "If not, and we are called
on to defend our liberties and privileges, I hope and believe we shall, one
and all, resist even unto blood; but I pray God Almighty this may never
so happen."[12]

Adams and Otis were chosen as part of a twenty-one-member committee that would pay Governor Bernard a visit at his home in Roxbury.
Bernard, who could see the carriage coming from a distance, became
anxious about his personal safety and feared that a mob was on its way.
Would his house be destroyed, as Hutchinson's mansion had been demolished by vandals four years earlier? To his great relief, the committee
members came peacefully. He invited Adams and the others in and
handed out glasses of wine, priding himself on his cordiality. He listened
carefully as the men explained that the seizure of Hancock's *Liberty* was
unconstitutional because the duties represented taxation without consent. They protested the impressments and demanded that Bernard call
for the removal of the *Romney* from the harbor.

The governor was polite but said he had no control of the British
navy. He sympathized with their complaints, he said, but unfortunately
could do nothing to help. He walked his guests to the door and expressed warm sentiments as they departed. Privately, Bernard wanted an
even stronger military presence in Boston to strengthen his hand. He
had secretly warned London that rebellion was on the horizon. Along
with the customs agents, Bernard sent a request to General Thomas
Gage in New York and Commodore Hood to send more soldiers and
ships for their protection.[13]

Samuel Adams guessed that Bernard would make this move. He directed John Adams to write instructions to the Boston assembly members that closed with "[e]very person who shall solicit or promote the

importation of troops at this time is an enemy to this town and province, and a disturber of the peace and good order of both."[14]

A week later, on June 21, 1768, Bernard ordered the assembly to rescind the circular letter and delete it from official records. This command came directly from King George III. The governor laid before the House the letter from Hillsborough, which carried the threat that if they failed to withdraw the circular, "it is the king's pleasure that [Bernard] should immediately dissolve them." Adams had finally gotten the attention of the "royal foot."[15]

Adams was now being labeled the "chief incendiary"[16] in the colonies. Yet a strong rebuff by the king, such as his disapproval of the circular letter, threatened to check his influence. Many leaders in Massachusetts, including John Adams, were already wondering if the protests had gone too far and had stirred too much anger.[17]

For more than a week, consternation grew in the assembly as debate over the circular letter continued. Bernard, growing impatient, sent a message that the assembly could not break until a decision was made. Samuel Adams urged members to stand firm. They could not back down after Connecticut, New Jersey, Georgia, and Virginia had passed petitions supporting the circular letter. Their credibility would be destroyed and pleas for future cooperation would be empty.

But the consequences of defying the king meant that not only battleships but troops would certainly descend on Boston.

Adams drafted a letter to Hillsborough for the House to consider as its public statement. What objections could there be to open communication between the colonies? he asked. Did Massachusetts not have a right to contact other legislatures for advice, news, and common concerns? Was this not the mark of a free people? He pointed out that the circular letter had merely informed the other colonies of Massachusetts' protests over the Townshend Acts; it did not ask them to take similar measures.

Adams stated that the recent petition to the king was within the colonists' constitutional rights and had legal precedence in English history. His argument was crafted in mild terms that even the most timid assembly member could not openly disagree with. The letter was read in a closed session of the body, which gave its approval by a vote of ninety-two to seventeen. Then it was sent to the British secretary to America without being made public. Even Bernard did not know the contents of the letter.[18]

But Adams wanted it disseminated to newspapers throughout the colonies. America was the audience his words were carefully aimed at, rather than Hillsborough, to whom they were formally addressed. Otis, however, wanted to relieve concerns from overseas. Unlike Adams, he harbored no desire for independence.

Informers told Governor Bernard that Otis and Adams argued over whether the letter should be printed before reaching Hillsborough. Adams, as the House clerk, felt he could publish any of its official statements without seeking authority from anyone else. Otis urged him not to send the letter to the *Boston Gazette,* asking: "Do you think it proper to publish it so soon, that [Hillsborough] may receive a printed copy before the original comes to his hand?"[19]

Adams replied, "What signifies that? You know it was designed for the people, and not for the minister." Otis grew indignant. "You are so fond of your own drafts that you can't wait for the publication of them to a proper time."

"I am clerk of this House, and I will make that use of the papers which I please."[20]

Aside from the decision regarding the petition to Hillsborough, the House still had to take up the separate issue of whether to rescind the circular letter, as ordered by the king. In a vote of ninety-two to seventeen, the assembly refused to renounce the circular.

Adams drafted a formal response to Bernard: "The circular letters have been sent, and many of them have been answered; those answers are now in the public papers; the public, the world, must and will judge of the proposals, purposes and answers. We could as well rescind those letters as the resolves; and both would be equally fruitless."[21]

He also protested Hillsborough's order to dissolve the assembly if the body refused to nullify the circular letter. "If the votes of the House are to be controlled by the direction of a minister, we have left us but a vain semblance of liberty." The stand taken by the assembly to support the circular was critical to Adams' dream to unify America: "A different determination [than reaffirming its support for the letter] would therefore have been to the last degree infamous, and attended with fatal consequences," Adams said. "Not only the right of the subjects jointly to petition for the redress of grievances, which all alike suffer, but also that of communicating their sentiments freely to each other upon the subject of grievances and the means of redress, which was the sole purport of the circular letter, would in effect have been given up."[22]

Before Bernard had a chance to dissolve the House in accordance with the king's orders, a committee worked frantically to draft a petition to the king for the governor's removal. The breakdown in Massachusetts' self-government meant that Bernard had lost his credibility with citizens. In line with the king's request, Bernard dissolved the Massachusetts House on June 31 in an act of what Adams called "despotism."[23] Massachusetts was then without a democratic form of government.

As the stand in support of the circular letter in Boston and Massachusetts was applauded in America, many in England were losing patience. The agent sent by Bernard and customs officials arrived in London on July 19, 1768, and heightened alarm with exaggerated accounts of the ruckus over the *Liberty* and the burning of the customs officer's boat, claiming open rebellion was at hand. The letter from the Boston customs agents warned of "a long concerted and extensive plan of resistance to the authority of Great Britain; that the people of Boston had hastened to acts of violence sooner than was intended; that nothing but the immediate exertion of military power could prevent an open revolt of the town, which would probably spread throughout the provinces."[24] British leaders ignored Adams' letters to the colony's London agent, which downplayed the fight over the *Liberty* and blamed the officers of the *Romney.*

Anxiety grew so great over a rupture in trade relations with America that stocks fell sharply in Britain. Americans owed English manufacturers and merchants £4 million for imported goods purchased on credit, a sum that would go uncollected if a break occurred.

British leaders believed force was needed to subdue agitation in Boston. On July 27, the cabinet agreed on a divide-and-conquer strategy that would single out Boston and strike fear into the rest of America. Two regiments, each with five hundred men, would be sent to the

Bay Colony along with another frigate. Hillsborough decided to take Bernard's advice and work to change the Massachusetts charter to strengthen the twenty-eight-member colonial council by requiring its members to be appointed rather than elected. Under the charter, council members in the upper House were voted on by the general assembly and members of the previous council. Bernard believed the assembly was under the control of Adams, who therefore also controlled the council.

The British ministry then turned its attention to the leading agitators in Boston. Bernard labeled Samuel Adams "one of the principal and most desperate of the chiefs of the faction."[25] Hutchinson concurred, calling him "the all in all," who needed to be "taken off." Hillsborough dusted off an antiquated law and sent orders to Bernard and Hutchinson to inquire "if any persons had committed acts which, under the statute of Henry VIII against treason committed abroad, might justify their being brought to England to be tried in the king's bench."[26]

In Boston, meanwhile, Adams encouraged merchants to sign on August 1 a non-importation pact that banned importation of all items subject to the Townshend Acts, along with a host of other British products except fishery supplies. The banned items included tea, paper, glass, and paints. The boycott would go into effect on January 1, 1769, and last until a repeal of the revenue acts. A month later, on September 5, New York tradesmen agreed to end business with any local merchants who did not support the provisions of the boycott agreement.[27]

Hutchinson soon began to seek out witnesses who might provide testimony of treasonable acts by Adams to trigger his deportation for trial. In a deposition given before Hutchinson by innkeeper Richard Sylvester, it was alleged that Adams urged armed attacks against crown officers during the commotion over the *Liberty*. Sylvester said he saw a group gathered in the streets of Boston's south end that day and went to investigate. According to his affidavit: "The informant heard the said Samuel Adams then say to the said party, 'if you are men, behave like men. Let us take up arms immediately, and be free, and seize all the king's officers. We shall have thirty thousand men to join us from the country.'"[28]

Commissioners reported to London that only the presence of the *Romney* prevented them from becoming hostages and that it would be impossible for them to set foot off Castle William Island and return to Boston until troops arrived.

Bernard could not officially call for troops without consent of the council, which was the upper House of the legislature. He suggested that Captain Corner station some of the *Romney* crew on Castle William Island. Corner challenged Bernard to make a formal request. The governor was afraid of reprisals from the Sons of Liberty, however, and refrained.[29]

"I think this proves the man very clearly," Admiral Hood said of Bernard. He reported to London, "What has been so often foretold is now come to pass. The good people of Boston seem ready and ripe for open revolt, and nothing, it is imagined, can prevent it but immediate armed force."[30]

By August, as rumors were growing that British troops were on the way, the mood in the town turned grim. Two British ships, the *Senegal* and the *Duke of Cumberland,* left port and sailed for Nova Scotia to transport troops to Boston. Bernard ordered the light on Beacon Hill to be dismantled to prevent signals from being relayed to the surrounding country in case of insurrection.

On August 9, the Boston town meeting selected Samuel Adams to participate in a committee "to consider the most wise, constitutional, loyal and salutary measures" to deal with the expected arrival of the troops.[31] The next evening, Adams, Otis, and others met at the house of Dr. Joseph Warren, a leading Whig. They decided that it was imperative that they garner support from the rest of the towns in Massachusetts. If military occupation led to violence, Boston did not want to stand alone against British troops. But with the assembly prorogued, how could they make a statewide appeal for help? Otis suggested holding a convention of towns to discuss the military occupation. The committee agreed, and began plans to hold a convention.

Informers told Bernard about the meeting at Dr. Warren's home, and he feared a conspiracy. In a letter to Hillsborough, he wrote that "the faction immediately took the alarm" on hearing that the troops were expected. According to Bernard, the meeting was for the purpose of hatching "a plan to surprise and take the Castle on the night following."[32] But Bernard had miscalculated. Adams' paramount goal was to unite others in their cause, not to make a desperate last stand by a force of arms.

But Adams and the other radicals did want a *show* of arms. Word was spread around town directing freeholders and residents to bring their hunting muskets and arms to the town meeting under the pretense that they believed war with France appeared imminent, and they were ready to support the mother country. At a somber Boston town meeting on September 13, four hundred muskets, including those stored for the militia, were stacked on the floor of Faneuil Hall. Emotions seemed ready to explode over the expected occupation. Adams and other leaders worked to calm fears rather than inflame the already heated passions. One Bostonian stood to urge an outright massacre of their enemies in self-defense on the grounds that liberty was as precious as life. Another man rose to say it was time to take power into their hands with the elected assembly officially dissolved. Otis exclaimed to the townspeople, "These are the arms. When an attempt is made upon your liberties, they will be delivered."[33]

Adams and the other leaders advised that the legal first step to be taken should be to petition the governor to call the assembly back in session. This was done, and Bernard refused. The following day, the plan for Boston to host its own de facto assembly through a convention of towns was introduced at the town meeting. Boston would invite delegates from sister towns in Massachusetts to formulate a plan to respond to the landing of troops. The proposal was accepted, and invitations were written up and sent out. As many as ninety-six towns pledged to attend the September 22 convention.[34]

Tories complained the Bostonians were going too far, calling the proposed convention of towns the most revolutionary act yet. "Boston," said General Gage, "is mutinous" and "its resolves treasonable and desperate. Mad people procured them; mad people govern the town and influence the province." Bernard declared the convention illegal and threatened legal action against participants if it proceeded.[35]

Soon after the convention opened on September 22, Adams realized that the delegates from the country towns were far less concerned with the pending threat of troops in Boston than the Bostonians. Before committing to a plan, they wanted to wait until the soldiers arrived to see how the situation would unfold. Frustrated that his efforts in other colonies were far more effective than in his own, Adams complained that the public mind was fickle. "I am in fashion and out of fashion," he said in dismay to his twelve-year-old daughter, Hannah.[36]

Yet he could claim a partial success at the convention. The delegates approved an Adams-authored petition to the king protesting the prospect of military occupation.

The ships carrying the British regiments from Halifax, Nova Scotia, arrived on September 28. On the first day of October, the soldiers disembarked. It was an otherwise quiet Sabbath. Under the command of Colonel William Dalrymple, red-clad Irish regiments made an impressive showing, marching to the sound of beating drums, with glistening, fixed bayonets at their sides. Each man carried a cartridge box of sixteen rounds, as if entering enemy country. The troops proceeded in sharp military order down the mile length of Long Wharf leading to the town. This display was joined by the battleship *Hussar* under the command of Captain James Smith, who ordered cannons loaded and springs rigged on cables with orders to fire on any resistance to the troops. Military occupation had formally begun.[37]

"The peaceable demeanor of the people was construed, by the party who had brought this evil on the city, as a mark of abject submission," wrote Mercy Otis Warren, the sister of James Otis. Bernard avoided the scene by traveling to the country. Dalrymple cursed the governor for "his want of spirit."[38]

Adams felt a deep resentment at the sight of the soldiers. He knew he would never be satisfied until America was independent. The British had answered legal petitions with a force of arms. He wrote to the London agent DeBerdt that the colonists would retaliate civilly, not by arms, but through an expanded boycott. Their goal was to prove that military occupation was unjustifiable. "The inhabitants preserve their peace and quietness," he wrote. "However, they are resolved not to pay their money without their own consent, and are more than ever determined to relinquish every article, however dear, that comes from Britain."[39]

Dalrymple's first task was to find quarters for his men. The Bostonians refused to accommodate the soldiers. General Gage arrived from New York soon after the troops landed. With the aid of Bernard, Hutchinson, and the sheriff of Suffolk, he commandeered quarters for soldiers in unoccupied houses in the town. With the assembly dissolved, the state House was converted into a barracks. Judges, magistrates, and members of the council had to attend their duties with the permission of armed sentinels.

Boston became an armed camp, and the public flogging of deserters became frequent at the Common. Within a month of landing, the regiments lost forty soldiers. To the horror of residents, one man was caught, shot, and buried at the Common. The wife of another soldier who had been sentenced to receive a potentially fatal number of lashes had heard that Samuel Adams was a sympathetic soul, although he was the last man who could curry favor from British authorities. Nevertheless, Adams made an appeal on behalf of the woman. To his surprise, the British granted his request to spare the soldier. Adams' daughter, Hannah, later said that the British were apparently trying to placate her father with this pardon.[40]

Adams told British officials that Boston was law-abiding, and there was no need for troops. By late 1768, General Gage reported that the town was pacified. Admiral Hood was less sanguine. He sailed to Boston to remain throughout the winter if needed. In November, he reported to London that Boston was quiet while waiting for a response from the petitions drafted by Samuel Adams. Hood noted a stiff resolve churning below the deceptively tranquil surface. "The spirit of opposition to the Acts of the Parliament of Great Britain is as high as ever," said Hood, "and general throughout the colonies."[41] The legislative council appealed to Gage to testify on the peaceful nature of Boston and to request that the troops be withdrawn. He acknowledged the tranquility but refused to lift the occupation.

Adams' favorite weapon continued to be his pen. In an October 17, 1768 article in the *Boston Gazette* read by colonists in Massachusetts and around America, he delivered a perspective on the British occupation of his city. His aim was to frame the issues and put the British on the defensive. He laid out a strategy of civil protest based on strict adherence to the law, clinging to the moral high ground to keep England "in the wrong."[42]

When the British crossed these boundaries, Adams' writings ensured that colonists were poised and fully informed. In Adams' view, military occupation would destroy the experiment of republican self-government in the colonies by creating a competing government and set of laws. Democracy relied on laws to protect individual rights. Adams quoted Locke: "Where law ends, tyranny begins."[43]

But the military is not a democracy, he continued. "Where military power is introduced, military maxims are propagated and adopted which are inconsistent with, and must soon eradicate, every idea of civil government." The British soldiers patrolling Boston streets were not subject to the city's laws. Their allegiance was to their commanders, not the people. "This may, in time, make them look upon themselves as a body of men different from the rest of the people; and as they, and they only, have the sword in their hands, they may sooner or later begin to look upon themselves as the lords, and not the servants, of the people."[44]

He also warned against rash acts. "It behooves the public, then, to be aware of the danger, and like sober men to avail themselves of the law while it is in their power. It is always safe to adhere to the law, and to keep every man of every denomination and character within its bounds. Not to do this would be in the highest degree imprudent."

The colonists needed to cling to the British constitution and the colonial charter, he argued. "Whenever it becomes a question of prudence, whether we shall make use of legal and constitutional methods to prevent the encroachments of any kind of power, what will it be but to depart from the straight line, to give up the law and the constitution, which is fixed and stable, and is the collected and long-digested sentiment of the whole, and to substitute in its room the opinion of individuals, than which nothing can be more uncertain," then "the safety of the people would probably be at an end."

6

PERSECUTION

His Majesty King George III was increasingly disturbed by reports from Governor Bernard, customs officials, and Admiral Hood that Boston was ripe for rebellion. He believed its defiance could easily spread to other colonies and chose to tighten his grip on North America. In his speech opening Parliament in November 1768, he warned of a "spirit of faction breaking out afresh in some of the colonies." The king warned the ministry to cut the stem of discontent in America: "Boston appears to be in a state of disobedience to all law and government, with circumstances that might manifest a disposition to throw off its dependence on Great Britain."[1]

Yet the king's attitude and the perceptions of English officials were based largely on exaggerated reports, rumors, and suspicions. Adams and the radical leaders had created a strategy of civil disobedience that left the British without an effective way to counter the defiance. In Boston, protesters were not breaking laws. British military leaders had to acknowledge that the city was tranquil even as they forecast rebellion. The British could not force the Americans to buy their products even at musket point. Adams' tactic to unite the colonies through a circular letter was legal, his deft use of boycotts unstoppable.

Yet it was the lawful protests orchestrated by Adams that brought the harshest condemnation from the British. The circular letter, the convention of towns, the boycotts and petitions to the king were viewed as signs of true rebellion, if not actual breaches of law. In Adams' view, these were moderate acts compared to the British response of military occupation and a naval blockade.

British officials were beginning to realize that Adams' strategies had outflanked them. The troops in Boston were having little, if any, intimidating effect and only fanned the spirit of political resentment. Meanwhile, English merchants were protesting loudly over the boycott, many claiming pending bankruptcy. The Townshend Acts were costing more revenue to the treasury than adding to its coffers.

In time, other colonies embraced Adams' circular letter, while Bernard had lost credibility. In public and world opinion, the British appeared more and more on the wrong side of the law. Even George Grenville, the architect of the Stamp Act, admitted that the order sent to the "Massachusetts assembly to rescind a vote under a penalty was illegal and unconstitutional."[2]

In London, the French ambassador, Count Du Chatelet, thought Massachusetts had stated its case firmly and convincingly. He believed coercive measures could only backfire. "Can the ministry reduce the colonies? Of what avail is an army in so vast a country? The Americans have made these reflections, and they will not give way."[3]

The French minister of war, Étienne François Choiseul, agreed that truculent British policies were unwise: "The Americans will not lose out of view their rights and privileges; and, next to fanaticism for religion, the fanaticism for liberty is the most daring in its measures and the most dangerous in its consequences."[4]

Yet British prime minister Lord Frederick North declared, "America must fear you before she can love you. If America is to be the judge, you may tax in no instance, you may regulate in no instance." He opposed repealing the revenue acts until "we see America prostrate at our feet." Lord North agreed with the advice of Bernard and Hutchinson. For Britain to regain the upper hand, the leading agitators and strategists must be "taken off." To the House of Lords, he declared, "The North Americans are a very good set of people, misled by a few wicked, factious and designing men." North urged the House to bring the Boston leaders to London for trial on charges of treason. This meant extending an antiquated law from the reign of Henry VIII to America that allowed charges to be brought against subjects who committed treason abroad.

The body gave its approval, but voices in the House of Commons questioned whether national pride was blurring judgment. "No lawyer will justify [extradition proposals]," said one stunned Member of Parliament. "None but the House of Lords, who think only of their dignity, could have originated them." Edmund Burke, a Member of Parliament, predicted that the strategy would fan growing unrest. "Suppose you do call over two or three of these unfortunate men; what will become of the rest?"[5]

In Boston, Tory leaders urged the ministry to shut down the radical *Boston Gazette,* the favorite vehicle of Adams' opinions. "There must be an abridgment of what are called English liberties," Hutchinson wrote to London. "The misfortune is that seven-eighths of the people read none but this infamous paper."[6]

British leaders drew up a list of radicals they wished to see brought to London for trial. On it were Adams, Otis, and Thomas Cushing, along with the publishers of the *Boston Gazette,* Benjamin Edes and Jonathan Gill, and several members of the Sons of Liberty. But this plan had to be abandoned when the British attorney general and the solicitor general found the charges lacked sufficient evidence of treason.[7]

Their legal reviews scrutinized the actions surrounding the September convention of towns in Boston, which had been portrayed as a conspiracy of treason. Under close legal examination, no acts of sedition could be found. The attorney general commented that the Boston leaders were well versed in crown law and knew exactly how to straddle the legal lines. He saw no treason, but "was sure they had come within a hair's breadth of it."

News of the plans to extradite the radicals reached Boston by early 1769, but came as no surprise; Hutchison's attempts to collect damaging testimony were already known. Adams, undeterred, stepped up his media campaign, furiously writing articles in the *Boston Gazette* and the *Evening Post.* From the solitude of his study, he sought to change the world. His wife would later recall the quiet hours late at night when the only sound to be heard was her husband's quill scratching across the pages of his essays. He often worked into the wee hours, the glow of his lamp visible from the street. Joseph Pierce, a friend of Adams whose business kept him regularly working past midnight, remembered frequent nights when that light still flickered as he passed Adams' home. Pierce was buoyed with the thought that "Sam Adams was hard at work writing against the Tories."[8]

With Benjamin Franklin still in England as a colonial agent and Deputy Postmaster for the colonies, no one understood the power of the press in America better than Adams. It was a critical part of his strategy of civil disobedience. "I esteem the liberty of the press (within its proper limits) as the greatest blessing to the good, and the severest scourge to the licentious; and in no other way will I ever use it," he told readers.[9]

Adams realized that the press was vital in winning political causes. He single-handedly made certain that an observant press kept churning out opinion and news about British policies and what he viewed as transgressions for the world to judge. He also recognized that fear of national embarrassment was the chink in British pride. A gifted polemist, Adams could dismantle British reasoning and portray actions in a way that often made them seem ridiculous.

He leveled his sights at the argument by Tory writers that if the Massachusetts charter did not acknowledge Parliament's right to tax, then the document was flawed and should be changed. If the charter was flawed, then so too was the cherished British Constitution, which also did not grant taxation without representation. Perhaps that should be changed, Adams suggested. He lambasted the argument of virtual representation, drawing into question whether most of Britain was therefore misrepresented and living under absolute rule. Proponents of this line of reasoning, he said, "would fain have us believe, that by far the greater part of the people in Britain are excluded the right of choosing their representatives, and yet are taxed; and therefore that they are taxed without their consent. Had not this doctrine been repeatedly urged, I should have thought the bare mentioning it would have opened the eyes of the people." He asked readers, "What else is it but that saying that the greater part of the people in Britain are slaves?"[10]

Adams' pieces, printed and reprinted in newspapers throughout the colonies, gave readers retorts to every loyalist claim. On March 18, 1769, the third anniversary of the repeal of the Stamp Act, the Sons of Liberty celebrated and Adams spoke to the crowd, summing up the crisis: "Our cities are garrisoned; the peace and order which heretofore dignified our streets are exchanged for the horrid blasphemies and outrages of soldiers;

our trade is obstructed; our vessels and cargoes, the effects of industry, violently seized; and, in a word, every species of injustice that a wicked and debauched ministry could invent is now practiced against the most sober, industrious and loyal people that ever lived in society."[11]

He urged steadfast adherence to the boycott as the only effective, peaceful leverage against the British ministry. As always, he urged the reliance on legal means. But he also hinted for the first time at independence: "I cannot but think that the conduct of Old England towards us may be permitted by divine wisdom and ordained by the unsearchable providence of the almighty, for hastening a period dreadful to Great Britain."

Despite the financial hardships of boycotts, colonists throughout America continued to pledge commitments. In March 1769, Philadelphia merchants finally joined the non-importation campaign. Baltimore merchants followed a few days later. In Virginia, George Washington stepped up in the House of Burgesses on May 7 with a resolution drafted by George Mason in support of Samuel Adams' circular letter and to voice opposition to extradition of Boston agitators for treason trials.

"Our lordly masters in Great Britain," Washington said, "will be satisfied with nothing less than the deprivation of American freedom. Something should be done to maintain the liberty which we have derived from our ancestors. No man should hesitate a moment to use arms in defense of so valuable a blessing. Yet arms should be the last resource."[12]

Virginia governor Lord Botetourt, Norbonne Berkeley, retaliated for the Washington-Mason resolutions by dissolving the House of Burgesses. The next day, its members met at the Raleigh Tavern in Williamsburg to endorse a Virginian non-importation agreement banning importation of all English goods and many European luxury items until the repeal of the Townshend Acts.

The largest colony's commitment to the boycotts encouraged others to even more stringent measures. At an informal, extralegal June convention at Annapolis, Maryland, an agreement was approved to shun British goods along with merchants who carried them. By October, the New Jersey assembly and merchants in Rhode Island both finalized boycott agreements. The North Carolina legislature signed on in November.

On May 13, 1769, faced with complaints by businesses and plummeting trade revenues from the colonial boycotts, Hillsborough and the English Board of Trade sent word to the colonial governors that the Townshend Acts would be repealed except for the duty on tea. That duty would be maintained to preserve the claim that England still affirmed a right to tax America.

These concessions were an endless source of political humiliation for British leaders. Twice in the last three years they had tried to tax the colonies, and twice strategies orchestrated by Samuel Adams had forced their repeal. Lord Hillsborough had to abandon his plans to change the Massachusetts Charter. General Gage was given permission to withdraw the troops from Boston if he so pleased. This was not his pleasure, however.

Governor Bernard was recalled to England in an effort to mend fences—not with Massachusetts merchants but with English ones, among whom his name had become poison. The ministry did not desert him or forget his loyal service; rather, he became the Baron of Nettleham.

In the three years since Adams launched the first boycotts, the efforts by merchants, legislatures, and colonists had shaken the empire. Along the way, Adams had united the disparate colonies along a harmonious theme of individual rights and a collective consciousness ardently fond of liberty.

But Adams believed the British had merely retreated to regroup. Just as the repeal of the Stamp Act came with the telltale Declaratory Act, the gutting of most of the Townshend measures, slated for spring 1770, came with the preservation of the tea tax. Adams feared that the partial victory would encourage merchants to relax the boycott. He urged fortitude until all the revenue acts were cancelled and Britain acknowledged that only colonial legislatures could authorize taxes in America.

Boston merchants met on July 27 and voted unanimously that the partial repeal was not enough. Accepting the duty on tea amounted to an acknowledgment that Britain could tax them. The shopkeepers resolved to order nothing from Great Britain except for absolutely vital items until this last levy was lifted. Residents agreed to shun the stores of merchants violating the boycott, whose names would be published.

Bernard left Boston four days later. He would remain governor for another year while in England, as British leaders thought that the immediate promotion of his replacement, Thomas Hutchinson, would spark protests if declared publicly. For the time being, Hutchinson was named as the acting chief magistrate of the colony.

Unlike the transplanted Bernard, who was born in England and set his sights on the other side of the Atlantic, Hutchinson was a native of Boston and descended from the earliest settlers.

Just weeks after Hutchinson officially took the helm, Otis was involved in a scuffle that permanently damaged his already fragile psyche and accelerated his deteriorating mental condition.

Even before this incident, signs of madness were becoming more pronounced. During a session of the assembly that year of 1769, Brigadier Timothy Ruggles, a staunch Tory, gave a speech that displeased Otis. As Ruggles closed, Otis sprang from his seat and yelled, "Mr. Speaker, the liberty of this country is gone forever, and I'll go after it!"[13] He then stormed out of the House. Some members stared in astonishment; others laughed.

Otis criticized customs officials in the newspapers after they had accused him of treason in letters to London. On September 5, at a café on King Street, Otis was confronted by a band of men that included customs officials. Harsh words led to punches. One customs official hit Otis. Others joined the melee, including military men who wanted to vent their frustration by striking a Whig leader. Otis, lanced in the head with a sword, was seriously wounded. He fell to the floor, blood streaming from his head. More devastating, however, was that his psyche was shattered forever.

"Though the wounds did not prove mortal," Mercy Otis Warren wrote of her brother, "the consequences were tenfold worse than death. The future usefulness of this distinguished friend of his country was destroyed, reason was shaken from its throne, genius obscured, and the great man in ruins lived several years for his friends to weep over, and his country to lament the deprivation of talents admirably adapted to promote the highest interests of society."[14]

She called him "the first martyr to American freedom."

7

THE BOSTON MASSACRE

James Otis remained a widely loved figure, and the attack on him sparked outrage. Royal and Whig leaders urged order, citing previous admonishments by Otis to remain within the law.

For the rest of his life, Otis drifted in and out of sanity, at times appearing quite lucid and in the next moment quite mad. Samuel Adams remained tender and respectful, humoring his friend's outbursts and protecting him from complaints that he should be removed from the leadership.

By the summer of 1770, Otis was forced to withdraw temporarily from public life. Adams pushed through a resolution at the Boston town meeting on May 8 that expressed gratitude for all his contributions.

On the streets and in the markets, the mood continued to be incessantly hostile to the British because of the occupation. The boycott forced many into economic restraint, placing a gloom over townspeople as they passed each other on the streets. Shopkeepers suspiciously eyed one another, watching closely for signs of breaches in the boycott. Townspeople scrutinized suspected informers, who were taunted and mocked even by boys. Merchants cursed the customs agents as spies and traitors. To discourage any disrespect, the commissioners responded with threats of surprise searches of homes and property.

The British soldiers—many young, bored, lonely, homesick, and frustrated with inactivity in a remote post—were often unruly and insulting toward residents, who targeted them for abuse. Commanders shielded the troops from prosecution under local laws, which inspired an attitude among the soldiers that fueled animosity.

Although townspeople did not resort to armed resistance against the military occupation, they kept up a daily barrage of verbal assaults, calling the men "lobster backs," "bloody backs," or cowards. The townspeople knew the soldiers could not fire or retaliate without a direct order from the governor. The uniformed intimidators were powerless. Many of the troops seethed with resentment and harbored feelings of helplessness and despondency, and residents played on the soldiers' anxiety. They claimed that everyone in town carried a pistol or knife concealed within their garments. Inhabitants waited for the signal to launch an all-out attack.[1]

Samuel Adams continued his barrage in the *Boston Gazette,* writing "An Appeal to the World," which criticized the British policy of stationing troops in an effort to discourage peaceful and lawful protests. Adams' critics accused him of escalating the tensions. But he felt he could not remain silent. Britain was singling out Massachusetts as part of a divide–and–conquer strategy in an effort to deprive the colony of help and support from the rest of America. Boston stood alone, in need of outside support, he wrote.[2]

By the end of 1769, incidents and demonstrations protesting the occupation began to grow violent. On October 28, townspeople assaulted a man who was suspected of tipping off customs officials about a shipment of wine smuggled from Rhode Island. The man was tarred, feathered, and carted through the streets for three hours. The angry crowd forced him to carry a large glass lantern to illuminate his humiliating ordeal.

In November, a British captain in the Twenty-ninth Regiment advised his men to kill any civilian who touched them. "If they touch you, run them through the body," he commanded.[3] Adams complained to royal officials that using a bayonet was no different than firing on residents. "Surely," said Adams, "no Provincial magistrate could be found so steeled against the sensations of humanity and justice as wantonly to order troops to fire on an unarmed populace."[4] The captain was indicted for his orders.

To exasperate feelings of ill will, the Massachusetts assembly was forced to remain closed. With its doors shut in the face of an angry populace, other means of protest were more likely to occur. Hutchinson was concerned that opening the assembly on schedule in January 1770 would give Adams the opportunity to round up legislative support to have the troops removed from the city. The lieutenant governor wrote to Lord Hillsborough, asking if the assembly should remain prorogued. "Adams has declared the troops must move to the Castle, and that it must be the first business of the court to remove them out of the town."[5] Hillsborough directed that the assembly should remain shuttered until March and then moved to Cambridge, four miles away.

Meanwhile, British leaders were still trying to find a way to indict Adams and others on charges of treason. "The talk is strong of bringing them over and trying them by impeachment," wrote one British leader to Hutchinson. "Do you write me word of their being seized, and I will send you an account of their being hanged."[6]

In a piece signed "Vindex," or defender, in the *Boston Gazette,* Adams wrote that closing the assembly meant denying self-government. Bernard read a copy of the article in London and passed it on to the ministry. Hutchinson wrote him, "'Vindex' is undoubtedly from Adams. It appears not only by the style, but from his having discovered just the same sentiments in company immediately after the prorogation of the court."[7]

On the cold winter morning of March 2, 1770, two British soldiers asked if they could earn some extra money at John Gray's rope plant. They were insulted by the workers and told to clean the outhouse, and a fight broke out. The soldiers, outnumbered, received a beating. They returned to their barracks and rounded up comrades to avenge their bruises, then returned to the plant and again were beaten by workers. Their humiliation inflamed the rest of the soldiers back at the barracks, who swore to take their frustration out on residents who insulted them.

The cold evening of Monday, March 5, was cloudless. The moon was bright enough to illuminate the thoroughfares, covered with a foot of freshly fallen snow. Throughout the evening small bands of marauding soldiers roved the streets, yelling at townspeople. About 9 P.M., a British officer crossed King Street, and a boy who served as a barber's assistant yelled, "There goes that mean fellow who had not paid my master for dressing his hair!"[8]

A sentry marched up to the boy and struck him. The boy ran away but returned with several friends to taunt the soldier, who lifted his rifle. This attracted the attention of several angry residents, who began to insult the soldier. The boys threw snowballs and ice at him. Fearing for his life, he called for help from soldiers at a nearby barracks. British captain Thomas Preston ordered his men from the Twenty-ninth Regiment out into the streets. About fifty residents soon surrounded the soldiers, who stood in a line in front of the sentry. The soldiers loaded their muskets, and a group of a dozen agitators challenged them to shoot, knowing that they were prohibited from doing so without orders from civil authorities.

In the confusion amid the yelling, shouts and insults, and snowballs and ice, the soldiers fired on the crowd. A second and then a third discharge of arms followed. Three people were killed at the scene, and two others were mortally wounded. Soon church bells rang out, and people poured out into the streets. Regiment drums sounded men to arms.[9]

Hutchinson rushed to the scene and appeared before the crowd from a balcony. He urged townspeople not to give in to passions and to trust that justice would prevail through legal means. He told the British officers to send their troops back to the barracks.

Samuel Adams watched authorities as witnesses were detained and statements were taken of the incident. At 11 o'clock the next morning, he could see sorrow and anger in the faces of residents who gathered at a town meeting called to deal with incident. The snow was still stained with blood. Two men were dying from their wounds. The Reverend Samuel Cooper opened with a prayer for their safety and that peace might be preserved in Boston. Adams helped craft a statement from the town: "The inhabitants and soldiery can no longer live together in safety; nothing can restore peace and prevent further carnage but the immediate removal of the troops."[10]

Adams was chosen as part of a group of fifteen selectmen to deliver the message to Hutchinson and the military leaders. Their demand came with a veiled threat: "The people not only in this town, but in all the neighboring towns, are determined that the troops shall be removed." Hutchinson, unmoved, replied, "An attack on the king's troops would be high treason, and every man concerned would forfeit his life and estate."[11]

Colonel Dalrymple said he would obey any order by civil authorities and offered to move the Twenty-ninth Regiment to Castle William Island. Although Hutchinson wanted to avoid another concession to his fellow colonists, he acquiesced to the conciliatory solution. It was agreed that the regiment would be evacuated, but the Fourteenth Regiment would remain in town and be restrained.

The town meeting was scheduled to reconvene in the afternoon. More than three thousand residents showed up, and the meeting had to be moved to the Old South meetinghouse. Adams was loudly cheered as their champion as he addressed the meeting. He read Hutchinson's statement offering to remove only one regiment and pronounced it unacceptable, calling it a half-measure that failed to lift the complete occupation. Shouts went up, "Both regiments or none."[12]

Adams and a seven-member committee were chosen to meet again with the acting governor and reissue the town's demands. As Adams rose to go to see Hutchinson, townspeople shouted encouragement. They believed he would not back down and looked to him as their undaunted champion. Mercy Otis Warren described Adams as the kind of man who was "too firm to be intimidated, too haughty for condescension, his mind was replete with resources that dissipated fear, and extricated in the greatest emergency."[13]

In a show of imperial power, Hutchinson met Adams and the committee surrounded by a phalanx of the highest officers of the British army and navy stationed in Boston, as well as the twenty-eight-member council. Hutchinson and the civil officials wore high white wigs and scarlet robes. The officers were adorned in full military regalia. But it was Adams who came determined to make knees quiver.

Adams was not intimidated by threats of treason charges. Hutchinson noted the same fearless determination in his penetrating blue eyes that he had displayed a dozen years before when he had threatened the sheriff of Suffolk to prevent the auction of his land. "It is the unanimous opinion of the meeting," Adams said in a forceful tone, "that the reply made to the vote of the inhabitants in the morning is unsatisfactory; nothing less will satisfy than a total and immediate removal of all the troops."[14]

"The troops are not subject to my authority," Hutchinson replied. "I have no power to remove them." Something in Adams' posture, the determination in his eyes, and the unmistakable tenor of his voice, conveyed the gravity of the moment. "If you have power to remove one regiment, you have power to remove both. It is at your peril if you do not," Adams threatened. He raised his arm as if alluding to the thousands of residents gathering outside. Messengers were already notifying the countryside and nearby towns to come to Boston's aid. The coiled energy pulsating within Adams made his hand shake like a live wire.

Adams continued: "The meeting is composed of three thousand people. They are become very impatient. A thousand men are already arrived from the neighborhood, and the country is in general motion. Night is approaching; an immediate answer is expected. Both regiments or none." Adam's eyes bored into Hutchinson's. The colony's chief magistrate recognized it as a unmistakable look of independence. "It was a strong expression," the lieutenant governor remembered, "of that determined spirit which animated all future measures."[15]

According to Adams' account of the moment, Hutchinson, surrounded by uniformed officers, lost his composure. "At the appearance of the determined citizens, peremptorily demanding the redress of grievances, I observed his knees to tremble," Adams recalled. "I saw his face grow pale, and I enjoyed the sight."[16]

Adams waited while Hutchinson, the council, and the military leaders deliberated in private. Hutchinson blamed Dalrymple for conceding during the early meeting with Adams by offering to remove one regiment. Hutchinson could no longer argue that they had no power to remove both regiments. "This was giving up the point," Hutchinson said. The council members were swayed by the sight of thousands of residents protesting the occupation. "They are people of the best characters among us, men of estates, men of religion," said one council member. "They have formed their plan for removing the troops out of town; and it is impossible they should remain in it. The people will come in from the neighboring towns. There will be ten thousand men to effect the removal of the troops, be the consequence what it may."[17]

Dalrymple said that military prudence forced him to withdraw his troops. His regiments, which consisted of about six hundred men, could not withstand ten thousand armed inhabitants. Hutchinson dreaded the thought of facing the town without the protection of troops but was forced to concede. He agreed that both regiments would evacuate Boston as soon as possible and move to the militia barracks at Castle William Island.

Adams and the committee returned to the town meeting and announced that the troops were ordered to leave the town's premises and would be gone within two weeks. Shouts of joy and celebration went up as residents cheered the victory, hailing Adams as a hero. Adams and others, including John Hancock and Dr. Joseph Warren, were appointed to head a civil guard to protect the town and maintain the show of strength that night. A watch was organized that continued for the eleven days the troops needed to pack up and evacuate.

Many in town breathed a sigh of relief, fully realizing that the crisis had come close to sparking a revolution. When news of the withdrawal reached London, the name that ministers whispered in hushed tones of exasperation was "Samuel Adams." Once again Adams had forced the British to retreat, to concede, to change their policy toward America. The plan to send troops was designed to intimidate Adams and the Boston assembly to rescind the circular letter. Yet the circular letter was not rescinded, and other colonies had joined the resistance movement. English merchants were complaining about the boycotts, and most of the Townshend revenue measures were being repealed. To insult injured British pride further, the troops themselves were held hostage on an island in the middle of Boston Harbor. Adams' strategies had produced a stunning political victory. Whenever British prime minister Lord North mentioned the troops stranded on Castle William Island, he referred to them as "Sam Adams' regiments."[18]

Adams' paramount concern in the wake of the event he called a "massacre" was that his adversaries would use the violence to discredit

Boston and the resistance movement. Yet he acted quickly to ensure that Captain Prescott and the soldiers who fired on the crowd would receive a fair trial. He believed it was crucial that Boston be exemplary in its handling of the situation.

Initially Captain Preston and the soldiers were unable to find a lawyer to take up their case. Adams was instrumental in getting some of the best legal talent around. He invited Josiah Quincy to his home to convince him to take the case. John Adams, as an officer of the court, was concerned about the sanctity of the courts and the rule of law and agreed to provide legal defense in a case that could hurt his popularity. "I had no hesitation in answering that council ought to be the very last thing any accused person should want in a free country," John Adams told Preston's representative, "that the bar ought in my opinion to be independent and impartial at all times and in every circumstance."[19]

Samuel Adams and other leaders at the Boston town meeting also agreed to place a local news embargo on reports of the shootings until after the trials. The town did publish a report on the incident for newspapers outside of Boston, including London publications. Some Boston papers obtained and printed the report before the trial.

Samuel Adams hoped that colonists would continue the boycott even after the British repealed most of the Townshend duties in April 1770. Just days after news of the repeal reached American shores, however, shopkeepers in Albany, Providence, and Newport dropped the prohibition on English goods, except for tea, which still carried a duty. The merchants placed orders for imported luxury items: fine lace and ruffles, leather work clothes, manufactured tools, linens and textiles, dinnerware and wine. In July, a poll of New York residents found strong support for dropping the boycott. Philadelphia soon welcomed English goods. Boston merchants felt they had to do the same or risk losing business.

Adams was disappointed, but admitted in a letter written later in the year to Stephen Sayre, an unofficial advocate for Massachusetts in London: "[Merchants] held it much longer than I ever thought they would or could. It was a grand trial which pressed hard upon their private interest."[20] Adams was concerned that the British still did not concede the right to tax America.

Adams thought that the boycott had made the colonies more self-reliant by boosting local ventures. At a town meeting, he remained fiercely opposed to renewing commercial ties with England. "Independent we are, and independent we will be," he declared.[21]

With the repeal of the Townshend taxes and the collapse of the boycott, many Whig leaders wanted to focus on their private lives. Hancock told Adams that he considered resigning his seat in the House and giving up politics because too many people publicly criticized him. Adams urged him to remain steadfast: "You say you have been spoken ill of. What then? Can you think that while you are a good man that all will speak well of you? If you knew the person who has defamed you nothing is more likely than that you would justly value yourself upon that man's censure as being the highest applause."[22]

During a June break from the assembly, Adams decided to take a ride in the country to help him relax. Stress agitated his palsy, and the tremor in his hand often made writing difficult. He invited John Adams to accompany him. As they rode through the winding, dusty roads on a bright, steamy Wednesday afternoon, Samuel confided that he did not worry much about money or where his next meal would come from. He was not concerned about building a large estate or leaving an inheritance for his children. None of that interested him. John shook his head in wonder. "He says he never looked forward in his life, never planned, laid a scheme, or formed a design of laying up anything for himself or others after him. I told him, I could not say that of myself," John recorded in his diary.[23]

Hutchinson was officially appointed governor and refused to call the assembly together as scheduled in spring. Sessions were postponed until summer, and the assembly again was moved out of Boston and reassigned to Cambridge, four miles away. "The further from Boston, the better," Hutchinson wrote to London. "The house will be sour and troublesome enough; but all they can do will be a perfect trifle compared with the trouble the town of Boston gives me." He urged the ministry to continue to target Boston: "Something may and must be done to humble the leaders of the people of the town, and so keep the inhabitants in order."[24]

Adams wanted to know why Hutchinson moved the assembly four miles from Boston. To attend sessions, he would be forced to spend time away from his family and be unable to keep in contact with city residents. He accused the governor of petty harassment. Hutchinson smugly replied that it was not his decision to make; it was "his majesty's pleasure." Hancock, Cushing, and Otis accepted this justification as within the king's right under the charter, and therefore beyond question or appeal. They made arrangements to travel to Cambridge when sessions began. Adams, who did not accept Hutchinson's justification, saw great leeway for abuse if the governor could write off every decision as "his majesty's pleasure." He believed that this allowed for arbitrary rule, despotism that required no rationalization to inhabitants.[25]

As clerk of the House, Adams demanded to see the order from the king or the British secretary to America. Hutchinson refused, saying disclosure was forbidden. Adams explained his dilemma in a letter to Sayre: "I must mention to you that the minister [secretary to America] has taken a method which in my opinion has a direct tendency to set up a despotism here, or rather is the thing itself—and that is by sending instructions to the governor to be the rule of his administration and forbiding [sic] him as the governor declares to make them known to us, the design of which may be to prevent his ever being made responsible for any measures he may advise in order to introduce and establish arbitrary power over the colonies."[26]

Writing as clerk for the assembly on August 6, 1770, Adams stated flatly, "This House has great reason to doubt, whether it is, or ever was his majesty's pleasure." But even King George III was not entitled to authority over the legislature in Adams' view. He demanded separation between government branches, and quoted John Locke: "Between an executive power in being with such a prerogative, and a legislature that depends upon his will for their convening, there can be no judge on earth." Adams saw no room for compromise: "We shall never except to the proper use of the prerogative: We hold it sacred as the liberty of the subject. But every abuse of it will always be excepted to, so long as the love of liberty, or any public virtue remains."[27]

His address was published in newspapers in America and London. He also wrote a series of articles under the name of "A Chatterer" in the *Boston Gazette,* detailing the dangers of blind obedience to sealed orders from the king. He pointed out that the king could not concern himself with all the political needs in a colony three thousand miles away, and scoffed at the notion that King George III was dictating Hutchinson's acts.

Hutchinson passed on the articles in the *Boston Gazette* to the ministry, writing in comment: "I doubt whether there is a greater incendiary than he in the king's dominions."[28]

While Adams wanted spotless legal standards to mark the trial, he fully believed the soldiers were to blame. He was disturbed when Captain Preston admitted that his affidavit had been altered from his original testimony. He questioned why the soldiers went to the scene with armed muskets, a claim Preston denied. Or why their guns were loaded to fire if they lacked the requisite order from civil magistrates and never sought one. Most of all, he questioned why they fired on an unarmed populace.

Adams also began a letter campaign to the new London agent for Boston—Benjamin Franklin. After Dennys DeBerdt's death earlier that year, Adams had initially opposed employing Franklin as the advocate for the colony. Franklin had been appointed deputy stamp master for America by the British ministry. His son, William Franklin, was the royally chosen governor of New Jersey. Furthermore, Franklin was not warm to the idea of independence and advised the British to populate the interior regions of North America to offset the power of radicals such as Adams. Yet Franklin proved an able lobbyist in his examination over the Stamp Act controversy. And no American was more famous or widely esteemed in the world than the venerated scientist, who was also the agent for Pennsylvania. The rest of the Massachusetts assembly wanted him, despite Adams' reservations.

Adams wrote to Franklin on July 13: "It affords very great satisfaction to the town of Boston to find that the narrative of the horrid massacre perpetrated here on the fifth of March last which was transmitted to London has had the desired effect; by establishing truth in the minds of honest men, and in some measure preventing the odium being cast on the inhabitants."[29]

Adams expressed suspicions that people or officials in Boston were providing the ministry with false damaging reports. In the wake of the Boston Massacre, Adams told Franklin: "We have observed in the English papers, the most notorious falsehoods published with an apparent design to give the world a prejudice against this town, as the aggressors in the unhappy transaction of the fifth of March."

After months of delay, the trial of Captain Preston was under way by late October. Samuel Adams was unable to attend because Hutchinson had reconvened the assembly, but moved sessions to Cambridge. John Adams, by all accounts, gave a brilliant summation. For the rest of his life, he would remember fondly the defense of Preston as one of his most selfless acts. "Facts are stubborn things," he told the jury, "and whatever may be our wishes, our inclinations or the dictates of our passions, they cannot alter the state of facts and evidence: nor is the law less stable than the fact."[30] Preston was acquitted on October 30 because of conflicting testimony.

The trial of the eight remaining soldiers began on November 27. During the trial of two of the British soldiers, Samuel Adams attended proceedings daily and took copious notes. All but two were acquitted of all charges in December. Hugh Montgomery and Matthew Killroy were convicted of manslaughter and sentenced to branding, which Suffolk County sheriff Greenleaf performed on their right thumbs. Preston sailed for England and was awarded £200 by the government for his troubles relating to the shooting.

Once the trial and decisions were over, Adams began a media campaign to absolve the town. In the *Boston Gazette* under his familiar pen name "Vindex," he wrote on December 10: "Whatever may be the sentiments of men of the coolest minds abroad, concerning the issue of this trial, we are not to doubt, but the court, the jury, the witnesses and the council on both sides have conscientiously acquitted themselves: To be sure, no one in his senses will venture to affirm the contrary."[31]

He was unhappy with the verdict, however. He believed that evidence had been suppressed, and he retried the case in the press with a series of articles. From December 10 until January 28, 1771, as Vindex, he wrote a piece each week in the *Boston Gazette* specifying minute details.

He maintained that Boston was not to blame for the incident and tried to refute claims that the town was unsafe and unruly.

Adams argued that the soldiers were not in mortal danger from snowballs and reviewed the truculent mood of the servicemen since the fight at the rope factory. The blame lay with British policy toward the town, he wrote: "Let me observe, how fatal are the effects, the danger of which I long ago mentioned, of posting a standing army among a free people!"[32]

8

STANDING ALONE

Adams grew concerned about the political lethargy in Massachusetts. A period of calm pervaded America as many colonists felt that the British had left them with little to complain about. Many leaders who had previously written protests over British tax measures wanted to restore harmony with England. Hancock remained aloof and uninterested in politics. John Adams, following the Massacre trials, retired from politics, vowing to spend his days as a yeoman farmer and lawyer on his Braintree farm. He wrote in his diary, "I shall be no more perplexed, in this manner. I shall have no journeys to make to Cambridge—no general court to attend—but shall divide my time between Boston and Braintree, between law and husbandry. Farewell, politics."[1]

Yet Adams believed colonists needed to continue their opposition to British authority. He wrote in a letter to Arthur Lee in London: "Affairs of America were in a more dangerous state; such is the indolence of men in general, or their inattention to the real importance of things, that a steady and animated perseverance in the rugged path of virtue at the hazard of trifles is hardly to be expected."[2]

His fears were not unfounded. Although British troops were ordered off the streets of Boston, the British ministry still could still control the harbor. Admiral Hood directed all British ships in North America to headquarter in the bay. By August 1771, a fleet of 12 warships with a total of 260 guns sailed into firing range of the town, commanded by Admiral Montagu. Nine months had passed since the ordeal of the

Boston Massacre trials ended. Bostonians were too worn out to protest. Battleships in the harbor no longer caused excitement. Hutchinson reported to London of "a disposition in all the colonies to let the controversy with the kingdom subside." He noted that "Hancock and most of the party are quiet; and all of them, except Adams, abate of their virulence."[3]

Adams feared that his goal of an independent America had lost momentum and could even die completely. He stayed awake at night trying to think of a way to reignite colonists with fervor for their rights, their self-governing institutions. The problem that he continually faced in trying to unite the colonies was the power colonial governors exercised in shutting down the legislatures. With each previous crisis, assemblies were closed and communication between popular leaders in each colony came to a halt. What if, he asked himself, these same leaders set up committees to exchange letters and information, to coordinate resistance, even when their representatives were barred from holding sessions? Royal authority would be powerless to stop them. Excited, he wrote the outline of the plan in a letter to Arthur Lee in September 1771: "In every colony societies should be formed out of the most respectable inhabitants, similar to that of the [English society of Bill of Rights], who should once in the year meet by their deputies, and correspond with such a society in London, would it not effectually promote such an union? And if conducted with a proper spirit, would it not afford reason for the enemies of our common liberty, however great, to tremble. This is a sudden thought and drops undigested from my pen. It would be an arduous task to awaken a sufficient number of colonies to so grand an undertaking. Nothing, however, should be despaired of."[4]

He dreamed of creating "committees of correspondence" in towns and villages and hamlets throughout America. Yet given the current apathy among Whig leaders, he wondered if the plan would fail. To persuade colonists of its dire necessity, he would need to launch a one-man media blitz to convince readers that Britain continued to pose a threat and that ultimately their safety rested in an independent America. As he outlined his thoughts, he began to believe that the political crises over the past six years lacked context for many colonists. The news they received on the Stamp Act, the Declaratory Act, the Townshend measures along with the various disputes with royal governors, and the military occupations of Boston and New York came to their attention in bits and pieces, with no overall context and theme. He needed to put the scattered pieces of the story together and demonstrate a pattern of British abuse and colonial success in preserving their rights.

He published the first of a series of articles in the *Boston Gazette* in September under the name "Candidus." He told readers that he would review what he called "the cause of American freedom." His underlying theme was the story of an emerging nation. He began by detailing the significance of the Stamp Act. After praising Patrick Henry's Virginia Resolutions of 1765, which opposed the tax, he recalled the role of the Stamp Act congress held in New York to unite the colonies in their grievances and he reminded readers that Britain retaliated with the Declaratory Act. "We cannot have forgotten, that at the very time when the Stamp Act was repealed, another was made in which the Parliament of Great Britain declared that they had right and authority to make any laws whatever binding on his majesty's subjects in America. How far this declaration can be consistent with the freedom of his majesty's subjects in America, let any one judge who pleases."[5]

Adams explained the history of the controversy over the circular letter (without crediting himself for the idea), reminding his audience that the British closed colonial legislatures that approved of the letter. In a series of articles, most more than 3,500 words, he explained the fundamentals of self-government, theories on natural rights and law, the separation of powers. He quoted the Magna Carta and William Blackstone's *Commentaries of the Laws of England,* explained John Locke, Montesquieu, and David Hume. After comparing the situation in America to that of Ireland, he wrote in opposition to an episcopate in America. Adams provided a historical analysis of slavery and how leaders tended to subjugate free people, comparing America with Rome. "Could millions be enslaved, if all possessed the independent spirit of Brutus, who, to his immortal honor, expelled the tyrant of Rome and his royal and rebellious race," he wrote. "The liberties of our country are worth defending at all hazards. If we should suffer them to be wrested from us, millions yet unborn may be the miserable sharers in the event. Every step has been taken but one; and the last appeal would require prudence, unanimity and fortitude. America must herself, under God, work out her own salvation."[6]

He produced these essays at a torrid pace, while balancing his writing duties in the House and keeping up his correspondence with writers in America and London. Nothing like his essays had ever appeared in America. By telling a distinctly American story about what he called the "American cause of freedom," he wanted to foster a national identity in the minds of colonists. In instilling pride in this struggle, he stoked patriotic feelings not toward Britain but toward America. The words "free" and "freedom" pervaded every one of his articles. He told readers that Americans "of all the people on the earth, [we] deserve most to be free."[7]

Adams' articles were reprinted throughout the colonies. Both supporters and enemies agreed the effect was remarkable. They were talked about in churches and meeting halls, and in taverns and dinner tables. Colonists without much formal education were suddenly quoting Locke, Montesquieu, and Voltaire. They began talking about their "natural rights," against what they now saw as a pattern of civil rights violations by Parliament and royal officials.

Hutchinson acknowledged the effect that Adams' words were having on the populace and employed a bevy of writers to counteract Adams' influence. The governor wrote to London: "Adams is the writer in the incendiary newspaper, and, I have no doubt, wishes to see the continent strike off their dependence upon Great Britain, and would push the colonies into a rebellion tomorrow, if it was in his power."[8] The governor called Adams' skill as a writer a "black art" and said that "long practice caused him to arrive at great perfection, and to acquire a talent of artfully and fallaciously insinuating into the minds of his readers a prejudice against the character of all whom he attacked, beyond any other man I ever knew."[9] In England, former governor Bernard seethed at the articles. A friend of the former governor commented, "Bernard used to damn that Adams. Every dip of his pen stung like a horned snake."[10]

The Whig leadership in Boston remained split, however. Hutchinson reported to London: "Hancock and Adams are at great variance," and "Some of my friends blow the coals, and I hope to see a good effect."[11] Hutchinson knew that the wealthy Hancock provided much of

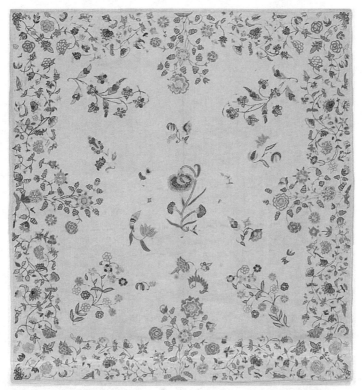

Samuel Adams' christening blanket, early eighteenth century. Photograph ©
Museum of Fine Arts, Boston.

Remick, Christian. "Perspective View of the City of Boston." 1768. Courtesy of the Massachusetts Historical Society.

"The Boston Massacre, 1770." Engraving by Paul Revere, hand-colored by Christian Remick. Photograph © Museum of Fine Arts, Boston.

Portrait of Samuel Adams, oil on canvas by John Singleton Copley, about 1772. Photograph © Museum of Fine Arts, Boston.

Portrait of James Otis, 1855 engraving by W. G. Jackman. Museum of Fine Arts, Boston. Harvey D. Parker Collection. Photograph © Museum of Fine Arts, Boston.

Portrait of John Adams, oil on canvas by John Singleton Copley, after 1783. Photograph © Museum of Fine Arts, Boston.

Portrait of Mercy Otis Warren, oil on canvas by John Singleton Copley, about 1763. Photograph ©
Museum of Fine Arts, Boston.

Portrait of John Hancock, oil on canvas by John Singleton Copley, 1765. Photograph © Museum of Fine Arts, Boston.

Portrait of Samuel Adams, circa 1794. Courtesy of the Emmet Collection, Miriam and Ira D. Wallach Division of Art, Prints and Photographs, The New York Public Library, Astor, Lenox, and Tilden Foundations.

the funding for the Whigs; his desertion could leave them unable to continue their protests. The governor took note of Otis' deteriorating mental health. "Otis was carried off today in a post-chaise, bound hand and
foot. He has been as good as his word—set the province in a flame, and
perished in the attempt."[12]

Samuel Adams tried to recruit his cousin John back into Boston politics. On the second anniversary of the Boston Massacre, he asked John
to say a few words. John declined, saying that his health was poor and
"rendered me quite willing to devote myself forever to private life. That,
far from taking any part in public, I was desirous to avoid even thinking
upon public affairs—and that I was determined to pursue that course,
and therefore that I must beg to be excused."[13]

Despite Hutchinson's efforts to woo him, Hancock reached out to
Adams to renew their friendship in the summer of 1772, hiring the celebrated painter John Singleton Copley to render portraits of both himself and Adams. At the time, Copley was sympathetic to the colonial
cause and greatly admired Adams. He chose to portray him at the cli-
mactic moment when Adams stood defiantly before the crown officials
and military officers the day after the Boston Massacre to demand the
end of military occupation. In Copley's portrait, Adams is shown in his
favorite red suit. It is the portrait of a middle-aged man softening
around the edges, his locks gray. But his blue eyes display the glare of
independence that Hutchinson had noticed that day. Adams stands
erect and fearless. One hand points a finger to Massachusetts' charter
and the other grips the instructions of the three thousand inhabitants
waiting for a response to their demands to remove the troops. The story
was the high point in the Adams legend at that time, a moment in
which he won the adoration of thousands and cemented his standing as
a popular hero.

By the autumn of 1772, Adams felt it was time to launch his plan
for the committees of correspondence. He had spent more than a year
laying the groundwork through newspaper articles and letters to like-
minded men, such as Richard Henry Lee in Virginia. Writing on October 5 under the name "Valerius Poplicola," or "friend of the people," he
reviewed colonial complaints and asked: "Is it not high time for the people of this country explicitly to declare whether they will be freemen or

slaves? It is an important question, which ought to be decided. It concerns us more than anything in this life."[14]

Thomas Cushing, the speaker of the House, doubted that the mood and timing were right for a call for committees of correspondence, as did Hancock and several Boston assembly members. They wanted to avoid any false steps. Cushing believed that America "must wait to grow more powerful."[15] Adams, who wanted to unveil his plan at an October town meeting billed to discuss the appointments of royal judges paid by the crown, launched a petition drive over the salary issue and collected 198 signatures. The event was poorly attended, and Adams, who knew his plan would lack credibility without the backing of a sufficient number of townspeople, adjourned the meeting on Wednesday, October 28. "There was a respectable appearance of the inhabitants," Adams wrote, "though not so full as has sometimes been on occasions of much less importance."[16]

Adams felt that the moment he had worked so hard for was slipping away. Knowing that a second chance might never appear again, Adams drafted a seemingly harmless inquiry asking Hutchinson if he planned to cancel the upcoming session of the House and requesting that it convene as scheduled on December 2. The statement was introduced at the October 28 Boston town meeting, approved by freeholders, and sent to the governor. Adams suspected that Hutchinson would likely respond in terms meant to impress London and the king. And indeed, Hutchinson answered that the decision to reconvene the assembly was the king's prerogative, which could not be influenced by petitions from any town meeting. Granting their request would only encourage pleas from other towns. Adams must have smiled when he read Hutchinson's reply. The governor was explicitly denying the right of the town meeting to make requests, thus rendering it powerless. Hutchinson was, in effect, proclaiming that the king turned a deaf ear to his subjects in Massachusetts. This, Adams knew, was more than the townspeople could abide.

Adams showed the reply to others, saying that the governor and king thought of them as slaves and expected them to abide all their decisions in silence. Anger replaced apathy at the Monday, November 2 town meeting attended by a large crowd, determined to make their voices heard. The body immediately passed a resolution that "they have ever had, and ought to have, a right to petition the king or his representative for a redress of such grievances as they feel, or for preventing of such as they have reason to apprehend, and to communicate their sentiments to other towns."[17] The town meeting record shows: "It was then moved by Mr. Samuel Adams, that a committee of correspondence be appointed, to consist of twenty-one persons, to state the rights of the colonists and of this Province in particular, as men and Christians and as subjects; and to communicate and publish the same to the several towns and to the world."[18] The debate over the proposal lasted until about ten o'clock that night. In the end, it passed unanimously.

Finding twenty-one men to fill the committee of correspondence took some prodding. Three of the four Boston assemblymen declined to serve, including Hancock and Cushing, who both cited pressing responsibilities. Two of the town's selectmen also found similar reasons to turn down the assignment. But twenty-one townspeople did step forward. James Otis was named chairman, an honorary title given his condition.

Hutchinson believed Adams' efforts would end in a humiliating failure. "Their scheme of keeping up a correspondence through the province," he wrote in a letter for the king's eyes, "is such a foolish one that it must necessarily make them ridiculous." Taking a swipe at Otis, he wrote to Bernard in London, "You may judge of this committee by their chairman, who is but just now discharged from his guardian, and is still once in a few days as mad as ever—the effect of strong drink."[19]

Adams called Boston's committee together on Tuesday, November 3. They agreed to keep their proceedings secret, except for information they all agreed to release. Adams believed the call to form committees should begin with towns in Massachusetts. They decided to issue a three-part statement, detailing their rights, British abuses of those rights, and the suggestion that other towns form committees and join the network. Drs. Joseph Warren and Benjamin Church volunteered to help write the statement. Adams wrote the section detailing their rights under the British constitution and the Massachusetts charter and as Christians. He expressly denied that Parliament had any authority in America. Warren produced a litany of British abuses that included taxation without consent, the closing of the assembly, the corruption of judges through

English salaries, military occupation, and courts of admiralty, among others.

Adams introduced the full statement at a packed town meeting on November 20 at Faneuil Hall. It was the last public meeting of Otis' distinguished career. His nerves were nearly uncontrollable and his mind wandered. The permanent gash in the skin of his head from the fight with British soldiers was big enough for a man to put his finger in. Otis sometimes joked that his friends thought he had a crack in his skull as well. Samuel Adams wanted his friend to exit the public stage in dignity, as part of the movement to foster American unity and in defense of the rights he had fought for for so long. Adams told those gathered at the meeting that Otis, as chair of the committee of correspondence, wanted their support in approving the statement. He gave his old friend credit for helping draft it, which seemed proof that Otis could still summon up his powerful intellect. Their work was published in a pamphlet by Benjamin Franklin in London and disseminated throughout America with Otis' name attached to it. John Adams later said the work contained all the ideas that eventually were expressed in the Declaration of Independence.[20]

Hutchinson viewed the report as a declaration of American sovereignty. He wrote to London: "[T]he grand incendiary of the province prepared a long report for a committee appointed by the town, in which, after many principles inferring independence were laid down, many resolves followed, all of them tending to sedition and mutiny, and some of them expressly denying Parliamentary authority."[21]

Adams hoped the invitation to other towns would spark debate over the issues with even greater success than the call to join the Stamp Act congress and his circular letter. Across the land, town meetings would be held to discuss committees of correspondence and consider Adams' statement spelling out their rights, followed by Warren's list of grievances with the British. He saw a potential to galvanize America like never before. Unlike the previous circular letter, the committee network would form a permanent framework for countless circular letters in the future.

Within days of receiving the invitation in December, the residents of Cambridge met and assigned their own committee of correspondence. They expressed "much concern to maintain and secure their own invaluable rights, which were not the gift of kings, but purchased with the precious blood and treasure of their ancestors." The committee from Cambridge wrote that they "discovered a glorious spirit, like men determined to be free."[22]

Suddenly the population was energized and passionate about their political autonomy. Nothing in the past year—event or crisis—could account for the mood shift except Samuel Adams' stream of published articles. A year earlier, many colonists, including Whig leaders, were unmoved by calls to maintain the boycott and demand their right to self-govern. Now they were once again poised to defend their rights.

Roxbury followed Cambridge, saying in words reminiscent of Adams' newspaper essays: "The rights of the colonists fully supported and warranted by the laws of God and nature, the New Testament, and the charter of the province. Our pious forefathers died with the pleasing hope that we their children should live free; let none, as they will answer it another day, disturb their ashes by selling their birthright."[23]

Adams' political opponents accused him of stoking discontent between the colonies and Britain. In January 1773, Tory loyalist Daniel Leonard described the remarkable reception the correspondence plan had received: "This is the foulest, subtlest and most venomous serpent ever issued from the egg of sedition. I saw the small seed when it was implanted; it was a grain of mustard. I have watched the plant until it has become a great tree."[24] Hutchinson wrote the British ministry in dismay over the popularity of the measure. He advised the king to prohibit the town meeting: "Adams brought about eighty towns to declare against the authority of Parliament. But his chief dependence is upon a Boston town meeting, where he originates his measures, which are followed by the rest of the towns, and, of course, are adopted or justified by the assembly."[25]

In early 1773, leaders from Rhode Island wrote Adams for help and advice. The previous June, the British Navy's armed schooner *Gaspee* ran aground in Narragansett Bay off the coast of the colony as it chased a ship transporting smuggled goods. An angry mob led by merchant John Brown rowed out to the trapped *Gaspee* and rescued the crew, then set the ship on fire. In response, Lord Sandwich, head of the British admiralty, vowed to revoke Rhode Island's charter and strip residents of any political rights.

Adams answered their call for help, lamenting "I have long feared that this unhappy contest between Britain and America will end in rivers of blood; should that be the case, America, I think, may wash her hands in innocence." He advised them to form a committee of correspondence immediately and strengthen the ties with the other colonies to garner support.[26]

Adams was jubilant about the response to the network. But he realized that Massachusetts stood in the same situation as Rhode Island: its charter was in danger of being revoked, and his colony might soon be forced to plea for support from other colonies. Would the southern colonies aid a northern one? Jealousies existed between the regions. The South was agricultural, and many plantation owners mistrusted merchants, who dominated Massachusetts. If the idea for a correspondence plan seemed to come from powerful Virginia, the largest colony, the South might be more inclined to pledge support. Adams wrote to Richard Henry Lee with updates on the successful spread of the plan, and Lee agreed to push a similar plan in the Virginia House of Burgesses. The Old Dominion followed Massachusetts' lead on March 12, 1773. The House approved an eleven-member committee, which then issued an invitation to the rest of the colonies to join in a common expression of grievances. Virginia assigned to its committee such rising leaders as Thomas Jefferson, Patrick Henry, and Richard Henry Lee.[27] By July, Rhode Island, Connecticut, New Hampshire, and South Carolina had formed committees as well. Adams and the Boston committee were overwhelmed with letters from more than eighty other towns in Massachusetts that expressed support and cooperation. The Boston committee met in the evening to draft inspirational exhortations to neighboring towns. Adams preached a constant message of unity. To Richard Henry Lee, he lamented that so often news from other colonies came through the intermediary source of English newspapers. "How necessary then is it; that all should be early acquainted with the particular circumstances of each, in order that the wisdom and strength of the whole may be employed upon every proper occasion."[28]

John Adams believed Samuel's committee of correspondence network began to crystallize a national consciousness. He later wrote in his work, *Novanglus:* "When a certain masterly statesman invented a committee of correspondence in Boston, did not every colony, nay every county, city, hundred and town upon the whole continent,—adopt the measure. I had almost said, as if it had been a revelation from above as the happiest means of cementing the union, and acting in concert? What proofs of union have been given since the last? Look over the resolves of the several colonies, and you will see that one understanding governs, one heart animates, the whole body. Assemblies, conventions, congresses, towns, cities and private clubs and circles have been actuated by one great, wise, active and noble spirit, one masterly soul animating one vigorous body."[29]

9

THE FUSE OF A REVOLUTION

In London, upon reading about the rising tide of resistance in America, Benjamin Franklin looked desperately for a way to play peacemaker. He had come to love England and its intoxicating cultural life with the best in art, music, theater, and literature, and where the towering scientific and intellectual community admired him as the scientist who tamed the heavens by inventing the lightning rod.

While many attractions pulled him toward England, he sympathized with the struggles of his homeland and native Boston and believed that the British ministry displayed "certain malice against us."[1] As an agent for Massachusetts and Pennsylvania, he stood at odds with the British leaders.

In the days before Christmas 1772, Thomas Whatley, a British treasury official, handed Franklin a packet of six private letters by Governor Hutchinson, Lieutenant Governor Andrew Oliver, and customs officials. They complained about the radical faction in Boston, pleaded for an end of liberties, and called for troops to subdue the populace. The letters were sent to British leaders, ultimately meant for the king's eyes.

Franklin was astonished as he read the lines written in the hand of the Massachusetts governor and his men. He quickly understood why British leaders thought Boston was controlled by agitators and traitors. Adams had told Franklin that the timing of British measures coincided with political battles with the governor. Hutchinson lived in fear that his reports to England might someday surface. The letters that had been given to Franklin contained several politically explosive passages. To Whately, Hutchison had written: "There must be an abridgment of what are called English liberties."[2]

Franklin felt that the real cause of resentment between Adams and the Boston radicals and England stemmed from Hutchinson's group. If Boston leaders knew the contents of the letters, he believed, blame might be diverted away from Parliament, the ministry, and the king. Responsibility for the contentious Anglo-American relations would fall wholly at the doorstep of the Massachusetts governor. To enlighten the colonists, Franklin secretly sent the letters to Thomas Cushing, Speaker of the Massachusetts House, asking that they remain strictly confidential.

When Adams, Hancock, and the Whig leadership received the packet of letters in early 1773, their greatest suspicions were confirmed. But what could they do? Franklin had asked that the letters be kept confidential and that they not be copied. Yet Adams wondered what use he could make of them if they remained buried. Why did Franklin send them if they could not be made public? Adams weighed his responsibility toward the residents of Boston against Franklin's wishes. Even though the letters provided documented proof that the governor and customs agents wanted to end their liberties and reintroduce military occupation, Adams decided not to disclose them.

Hutchinson, meanwhile, decided to counter the effect of Adams' newspaper articles with an essay that he believed would lay to rest any questions over British rule in America. Although he was not an attorney, Hutchison had spent years on the bench as chief justice, reading law and writing history. In writing his treatise, he sought input from the state's attorney general, Jonathan Sewall, and leading crown barristers. He called the assembly into session in January in the hope that many Bay Colony towns would decide it was unnecessary to form correspondence committees with the House proceedings under way again. Hutchinson referred to the Adams-authored "Rights of Colonists" as "the declarations against the authority of Parliament." His own report, he said, would "make apparent the reasonableness of coercion, and justify it to all the world."[3]

On January 6, Hutchinson addressed the legislature. He argued that the first settlers and succeeding generations did not question the authority of Parliament. Such a stance had surfaced only in the past decade. He rattled off a list of precedents stating, for example, that the charter did not exempt the settlers from the authority of Parliament but merely laid out the rights common to subjects of the British Empire, whether on land or the high seas. Subjects in far outposts or somewhere sailing about the Atlantic were still subject to Parliament, whether they were directly represented or not. He reasoned that the charter was granted to the Massachusetts Bay Colony for the purposes of a financial company and was never intended as a constitution for a colony. Samuel Adams and other radicals erred in failing to consider that it was the settlers who removed themselves from the voting districts in England to come to America. If they returned to Britain, they could enjoy the same rights of representation as those living in the mother country. Nothing had been taken from them that they had not forfeited voluntarily.[4]

Hutchinson concluded by saying that the supremacy of Parliament could not be denied and the so-called grievances of the colonists should be forgotten. Confident that his logic was irrefutable, he challenged Adams and the radical leadership to respond to his arguments. His statement was published in newspapers throughout the colonies and in England, where many felt it would effectively silence complaints from Boston or America. Referring to himself in the third person, Hutchinson proudly wrote to the secretary to America and others in England that "it was the general voice in both houses of the assembly that the principles he had advanced were not to be denied."[5]

Adams drafted the response for the Massachusetts House. He wrote to a friend that he was prepared to "to take the fowler in his own snare."[6] In preparing the work, he wrote to his cousin John, who was still retired from politics, for help: "I am sorry to trouble you at a time when I know you must be much engaged, but to tell you a secret, if there be a lawyer in the House in Major Hawley's [Joseph Hawley, a Whig assemblyman from Northampton] absence, there is no one whom I incline to confide in."[7]

Samuel Adams presented the first of two lengthy papers, which were approved unanimously by ninety-seven votes in the House on January 26, 1773. In them, he agreed with the governor that "indeed, it is difficult, if possible at all, to draw a line of distinction between the universal authority of Parliament over the colonies, and no authority at all."[8] For this very reason, the charter of the colony gave the early settlers the right of self-government. The patent from the king stated that the settlers could pass laws "not repugnant to the laws of England." In Adams' view, this was a clear indication that English and colonial laws were separate and that the local assembly stood outside of Parliament's promulgations. Their mandate directed: "The laws of the colonies should be as much as possible, conformable in the spirit of them, to the principles and fundamental laws of the English constitution, its rights and statutes then in being, and by no means to bind the colonies to a subjection to the supreme authority of the English Parliament." Adams continued with his own list of precedents and showed the same pattern in other colonies. "The several charters conveyed to the grantees, who should settle upon the territories therein granted, all the powers necessary to constitute them free and distinct states."[9]

Hutchinson erroneously maintained that previous generations viewed the colonies in the same light as counties in England, Adams wrote. He quoted King James I, who said, "America was not annexed to the realm, and it was not fitting that Parliament should make laws for those countries." Adams drew a distinction between the colonies and the mother country. "If they are not now annexed to the realm, they are not a part of the kingdom, and consequently not subject to the legislative authority of the kingdom. For no country, by the common law, was subject to the laws or to the Parliament, but the realm of England."[10]

Adams rejected the notion that the settlers gave up the right of self-government by migrating to America and beyond the constituencies in England. "For nothing is more evident than that any people, who are subject to the unlimited power of another, must be in a state of abject slavery." The crux of his message was that the colonies had always been independent and sovereign.

Adams introduced a second rebuttal on March 2. Here he argued that Hutchinson's precedents were drawn from medieval times, and he ridiculed the governor for citing an antiquated form of government: "We trust your excellency does not mean to introduce the feudal system in its perfection." Adams pointed out that changes to the constitution, beginning with the Magna Carta, greatly enlarged the liberties of the people and that arguing past precedents was meaningless.[11]

Adams' dismantling of Hutchinson's logic forced colonial readers loyal to Parliament to rethink their allegiance. His arguments were printed throughout America, debated by neighboring committees of correspondence and legislatures, and discussed daily at workplaces, churches, homes, and meeting places.

From London, the Virginian Arthur Lee wrote Adams: "Your reply to the governor's second speech is certainly unanswerable."[12]

Adams' responses also were printed in England, and the ministry criticized Hutchison for reopening the debate. Ministry leaders thought it presumptuous and inappropriate that a colonial governor should champion Parliament.[13]

Adams still held the letters written by Hutchinson and other royal leaders in Massachusetts that Franklin had passed onto him. The most damaging accusations against Boston were leveled in letters written by Lieutenant Governor Oliver, who recommended changes in the charter and arrest of the "principal incendiaries."[14] Oliver, Hutchinson's brother-in-law, proposed creating a colonial aristocracy that would pack the council with appointed loyalists and offset the power of the democratic assembly, the lower house of the legislature. A letter by the customs official Charles Paxton demanded that two or three regiments be again stationed in the town for the protection of his office.

Adams finally believed that he had little choice but to break Franklin's confidence. Disclosure was critical to the public welfare. He could not justify concealing evidence that the governor and his allies wanted troops to descend on Boston and revoke Massachusetts' charter. In May, he helped draft an appeal to the king to remove Hutchinson, which was to be sent to Franklin in London. The statement explained that the governor's credibility with the people in Massachusetts was destroyed beyond repair.

Adams had kept the letters secret for two months. By late May 1773, he decided they should be read to the assembly. Addressing the body, John Hancock announced the existence of the letters and stated that the contents would be unveiled to delegates within forty-eight hours. Word spread that the governor's true intentions would be unmasked. In a closed session of the House, Adams rose to say that he held letters written in the hand of the governor and other crown officials that were libelous to Massachusetts. He had permission to read them to the assembly, but his source demanded that the letters not be copied. Silence fell as members leaned forward to listen. Adams read each note, emphasizing the explosive words that called for troops and an end to liberty in Boston. Listeners became incensed, shouting for a petition to remove Hutchinson. Others called him a traitor to his hometown. Adams called for a vote condemning the letters as acts detrimental to the colony. Members overwhelmingly approved a statement, by a vote of 101 to 5, that the "design and tendency of them is to subvert the constitution and introduce arbitrary power into the province."[15]

When Hutchinson denied that the letters made these accusations, Adams, as clerk of the House, furnished him with the dates of the letters and challenged him to release copies. Hutchinson refused and quickly dispatched instructions to a friend in London to burn his letters, saying "I have wrote what ought not to be made public."[16]

Finally, on June 2, Samuel Adams told a House committee that since copies of the letters were being distributed abroad among crown officials and others had been leaked in Boston, secrecy was no longer an issue. They were, in effect, part of the public discourse even if they were not publicly available. He recommended that the letters of Hutchinson, Oliver, and the others be printed. The assembly agreed. Before the letters were published, however, Adams and the assembly published their own spin on the letters to make certain that readers would interpret the governor's correspondence in the harshest light. The assembly then approved the petition to London for the removal of Hutchinson, Oliver, and others in a vote of eighty to eleven. Adams wrote to Arthur Lee: "I should think enough appears by these letters to show that the plan for the ruin of American liberty was laid by a few men born and educated amongst us and governed by avarice and a lust of power. Could they be removed from his majesty's service and confidence here, effectual measures might then be taken to restore 'placidam sub libertate quietam [peace under liberty].'"[17]

Hutchinson's political career was crippled. The populace in Massachusetts considered him "odious,"[18] blaming him for all the misery in their struggles with Britain, including the military occupation from 1768 to 1770. His reputation was damaged in England because of the criticism over his failed attempt to convince colonists of the supremacy of Parliament. John Adams expressed the thoughts of many in an article written for a newspaper. He wrote as the ghost of Crispus Attucks, the first victim in the Boston Massacre: "You will hear from us with astonishment. You ought to hear from us with horror. You are chargeable before God and man, with our blood."[19]

Samuel Adams felt it was time to make a call for America to unite. Committees of correspondence were operating throughout the continent. He sat down in his second-floor study and began to consider what steps the colonies should take. Ever since the Stamp Act congress, he had dreamed of an annual convention of colonial leaders that could stand as a united chorus in opposition to Britain. What could such a body be called? A colonial congress? As Adams did not envision them as colonies but as independent states, he settled on a "congress of American states," a term he included in an article prepared for the Boston Gazette.

Writing under the title "Observation" and published on September 27, 1773, Adams laid out his plan: "As I have long contemplated the subject with fixed attention, I beg leave to offer a proposal to my countrymen, namely, that a CONGRESS OF AMERICAN STATES be assembled as soon as possible; draw up a Bill of Rights, and publish it to the world; choose an ambassador to reside at the British Court to act for the united colonies; appoint where the congress shall annually meet, and how it may be summoned upon any extraordinary occasion, what farther steps are necessary to be taken."[20]

With these words, Samuel Adams became the first leader in America to call for the Continental Congress and nationhood. For the first time, he wrote openly that he believed the only security for American freedom lay in the creation of a new nation. In the October 11 issue of the Boston Gazette, he wrote: "But the question will be asked, 'How shall the colonies force their oppressors to proper terms?' This question has been often answered already by our politicians, viz: 'Form an independent state,' 'AN AMERICAN COMMONWEALTH.'"[21]

Adams' articles were reprinted in papers in several colonies, and leaders began to discuss the possibility of a continental congress. As before,

Adams believed that the call for such a body would be more successful if sounded by another colony; leaders elsewhere feared that Adams and Boston wanted to break from England so Massachusetts could lead America. Through the Boston Committee of Correspondence, Adams emphasized the need for a congress to leaders in other New England states, hoping his neighbors would demand a congress of all the colonies.

The articles infuriated Hutchison, who had known since 1765 that Adams wanted to prod the colonies toward independence. He wrote to London, complaining about the Whigs and Adams' leadership: "They have for their head one of the members from Boston, who was the first person that openly, in any public assembly, declared for absolute independence, and who, from a natural obstinacy of temper, and from many years' practice in politics, is, perhaps, as well-qualified to excite the people to any extravagance in theory or practice as any person in America." He wrote that Adams had an almost autocratic hold over Boston and accused Adams of single-handedly preventing harmony in English–American relations. "Whenever there appears a disposition to any conciliatory measures, this person, by his art and skill, prevents any effect; sometimes by exercising his talents in the newspapers."[22]

British leaders were curious about Adams and were surprised to learn that he was not an eminent lawyer or well-off businessman but a nearly penniless former tax collector and failed brewer. Leaders in London proposed bribing Adams with an appointment. Hutchinson wrote Lord Dartmouth that he doubted Adams would accept a royal post; besides, the power of a high office would be dangerous in his hands.

In the early autumn of 1773, Adams' hopes for the establishment of an American congress, however, seemed a remote possibility. What was lacking was a crisis that would trigger such a plan. Then in October, news arrived in Boston of the Tea Act.

In early 1773, the British decided to prop up the financially ailing East India Company, which was teetering on bankruptcy because of the American boycott of tea. The act placed a three-pence duty on each pound of tea but allowed the East India Company to sell leaves directly to America and bypass middlemen wholesalers in England. As a result, the tea could be sold at a discount rate that even smugglers could not match. If colonists bought the dutied tea to save money, it would establish a tax in America and break the leadership of radicals like Samuel Adams. Prime Minister Frederick North stated the challenge bluntly when the Tea Act was signed the previous May: "It is to no purpose the making objections, for the king will have it so. The king means to try the question with the Americans."[23]

On October 21, Adams sat down to write his regular circular letter to be disseminated to other committees across America. In it, he warned about the tea tax: "It is easy to see how aptly this scheme will serve both to destroy the trade of the colonies & increase the revenue. How necessary then is it that each colony should take effectual methods to prevent this measure from having its designed effects."[24]

The British did not realize the effect the committees of correspondence were having in uniting the colonies. Americans were poised to fight the tea tax. Just two years earlier, the boycott of English goods had collapsed and popular leaders sought to placate the British. By late 1773, however, the mood had been completely transformed. Newspapers across the continent railed against the dangers of the Tea Act. Reports filtered from New York and Philadelphia of vigorous efforts there to force consignees, or tea agents, to resign and get the tea shipments cancelled.

But the issue was more complicated in Boston. Hutchinson could not afford another embarrassing capitulation to Adams. His two sons were stockholders in the shipment of tea, and he had the backing of the British navy's North American fleet, which was still headquartered at Boston Harbor. Troops were stationed on William Castle Island. If Boston's tea agents were allowed to land the goods under the protection of the royal governor, the tea tax would have an irreversible foothold.[25]

Adams held conferences in homes and meeting halls to come up with a solution. He met with members of the Sons of Liberty in secrecy. Many of the details of their plans were not recorded and can only be imagined. But late in the evening on Monday, November 1, two men were sent out with a message for the Boston agents of the East India Company.

Tea agent Richard Clarke was awakened at 1 A.M. by a threatening knock at his door. Two men appeared in his courtyard, silhouettes in the moonlight, and left a written demand that the consignees appear at the Liberty Tree on Wednesday and resign their commissions. On Tuesday, notices of the meeting were posted around town with the threat: "Show me the man that dare take this down."[26]

On the day of the Liberty Tree meeting, a large flag was unfurled and hoisted to the top of a tall pole, the town crier called for townspeople to gather, and church bells tolled uninterrupted for an hour before the meeting. Adams, John Hancock, and a crowd of about five hundred impassioned residents waited, but the consignees did not show up.[27] *The Massachusetts Spy*'s Thursday edition printed a letter from Philadelphia that predicted violence if tea were landed at the Pennsylvania port.[28] In other towns, merchants cynically wondered if Boston would prevent the tea from being docked. More tea, mostly smuggled, was channeled through Boston than any other port. It was vital to the town's economy. If Boston failed to turn the tea back, the city's credibility for patriotism would be destroyed, and Adams' leadership would be crippled.[29]

The next day, October 5, Adams oversaw a town meeting to discuss the issue. Some of the tea agents attended, and Adams asked for a vote to determine if the people approved Philadelphia's move to force tea its agents to resign. The resounding answer was yes. The Boston agents at the meeting, however, remained resolute and refused to lay aside their commissions. Adams and a delegation were sent to find those consignees who had not attended the meeting—the governor's sons. Adams found them and demanded that they quit their commissions, but they also refused.

A few days later, John Hancock's ship, the *Hayley*, arrived in Boston Harbor direct from London. Captain James Scott told city leaders that he had refused to carry any of the East India tea, but vessels carrying the tea sailed down the English Channel the same time as his, and four were bound for Boston. The cargo was already on its way somewhere over the Atlantic.[30]

Word that the ships' arrival was imminent spread. That night, angry residents gathered at Richard Clarke's home, pounding on his door while unleashing the unnerving alarm of horns, whistles, and shouts, forcing the family to seek shelter on the second floor. One of Clarke's sons sent a warning shot into the air. This incited the mob to smash windows and throw rocks and debris into the home, injuring family members, before dispersing.[31]

Adams wanted to prevent protests from exploding into violence, but he also realized that time was running out. He needed to know if neighboring towns supported Boston's opposition to the tea tax, and would lend support if the crisis came to open defiance. After inviting members from the committees in Dorchester, Roxbury, Brookline, and Cambridge to meet at the selectmen's chamber in Faneuil Hall in Boston, Adams laid the question before them: "Whether it be the mind of this committee to use their joint influence to prevent the landing and sale of the teas exported from the East India Company?" The unanimous answer was yes.[32]

As townsfolk solemnly gathered for church services on Sunday, November 28, excited cries were heard from the streets. The cargo ship *Dartmouth* had appeared in Boston Harbor, carrying 114 chests of East India tea among its freight. Hearts sank. Under British law, the ships were required to be unloaded and all cargo duties paid within twenty days after the vessel entered the harbor and the captain registered its arrival. That grace period ended December 16. Adams and the town selectmen held a noon meeting that day and launched a fruitless search for the consignees, who had already taken sanctuary at Castle William Island.[33]

On Monday, an overflowing crowd crammed into Faneuil Hall, which could hold thirteen hundred people. When thousands more arrived, the meeting was moved to the Old South meetinghouse, which accommodated the throng of more than six thousand. Adams introduced a resolution that passed unanimously: The tea should be sent back to England without paying the import duty. The consignees who attended the meeting asked for time to prepare their answer. The meeting was adjourned until the evening to give them time to consider resigning with public opinion laid before them. At the second session, the body demanded that the *Dartmouth's* owner, Francis Rotch, refrain from registering the tea with customs and that Captain James Hall not allow any of the merchandise to be unloaded. Twenty-five men were appointed to guard the ship to prevent a clandestine unloading of the tea. The consignees answered that they had no power to send the tea back, but offered to warehouse it and refrain from making sales. Another vote was taken. The unanimous results were the same: the tea should be sent back rather than stored.

On Thursday, December 2, the ship *Eleanor* arrived with more tea and was anchored next to the *Dartmouth*. The *Beaver,* the third tea ship, was spotted off the coast of Boston on Tuesday, December 7.

Hutchinson, meanwhile, sent a command to harbor officials to load guns at the Castle William Island so that no ships could sail out of the harbor unless the captain presented proof that the duties had been paid. Newspapers already reported that tea agents had resigned in New York. Now a letter from Whig leaders in Philadelphia said its agents had resigned. The showdown over the tea would occur in Boston, before the British navy and the troops stationed on William Castle Island.

On Tuesday, December 14, Adams watched as inhabitants from a twenty-mile radius gathered at the Old South meetinghouse to address the crisis. A proposal was supported to order Rotch to make a formal request to custom officials for a clearance to return to England with the tea still aboard. Rotch agreed, and ten men were appointed to accompany him on the errand. At 10 A.M. the following day, Rotch was escorted to the custom house, where the collector and comptroller unequivocally and finally refused his ship a clearance until the tea was unloaded.

Nine days before Christmas in 1773, warships lined Boston Harbor with cannons trained on Griffin's Wharf, their heavy black guns visible from shore. The seamen aboard the towering frigates—the largest in Britain's North American fleet—stood watch with cannon springs and cables rigged, ready to fire, guarding the three cargo vessels laden with 342 chests of Bohea tea sent by the East India Company. The British seamen had orders to fire on any colonists who made a stand to prevent the unloading of the tea.

The grace period ended at midnight, and Adams was running out of options. Seven thousand people gathered in Boston from Charlestown, Cambridge, Brookline, Roxbury, and Dorchester to address the crisis. Captain Rotch informed them that he had applied to the customs collector for a clearance, but the official said he could not avert his duty and grant one until the ship was emptied of the taxable goods. A cry went up demanding that Rotch protest the refusal because of the extraordinary circumstances. The captain agreed to appeal directly to Governor Hutchinson for a permit to sail out of the harbor with the tea and pass the cannons safely. Rotch left to make his way to the governor's office.

The meeting reconvened at 3 P.M., and the immense crowd waited for Rotch's return. The sun had nearly set by 5:45 when the captain appeared, saying that Hutchinson had refused to grant him a permit. Cries went up for "a mob, a mob," but Adams quieted the crowd. Rotch was asked if he would order his ship back to England with the tea aboard. He answered that this was not an option. Did he intend to unload the tea? he was asked. He said he would do so only if forced by authorities. No one doubted that British officials would insist that the cargo be unloaded the next morning.[34]

Now all eyes turned to Samuel Adams, his face illuminated by candlelight. Around him, he could see the expressions of anticipation. If he lifted a finger, he knew the crowd would burst from the meetinghouse and race to destroy the three ships. The fourth vessel had already been wrecked on the rocks on the back of Cape Cod, an incident in which some saw a providential hand. This was the decision Adams had agonized and worked to avert. Life in his hometown would change forever if cathartic passions were heeded. Boston would be turned upside down and subjugated if it defied the British government. Troops would march through the streets again, as in the days before the Boston Massacre. Soldiers would have free license to insult, to plunder, to violate. Martial law would likely be imposed. King George III would surely make an example of Boston. Men whom Adams thought of as patriots would be branded traitors, and traitors would be deemed patriots.

What of his own fate and the future of his family? He would be an outlaw, the leading traitor to the most powerful empire Europe had seen since Rome. He was fifty-one years old, nearly penniless, and would face life as a fugitive if he gave the order to defy the king. As the leader of the radical faction, his life was at stake.

In his own mind, Adams placed blame for the crisis completely on the governor, the customs officials, and the tea agents for refusing any chance to prevent the tea from being returned to London. He felt that both he and the inhabitants were absolved of instigating the conflict. After indefatigable efforts, the people found "all their endeavours for this purpose totally frustrated," he thought. "It cannot therefore be fairly said that the destruction of the property was in their contemplation."[35]

Yet there were only two options: destroy the property and step outside the law, or give up the fight. As night set, it was apparent that no resolutions, no arguments, no negotiations remained to remedy the situation. In the morning, British authorities would demand that the tea be unloaded. The deadline had come. The grace period was over.

Adams looked out at the thousands of questioning faces. He knew he held the fuse of a revolution in his hand. The fate of America and the British Empire lay in his next few words. With resignation, he composed himself and said that they had done all that could be done. "This meeting can do nothing more to save the country," he said. He adjourned the meeting.[36]

When a cry went up "Boston Habor a tea-pot tonight"[37] from a group of about forty men standing in the doorway of the meeting hall, those listening quickly realized that Adams' words were a coded command. A covert plan had been in the works for weeks. The idea had first come up at the November 29 meeting, but for all appearances it had been shelved. The group of men carried blankets and hatchets and were disguised as Mohawk Indians with painted faces. A line of men formed and headed toward Griffin's Wharf and the *Dartmouth,* the *Beaver,* and the *Eleanor.* Soon the posse swelled to eighty men, who headed two by two through the darkness, guided by a bright moon. The weather was unseasonably tranquil.

Three leaders stepped forward at the wharf and divided the men into three detachments, one for each ship. They boarded the vessels quietly. Orders were given to open the hatches, remove all the chests of tea, and toss them into the harbor. The men split the wooden chests with their tomahawks so that they would take on water, saturating the contents. In roughly three hours, all 342 chests of tea were thrown overboard.

Admiral Montagu of the British fleet watched the scene from his warship, unable to act. Firing would destroy the cargo vessels and kill the many innocent spectators who had gathered at the wharf. Montagu decided that it would be a political disaster to board the ships and attack those taking part in the act.

Adams and others knew that they had crossed the Rubicon. Beneath their spirit of excitement lay foreboding. Governor Hutchinson realized that war was now inevitable. The first blow had been struck. He believed his longtime nemesis, Samuel Adams, had orchestrated this defiant act to fully implicate and wed the citizenry to his cause.

"This was the boldest stroke which had yet been struck in America," Hutchinson commented. "The thing was done: there was no way of nullifying it. . . . To engage the people in some desperate measure had long been their plan."[38]

New York threw a tea party of its own the following April. Militias began to form. Arms were collected and stockpiled. "It is certain that ever after this time an opinion was easily instilled, and was continually increasing, that the body of the people had also gone too far to recede, and that an open and general revolt must be the consequence," Hutchinson wrote. "And it was not long before actual preparations were visibly making for it in most parts of the province."[39]

Writing to the town of Plymouth the morning after the tea party, Adams reported, "We inform you in great haste that every chest of tea on board the three ships in this town was destroyed the last evening without the least injury to the vessels or any other property. Our enemies must acknowledge that these people have acted upon pure and upright principle."[40] To Arthur Lee in London, he wrote that the tea party was a proud moment in Boston: "You cannot imagine the height of joy that sparkles in the eyes and animates the countenances as well as the hearts of all we meet on this occasion."[41]

10

PORTENTS OF WAR

Benjamin Franklin was forced to admit that he disclosed the Hutchinson letters in a 1773 Christmas Day article in London's *Public Advertiser* after false accusations led innocent men to duel with pistols to preserve their reputations. In January 1774, Franklin was summoned before the Lords Committee of His Majesty's Privy Council for Plantation Affairs, just days after news reached London that the inhabitants of Boston had thrown the tea into the harbor, destroying it.

Franklin stood before the council, the Adams-authored petition requesting Hutchinson's removal as governor in hand. Alexander Wedderburn, the solicitor general representing Hutchinson, unleashed his pent-up rage over Boston on Franklin. In the name of the king, Wedderburn pounded on a table and vilified Franklin in a dressing down that lasted nearly an hour. After the tirade was over, Franklin turned to Wedderburn and whispered: "I will make your master a little king for this."[1]

In the streets of London and the halls of Westminster, a public cry of exasperation erupted over news of the Boston Tea Party. British leaders believed Boston was controlled by mobs in the throes of rebellion. Courtiers and ministry officials renewed calls to bring Samuel Adams and Boston's radical leadership to London to be tried on charges of treason. General Thomas Gage, the commander of British forces in the American colonies, recommended sending over four regiments of British regulars. Benjamin Franklin was mortified at the news, calling the destruction of tea "an act of violent injustice."[2] He wrote urgently to

Samuel Adams and the town's Whig leaders, pleading with them to repay damages for the lost tea. Sensing the mood in America, Adams dismissed the advice, saying "Franklin might be a great philosopher" but he was a "bungling politician."[3]

Adams believed that condemning the dumping of the tea would be paramount to rescinding the circular letter after neighboring colonies had pledged their support. For Adams, the bold act was a galvanizing moment, not a time to step back. The act signaled that the public was ready for revolution, he believed. Many Americans, both Whigs and Tories, feared war could not be avoided much longer.

Parliament retaliated for the tea party on Thursday, March 31, by passing the Boston Port Bill, which prohibited all commercial shipping in Boston Harbor save a few authorized shipments of food and fuel to keep the residents from starving in economic hard times that were sure to follow. The act put 3,500 men out of work immediately: sailors, ship-yard workers, rope makers, fishermen, mercantile workers, clerks. Any ship entering Boston Harbor would be confiscated by British authorities and become property of the crown. Parliament's act came with an ultimatum: the Port Bill would remain law unless Massachusetts provided restitution for the destruction of the tea. Only then would commercial traffic in the harbor resume.

Adams believed that any strident measures were likely to backfire. He wrote to Arthur Lee in London on April 4: "If the British administration and government do not return to the principles of moderation and equity, the evil which they profess to aim at preventing by their rigorous measures, will the sooner be brought to pass, the THE ENTIRE SEPARATION AND INDEPENDENCE OF THE COLONIES."[4]

Adams thought that Boston had already been tried, condemned, and sentenced without the opportunity to state its case to British leaders. He called together eight committees of correspondence from Massachusetts and representatives from thirteen others from Rhode Island for a meeting at Faneuil Hall. The body vowed to support Boston. The crucial question to Adams, Whig leaders, and the swelling ranks of the unemployed was: Did the other colonies feel sufficient sympathy for their plight, or was sentiment beginning to side with the British?

On May 13, Adams watched troops arrive in Boston. General Gage arrived to replace Hutchinson as governor. Bostonians kept a civil air while coolly assessing him. They were familiar with Gage; he had served as the British commander-in-chief of America since 1763.

Gage seemed confident of his power. He was certain that Boston could not pose any problems for him. The inhabitants seemed subdued. The townspeople hosted an elegant display of entertainment at Faneuil Hall to welcome the general, who was escorted by a company of polished cadets led by John Hancock. Magistrates and principal leaders of the town welcomed him with great deference.

Despite appearances, however, animosity boiled below the surface. Mercy Otis Warren noted, "Though jealousy, disgust and resentment burnt in the bosom of one party, the most unwarrantable designs occupied the thoughts of the other, yet the appearance of politeness and good humor was kept up through the etiquette of the day."[5]

Gage announced that four regiments of British soldiers were on their way to join him and suspended the legislature until June. This suspension prevented Adams from issuing an invitation to other colonies to form a congress or for his own assembly to choose delegates. On the same day as Gage's arrival, Adams sent out letters to all the other colonies, detailing the Port Bill and revealing that military occupation was to follow. He pleaded for help: "The Town of Boston is now suffering the stroke of vengeance in the common cause of America. I hope they will sustain the blow with becoming fortitude; and that the effects of this cruel act, intended to intimidate and subdue the spirits of all America, will by the joint efforts of all be frustrated."[6]

The closure of Boston Harbor could mean windfall profits for other American ports, such as Philadelphia, Charleston, and New York, if they did not support Boston. Adams believed it critical that these other towns join the boycott. In a letter to Philadelphia's committee of correspondence, he warned that Britain was trying to divide and conquer the colonies by making an example of Boston: "The single question then is whether YOU consider Boston as now suffering in the common cause, and sensibly feel and resent the injury and affront offered to her? If you do (and we cannot believe otherwise) may we not from your approbation of our former conduct in defense of American liberty, rely on your

suspending your trade with Great Britain at least, which, it is acknowledged, will be a great, but necessary sacrifice, to the cause of liberty, and
will effectually defeat the design of this act of revenge?"[7]

Boston Whig Paul Revere took to horseback to bring Adams' letters
to the correspondence committees in Connecticut, New York, New Jersey, and Philadelphia, and from Pennsylvania word spread to the southern colonies. Support for Boston was immediate, if somewhat cautious.
Calls for a congress were shouted, in effect simultaneously, given the
method by which news disseminated throughout the colonies. On Tuesday, May 17, the citizens of Providence, Rhode Island, were the first to
officially propose an intercolonial congress to defeat the coercive acts.
Philadelphia followed with the same proposal on May 21, and New York
did the same on Thursday, May 23.[8]

Moderates as well as radicals called for a convention. Many Americans wanted to avoid another boycott and desperately wanted to avert
the looming prospect of war. Concerns that the resistance movement
could lead to independence bolstered support for a congress as a vehicle
to discuss alternatives and redirect the debate.

For its part, Parliament continued to use Boston to demonstrate the
price of continued defiance. Another series of coercive acts was approved
on Friday, May 20. Royal officials in Massachusetts were given shelter
from legal suits in colonial courts. The colony's charter was gutted by
making the upper council appointed rather than elected. Juries were to
be selected by the sheriff instead of the townspeople. Town meetings
could be held only with the written consent of the governor.

Other colonies responded immediately to the plea for support.
When news of the Port Bill reached Virginia, House of Burgesses members Thomas Jefferson, Patrick Henry, Richard Henry Lee, and a few
others launched a continental appeal to Heaven. They asked that each
colony declare June 1, the day the Port Bill was to take effect, as a day of
prayer and fasting in support of Massachusetts. "We were under conviction of the necessity of arousing our people from the lethargy into which
they had fallen, as to passing events," Jefferson wrote.[9]

Virginia appointed deputies to attend the Continental Congress to
be hosted in Philadelphia. Dunmore, the royal governor of the Old Dominion, retaliated by dissolving the House of Burgesses. Its members

gathered the next day at Raleigh Tavern in Williamsburg, vowing to support the Congress and sending letters urging the rest of America to do the same. With its legislature closed, Virginia's committee of correspondence stepped in to provide leadership in its absence.

The Virginians asked the colonies throughout America to declare "a day of fasting, humiliation and prayer, to implore Heaven to avert from us the evils of civil war, to inspire us with firmness in support of our rights, and to turn the hearts of the king and Parliament to moderation and justice," Jefferson wrote.[10]

On Wednesday, June 1, colonists across America prayed to avert the looming crisis. They fasted and met at churches and homes, many bowing on bended knees, contemplating in silence the dire options before them. Colonial liberty appeared to be under heavy assault, and resistance meant military occupation and bloodshed. The options were reduced to two: defy the greatest army in the world or submit to it. Thoughts turned toward Massachusetts and the suffering workers, the idle fisherman, the docked sailors, the empty store shelves, the moored boats, the hungry residents.

Jefferson described the effect of the day of fasting as being "like a shock of electricity, arousing every man, and placing him erect and solidly on his center."[11]

On Thursday, June 2, Parliament bolstered the 1765 Quartering Act, applying it to all of the colonies. British troops would be assigned lodgings in homes, taverns, and unoccupied buildings.

Tories in Massachusetts felt that with Gage stationed in Boston and troops sailing to the rescue, Samuel Adams' hold over the assembly could finally be broken. If Adams and his supporters made any attempt in the legislature to choose congressional delegates, Gage could shut the House down. Failure to appoint delegates to the Continental Congress would be disastrous for Samuel Adams, who was working with leaders in Virginia to leverage support for the event. Adams knew that his adversaries were watching him closely. He and Dr. Joseph Warren arranged for a few select assemblymen to meet in secret and form a strategy to jettison through the assembly a measure to pick congressional delegates.

Adams and other Massachusetts' House members, including John Hancock, Thomas Cushing, Joseph Hawley, Robert Treat Paine, and

Benjamin Greenleaf, created a detailed plan to be carried out like a military assignment. They decided who would be sent as delegates to the Continental Congress and how to raise money for the trip in a way that Gage could not cancel. They were not sure if they had enough votes in the House, however. The secretly canvassed members they believed they could count on to support the Congress.

The House reconvened in June. Members gathered in Salem, silent as to their intentions. Adams was inexplicably absent and rumors flew that he had finally been arrested. The Whigs, who long feared that Adams would one day be placed in irons and sent to England, grew frantic. Finally, after several hours, Adams appeared, to the great relief of Whig members, apologizing that work with the committee of correspondence had detained him.

Adams remained quiet for several days as the House deliberated conciliatory measures in an apparent effort to mend ties with Britain. To all appearances, he seemed defeated and willing to retreat from hard-line positions. This was a ruse. A political machine had been set in motion.

On Friday, June 17, Adams rose as chair of a committee reporting on the state of Massachusetts. He looked over the body of 129 assembly members, then ordered that the doors be shut and locked until urgent business was decided. Tory eyes rose in concern. The doorkeeper was ordered to let no one leave or enter until the present business was adjourned. Then, to the shock of loyalists, Adams quickly laid before the House a series of stunning resolutions, including proposals to designate himself along with Whig House leaders James Bowdoin, Thomas Cushing, John Adams, and Robert Treat Paine as delegates to a continental congress to meet September 1 in Philadelphia.

An uproar exploded. Loyalists tried to storm from the room; others tried to fight the resolutions on a parliamentary front. But Adams and others had carefully chosen lieutenants to carry out the plan with clockwork precision. Every Tory objection had been anticipated, every step had been worked out ahead of time. Adams had orchestrated the proceedings too masterfully to be countered, moving too quickly to be stopped. He was given the key to the door and deposited it in his pocket.

During the debate, one loyalist did manage to escape, racing to Governor Gage with the news that the assembly was appointing members to a national congress. Gage immediately gave orders to shut down the House. The command was dispatched to the assembly hall, but the messenger, Thomas Flucker, was locked out. He ended up reading Gage's orders to a bolted door, where several others Tories who were barred from entering waited.

In the political storm inside the chamber, Tories began to wilt and Adams' series of resolutions was passed by the majority. Since no money could be drawn from the treasury without Gage's approval, each town was assigned a sum to fund expenses for the delegates' journey. Resolves were also passed for the financial relief of Boston and Charleston, situated along Boston Harbor. The House approved an expanded boycott of English goods and pledged support for home manufacturers. After all the proposals were approved, Flucker was admitted into the chamber to shut down the assembly.[12]

Over the summer, legislatures across the continent met to appoint delegates to attend the Congress. By August, all of the colonies had appointed representatives except Georgia. The issues over British rule were being hotly debated in every town, village, and hamlet.

Pamphleteers churned out opinions, including the influential work by Philadelphia attorney James Wilson entitled *Considerations of the Nature and Extent of the Legislative Authority of the British Parliament.* In what became known as the dominion theory, Wilson urged loyalty to the king but not to Parliament. Jefferson echoed this view in his pamphlet *Summary View of the Rights of British America,* as would John Adams in his *Novanglus,* or "New England" letters, later that year and in the spring of 1775.[13]

As popular support for the Congress became bolder and more vocal in Massachusetts, Gage decided that Samuel Adams had to be dealt with. As governor, Gage had the power to arrest Adams, but refrained from doing so because it would almost certainly have ignited a popular uprising. His troops, with only a toehold in Massachusetts, could not withstand an all-out battle with armed inhabitants.

Hutchinson had doubted that Adams' loyalty could be bought, but Gage wanted at least to extend an offer. He sent a Colonel Fenton, who commanded one of the newly arrived regiments, to Adams with a discreet message filled with promises of pecuniary rewards as well as public advancement in exchange for his cooperation. Among the perks, it is believed that Adams was offered a yearly salary of 2,000 guineas and a patent of nobility in the American peerage that England would establish. In making the offer, Fenton gave Adams some frank advice from General Gage. He should not provoke his majesty King George III any further. Adams listened quietly and then replied, "Sir, I trust I have long since made my peace with the king of kings. No personal consideration shall induce me to abandon the righteous cause of my country. Tell Governor Gage it is the advice of Samuel Adams to him no longer to insult the feelings of an exasperated people."[14]

With the House shuttered, Adams and the Boston committee of correspondence sent out invitations for another convention of towns in Suffolk County, Massachusetts to meet in September in Dedham, a small town about ten miles outside of Boston. Adams conceived a radical plan to disable the royal government, which he believed could no longer claim constitutional authority with the Charter gutted. He wanted the Suffolk County Convention to endorse the idea of forming an independent provincial congress to meet in mid-October, the first of its kind in America, with allegiance to the national Continental Congress rather than Britain. For Massachusetts, at least, this amounted to a declaration of independence. As a former tax collector, Adams knew that withholding taxes from royal officials would cripple British authority in Massachusetts. Since Adams would be in Philadelphia attending Congress during the Suffolk Convention, he met with Dr. Joseph Warren, who drafted a series of proposals with Adams' help to introduce at the September event, and formed a plan to send the convention's resolutions on to the Continental Congress. Adams and Warren agreed that the Boston Port Bill, along with the changes to the colonial Charter and Britain's other coercive measures, should be "be rejected as the attempts of a wicked administration to enslave America."

They drew up proposals that Massachusetts' residents should deny the authority of the royal judges, and sheriffs should not be held responsible for failing to carry out the orders of "unconstitutional" courts. Adams and Warren proposed a demand that any appointed member of the Massachusetts council should resign and that residents should arm themselves and form militia companies, with the "utmost diligence to acquaint themselves with the art of war as soon as possible," and fight only if attacked. They proposed that taxes be withheld until a constitutional government could be restored by the proposed provincial congress, and to renew their boycott of trade with Great Britain, Ireland, and the West Indies. Adams and Warren also wanted the convention to endorse an unequivocal statement denouncing vandalism or lawlessness. Warren's draft of the proposal admonished: "We would heartily recommend to all persons of this community, not to engage in any routs, riots, or licentious attacks upon the properties of any person whatsoever, as being subversive of all order and government."[15]

As the sweltering month of August came, Adams began to plan for the trip to Philadelphia, his first-ever extended journey away from his hometown. Many grateful residents believed it was the time to repay his years of service. Neighbors came together to make repairs on his home. They built a barn for him. A collection was taken for the tailor to produce a new set of clothes to replace the favorite red coat he had worn for the Copley portrait. Replete with his new attire, he bade an emotional farewell to his family on August 10: his son and namesake, twenty-three-year-old Samuel, was a Harvard graduate studying medicine with Dr. Warren; Hannah, age eighteen, was a blossoming young woman; his wife, Betsy, retained his affections after nearly a decade of marriage.

He watched them fade into the distance as he rode in a coach with the colony's other delegates. James Bowdoin, who had also been chosen to represent Massachusetts, was forced to withdraw because of his wife's ill health. They left the town amid cheers, escorted by two armed riders and two footmen, passing by five of regiments of curious British soldiers.

All along the three hundred-mile trip, inhabitants came out to meet them, expressing their concern and a willingness to support a boycott. By August 16, they had reached New Haven. Connecticut was sending a steady stream of provisions to Boston, often smuggled under the cover of night, to provide relief. The reception in New Haven was encouraging: town bells rang out, residents stood on doorsteps and waved through windows, children lined the streets and ran alongside their carriage, the town's cannons were fired in salute. To John Adams, it felt as if it were a coronation.[16] Samuel Adams knew that much depended on them as delegates. He could see on the faces expressions of anxiety over a looming war, military rule, economic hardship, and estrangement from the empire. He saw apprehension in many eyes.

They arrived at Trenton on the Delaware by August 29, then ferried across the Delaware River into Pennsylvania and arrived near Burlington, about twenty miles from their destination. There Samuel Adams glimpsed passenger wagons for the first time: these were the horse-drawn buses of the day, elongated to accommodate as many riders and bags as possible.

They made their way to Frankfort, about five miles from Philadelphia. Samuel could see clouds of dust rising in the summer heat. A parade of carriages of congressional delegates eager to introduce themselves came to meet them. For the first time, faces and voices could be matched with names signed to correspondences. The Massachusetts delegates met John and Edward Rutledge and Christopher Gadsden of South Carolina, John Sullivan and Nathaniel Folsom from New Hampshire, as well as many Philadelphia city leaders. John Witherspoon, the great educator, came to welcome them. They also met Charles Thompson of Philadelphia. "This Charles Thompson is the Sam Adams of Philadelphia—the life of the cause of liberty, they say," John Adams noted.[17]

The Massachusetts delegation, dirty, ragged, and exhausted, was escorted into Philadelphia. Feelings of brotherhood ran high as they gathered at a quaint tavern. Some of the brightest legal minds had gathered for the Congress. Thomas McKean of Delaware estimated the body would include fifty-six members, twenty-two of whom were lawyers.[18]

Dr. Benjamin Rush, a Philadelphia physician, pulled Adams and the Massachusetts delegation aside for a private conversation. They withdrew to an empty room where Rush sat down, joined by a few of his colleagues. Rush told them bluntly that not everyone in the Congress welcomed their arrival, despite the air of civility. Their enemies back in Boston had sent reports ahead to warn delegates to be wary of Samuel Adams and the Massachusetts representatives. According to folks in Boston, Samuel was cunning and crafty, but impoverished and completely dependent on his popularity with the vulgar underclasses to maintain a living. Cushing was in the same situation. John Adams and Robert Treat Paine were young lawyers trying to ride a popular wave.

Rush advised them to tread carefully: "You must not utter the word independence, nor give the least hint or insinuation of the idea, either in congress, or in any private conversation. If you do, you are undone; for independence is as unpopular in all the middle and south as the Stamp Act itself. No man dares speak of it."[19]

Samuel Adams had anticipated this. He had worked under the assumption that both he and Massachusetts must take a subordinate role if his dream of independence was to be fulfilled. He also knew delegates supporting reconciliation needed to distance themselves from him to appease London.

Boston Tories had their connections in Philadelphia, but so, too, did he. His writings to other colonial leaders over the years and his many newspaper essays paid off. He found a well of support for beleaguered Boston. He wandered among the delegates, meeting them on Philadelphia's streets, at cafés and dining halls, in Carpenter's Hall, where the Congress convened. He acquainted himself with each of the members, learning their names and faces and shaking their hands. Just as he knew every face on the streets of Boston, he personally made contact with every delegate in Philadelphia. With just a few words, he won over advocates and defused notions about runaway ambitions in Massachusetts. He was careful not to offer opinions.

Joseph Galloway, a Pennsylvania delegate, wrote to Benjamin Franklin's son William Franklin, the loyalist governor of New Jersey: "The Boston commissioners are warm, and I believe wish for a non-importation agreement, and hope that the colonies will advise and justify them in a refusal to pay for the tea until their [grievances] are redressed. They are in their behavior and conversation very modest, and yet they are not so much so as not to throw out hints, which, like straws and feathers, tell us from which point of the compass the wind comes."[20]

Thanks to Adams' relationship with Richard Henry Lee, Virginia stood solidly behind Massachusetts. Thomas Lynch Sr. of South Carolina relayed a story about George Washington to Samuel and John Adams. The day after the House of Burgesses was closed by the governor, Colonel Washington was said to have proclaimed, "I will raise 1,000 men, subsist them at my own expense and march myself at their head for the relief of Boston."[21]

Samuel was determined to place Virginia at the pinnacle of congressional leadership to cement America to Massachusetts' cause. After learning that Peyton Randolph was generally regarded as the most formidable legal mind among Virginia's delegates, he began to orchestrate Randolph's nomination as chairman of the Congress by suggesting to Lynch that if his South Carolina delegation nominated Randolph, Massachusetts would support the motion. Eager to curry favor and forge an alliance with Virginia, South Carolina's delegate quickly agreed. Adams' gesture was also designed to offset fears in South Carolina that New England was intent on leading the Congress. When the sessions convened on September 5 in Carpenter's Hall in Philadelphia, Lynch rose on cue to nominate Randolph as chairman. Massachusetts supported the motion, which then passed unanimously.[22]

Adams knew that many in the Congress mistrusted Massachusetts on religious grounds. Massachusetts Puritans had historically been intolerant of various sects, especially the Anglican Church, which was popular in several southern colonies. Adams had written in opposition to the establishment of an episcopate of the English church in America because it would strengthen British authority. When the Continental Congress opened, Adams directed Thomas Cushing to make a motion that proceedings begin each morning with a prayer. John Jay of New York immediately rose in protest, followed by Edward Rutledge of South Carolina. The colonies were divided into at least five religious denominations: Anglicans in the South; Quakers in Pennsylvania; and Anabaptists, Presbyterians, and Congregationalists throughout. Jay, a religious man, objected that the delegates could not share a common prayer with such a variety of faiths.[23]

Adams drew curious looks as he rose to speak. He knew he had to somehow clarify his views. He declared before the delegates that he was no religious bigot and would bow in prayer with any pious, virtuous supplicant who loved his country. What the other delegates did not know was that he had already sought out a Philadelphia clergyman to nominate as a leader for the prayer. Adams confessed that although a stranger to the city, he had been told by good authority that Jacob Duchè, the assistant rector of the United Parishes of Christ's Church and

St. Peter's in Philadelphia, was a true patriot. Adams proposed that Duchè be appointed to lead the prayers, John Adams seconded the motion, and the body agreed.[24]

Adams' gesture did much to ease divisions within the Congress. Joseph Reed, Philadelphia's leading lawyer, told the Massachusetts representatives that they "never were guilty of a more masterly stroke of policy, than in moving that Mr. Duchè might read prayers. It has had a very good effect."[25]

The next morning, a news express arrived via New Jersey that Boston was under siege. The alarming reports were ambiguous. By some accounts, British soldiers seized the gunpowder in a town near Boston, and six inhabitants were killed in fighting. Claims floated that Boston had been leveled to the ground after being cannonaded an entire night by the British. The delegates were in shock. Samuel Adams' heart sank. He had no news of his wife, his son or daughter, his friends in Boston, his home. The news was too tragic to be true. He prayed that his loved ones were safe.[26]

The church bells that tolled throughout Philadelphia could only heighten his anxiety. Delegates gathered at nine o'clock on the morning of September 7. The Reverend Duchè rose to read several prayers, including a passage from Psalms 35.[27] "Plead my cause, O LORD, with them that strive with me." Duchè recited "Fight against them that fight against me."

More accurate reports followed days later. On September 1, the British had seized an arsenal of weapons stockpiled by the Sons of Liberty and inhabitants at Charleston, across the bay from Boston. Thousands of militiamen rushed to the scene, but no one was wounded. Colonial officers appointed by the Massachusetts Committee of Safety restrained the newly formed legions of minutemen eager to force Gage to surrender the powder. The radical leaders adhered to a strict defensive stance that mandated that no one should fire unless fired upon.

Because of the trouble in Boston, Samuel Adams could not placate the moderates and hold his opinions to himself. He needed to urge a strong response by the Continental Congress. Many delegates were sympathetic; Gage's act erased some of their mistrust toward Adams and the radicals.

On September 9, the convention of towns in Suffolk County, Massachusetts, passed resolutions drawn up earlier by Samuel Adams and Joseph Warren. Paul Revere carried the Suffolk County Resolves from Massachusetts on a dashing ride, covering the three hundred miles to Philadelphia in six days. This gave Samuel Adams a chance to present them before the Continental Congress, which was suddenly poised to act.[28]

On September 17, the Suffolk Resolves were read before the delegates of the Continental Congress with "great applause," according to Adams. Many listeners were moved by the news that General Gage had fortified Boston Neck by placing troops and 28 cannons along the strip. The 120-yard-wide neck was the only way to get supplies into Boston without a boat. Delegates were also outraged that the British had seized the supply of privately-owned gunpowder at the community magazine in Charleston, and had prevented anyone in Boston from removing their powder from their town's magazine.

That same day, the Continental Congress unanimously endorsed the Suffolk Resolves and ordered that they be published in newspapers with a congressional endorsement. The resolutions of the Continental Congress were secret unless otherwise ordered.[29] It was a resounding victory for Adams. Writing to a friend in Boston, he reported the reaction to the resolves in the Continental Congress: "They were read with great applause, and the enclosed resolutions were unanimously passed, which give you a faint idea of the spirit of the congress. I think I may assure you that America will make a point of supporting Boston to the utmost."[30]

On Friday, September 30, the Continental Congress followed the lead of the Suffolk Resolves by halting all American trade with Great Britain, Ireland, and the West Indies, and approved an association on October 18 to enforce the boycott and embargo.[31]

As a result of Adams' strategies, royal government in America began to collapse. Without tax receipts, crown officials had no funds to run civic offices. The shuttered legislatures would never reopen. In a letter to Warren, Samuel Adams said the attitude in the Congress changed after General Gage seized the gunpowder in Charleston: "Heretofore we have been accounted by many, intemperate and rash;

but now we are universally applauded as cool and judicious as well as spirited and brave. This is the character we sustain in congress. There is however a certain degree of jealousy in the minds of some that we aim at total independency not only of the Mother Country but of the colonies, too: and that as we are a hardy and brave people we shall in time over run them all. However groundless this jealousy may be, it ought to be attended to."[32]

The speed with which news traveled between Adams in Philadelphia and the Boston committee—thanks to couriers such as Paul Revere—led Samuel Adams' opponents to cry that he had set up an intelligence network to sustain an air of crisis and foster support for Boston. He knew that it was critical to obtain intelligence faster than the loyalists. Pennsylvania delegate Joseph Galloway believed that Adams controlled not only the Congress but events back in Massachusetts. When the Continental Congress opened in September, two factions emerged, loyalist moderates and radical separatists. Moderates wanted to establish colonial rights and return to harmony with Britain. Galloway wrote in criticism of Adams: "The [radicals] consisted of persons, whose design, from the beginning of their opposition to the Stamp Act, was to throw off all subordination and connection with Great Britain; who meant by every fiction, falsehood and fraud, to delude the people from their due allegiance, to throw the subsisting governments into anarchy, to incite the ignorant and vulgar to arms, and with those arms to establish American Independence."[33]

The moderates were men of principles, Galloway explained, possessing the greatest fortunes. The radicals were "congregational and Presbyterian republicans, or men of bankrupt fortunes, overwhelmed in debt to the British merchants." Galloway noted that "continual expresses were employed between Philadelphia and Boston. These were under the management of Samuel Adams."

Across America, leaders in committees of correspondence were raising militias and taking over the reins of government from royal officials. After watching the mobilization in Virginia, the royal governor John Murray, Earl of Dunmore, reported to London that by the end of 1774, every county was "arming a company of men for the avowed purpose of protecting their committees." He noted that he no longer controlled the government. "There is not a justice of peace in Virginia that acts except as a committee man."[34]

The committees allowed Adams to monitor the activities and mood of the country better than any man in the Continental Congress. To opponents, this intelligence network gave the impression that he was directing events rather than responding to them. Through his correspondence, he received information from across the continent. Many members in the Continental Congress recognized that Samuel Adams and John Adams together formed an unequaled team. John Adams became a champion on the floor; Samuel controlled activity from behind the scenes. He spoke little on the floor, preferring to work in a way that often left no fingerprint on plans he directed. Yet Patrick Henry detected his influence, saying "the good that was to come from these congresses was owing to the work of [Samuel] Adams."[35]

11

REVOLUTION

When Samuel Adams returned home in November 1774, Boston was caught up in a martial frenzy. The Committee of Safety, formed by Adams and the radical leaders, was under the direction of John Hancock, who was coordinating efforts to train militia units. Adams could see new recruits marching along the greens to sharp staccato beats of drums and the shouts of company commanders in daily drills. Colonists were stockpiling weapons and gunpowder in neighboring villages, hiding muskets and balls in barns, woodsheds, concealing flour and provisions in cellars. The very best of the militia had been assigned to special units and dubbed "minutemen," trained to jump into action in sixty seconds. Adams was pleased to learn that his townsmen—the farmers, shipyard workers, merchants, and laborers—were not completely devoid of military skill. Several veterans from the French and Indian war had stepped forward to offer help. Massachusetts hoped to raise a fighting force of twelve thousand by January 1775, and put out a call for other colonies to raise another twenty thousand men to send to Boston.

The inhabitants had also taken over the reins of government as a result of the Adams-Warren Suffolk Resolves. As directed under the resolves, tax collectors withheld monies collected from royal officials. The old general assembly and council, under the authority of General Gage as acting governor, was closed. Towns in Massachusetts had sent delegates to the independent provincial congress that met in Concord in October. This was the first non-royal state government in America. John

Hancock was named as its president. Reports arrived that other colonies were following close behind: committees in each colony were arranging conventions and unveiling plans for state governments.

The air of military fervor emboldened the New England colonies of Maine, New Hampshire, Connecticut, Vermont, and Rhode Island. At Portsmouth, New Hampshire, John Sullivan led a company that captured the local fort and hauled away one hundred barrels of gun powder along with a several cannons. At New Port, Rhode Island, militiamen seized forty-four artillery guns and carted them to Providence. In Connecticut, the assembly called on residents to double the supplies of ammunition and to step up military training and artillery.

In December, a Maryland provincial convention recommended that inhabitants form companies, each of sixty-eight men.

Adams wrote colonial leaders in February that Boston was taking the brunt of "ministerial vengeance" for the colonies: "While America bears them witness that they suffer in HER cause, they glory in their sufferings. Being thus supported by HER liberality, they will never ungratefully betray her rights. Inheriting the spirit of their virtuous ancestors, they will, after their example, endure hardships, and confide in an all-gracious Providence. Having been born to be free, they will never disgrace themselves by a mean submission to the injurious terms of slavery."[1]

Facing deprivation and starvation from the closed port, the city survived through a stream of donations from neighboring towns that were smuggled in at night. Adams coordinated a committee to distribute relief in the form of money or crops. Bushels of rye and Indian corn came from Farmington. Marblehead sent olive oil, money, and barrels of fish. Brookfield sent 8 bushels of rye and 10 bushels of Indian corn. As winter wore on, New York sent more than £1,000 worth of flour. Norfolk and Portsmouth, Virginia, sent a ship carrying 715 bushels of corn, 33 barrels of pork, 58 barrels of bread, and 10 barrels of flour. Henrico County, Virginia, sent 329-½ bushels of wheat, 135 bushels of corn, and 23 barrels of flour.[2]

Adams wrote notes expressing gratitude to each town that sent supplies. To New York, he wrote: "I am directed by the Committee to request that you would assure our benefactors, the citizens of New York, of their warmest gratitude for the very seasonable relief they have af-

forded to their afflicted brethren in this place, by such generous donations, in this most difficult time of the year. While we acknowledge the
superintendency of divine Providence, we feel our obligations to the sister Colonies. By their liberality, they have greatly chagrined the common
enemies of America, who flattered themselves with hopes that before this
day they should starve us into a compliance with the insolent demands
of despotic power."[3]

King George III retaliated by prohibiting New England from trad-
ing with any other country and forbidding the region's fishermen from
casting nets in the North Atlantic. When he learned that provincial conventions had sprouted up in other colonies, the king ordered that ports
and fishing waters also be closed to Maryland, New Jersey, Pennsylvania,
South Carolina, and Virginia.

Defiance was no longer limited to New England, and other colonies
continued to stand by the Bay Colony. When news of Parliament's reaction reached Richmond, Virginia, Continental Congress delegate Patrick
Henry rose defiantly at a provincial convention to proclaim "Give me
liberty, or give me death."[4] By April, all thirteen colonies had approved
the Continental Association, which was created by the national Continental Congress as part of the Suffolk Resolves to enforce the continen
tal boycott and trade embargo on British goods.

Adams believed that the British would soon use military force. He
received a dispatch from friends in Montreal that a British invasion
could be launched from the north through Canada. Adams was advised
to send troops to seize two essential points considered the "keys to
Canada," Ticonderoga and Crown Point on Lake Champlain. Benedict
Arnold, an ambitious militia company leader camped out around
Boston, volunteered for the project along with Ethan Allen, who commanded the "Green Mountain Boys."[5]

With war plans gearing up, the Whigs lived in daily fear that Adams,
Hancock, Dr. Warren, and other provincial leaders would soon be ar-
rested or perhaps shot. Gage held warrants for the arrest of Adams and
Hancock. Adams suspected that as soon as more regiments appeared in
Boston, they would be arrested, chained, and sent to England.

A group of British soldiers hatched a plan to trigger a fight during
the commemoration service marking the fifth anniversary of the Boston

Massacre and assassinate Adams, Hancock, and Warren. In the confusion, they would draw swords and then blood. Hundreds of soldiers—almost a full regiment—agreed to take part in the attempt. One soldier volunteered to carry an egg to the meeting and throw it at anyone who spoke against the king. This would begin the attack.[6]

On March 5, 1775, the day of the service, a group of about three hundred uniformed British soldiers pushed their way into the Old South meetinghouse where thousands of residents were gathered. Adams tried to ease tensions by asking those seated in the front rows to surrender their seats to the soldiers.

"I took care," Adams wrote afterward, "to have them treated with civility, inviting them into convenient seats that they might have no pretence to behave ill, for it is a good maxim in politics as well as war to put and keep the enemy in the wrong."[7]

Dr. Warren, the featured speaker, arrived late, dressed as Cicero, with a fleece-white toga draped over his suit. The large crowd made it impossible for him to enter the hall through the front door, and he was forced to circle the building to find a window to climb though. Warren finally emerged, framed by the window, dragging his flowing toga, to the sound of enthusiastic cheers. A British captain rose from the front row with a menacing look. He held out his hand, cupping five musket balls, for Warren to see. Unfazed, Warren dropped his handkerchief over the extended hand to the laughter of onlookers.

Warren gave a spirited oration. According to a Tory newspaper, his speech "was applauded by the mob, but groaned at by people of understanding." Adams then rose and introduced another speaker to say a few words about the tragic "Boston Massacre." This phrase infuriated the soldiers. A serviceman yelled "fire," causing the crowd to panic. People jumped from windows and pushed through doors in a desperate attempt to reach safety. Adams shouted that the solider would be reported for falsely yelling "fire" in a crowded hall. The officer shouted back and challenged him to fight. The two nearly came to blows before order was restored. Soon the meeting broke up, and the soldiers failed to follow through with their plan.[8]

An English colonel sent Hutchinson, in London, news about the egg plot. A newspaper account reported why the murder attempt failed: "He who was deputed to throw the egg fell in going to the church, dislocated his knee, and broke the egg, by which means the scheme failed."[9] A week after the incident, a band of soldiers broke into Hancock's mansion with the intent of shattering windows and vandalizing the furniture. He demanded they leave. They did so, after responding that his house and stables would soon be theirs.

Adams and Hancock decided to keep their movements secret to avoid arrest or another assassination attempt. They stayed in Lexington, twelve miles north of Boston on the road to Concord, at the home of the Reverend Jonas Clarke. In April, they planned their trip to Philadelphia for the Continental Congress session that began in May and went over details concerning the invasion of Canada.

In London, Lord William Dartmouth, secretary to America, meanwhile grew concerned about reports of the growing ranks of militia in Massachusetts and of stockpiles of munitions. He ordered a preemptive strike, allowing Gage to use whatever force was necessary to disarm the colony. Gage decided it was time to arrest Adams and Hancock. Spies informed him that the men had been spotted in Lexington. Hancock's role in forming and drilling the militiamen put him alongside Adams atop Britain's "most wanted" list. Informers also reported that patriots stockpiled military weapons and ammunition at Concord, eighteen miles northwest of Boston.

The Sons of Liberty and the Committee of Safety arranged watches to monitor the movements of troops stationed in Boston. As a cool spring evening fell on April 18, Dr. Warren, in charge of the Committee of Safety in the absence of Adams and Hancock, noticed that several British troops were absent from their posts. He wandered the winding streets of Boston searching for the men. Most were in their barracks, preparing for a march. Warren immediately sent for Paul Revere, who reached him at 10 P.M. Warren instructed Revere "to go to Lexington, and inform Mr. Samuel Adams and the Hon. John Hancock Esq. that there was a number of soldiers, composed of light troops, and grenadiers, marching to the bottom of the common, where there was a number of boats to receive them; it was supposed that they were going to Lexington by the way of Cambridge River to take them, or go to Concord to destroy the colony stores."[10]

Revere met a friend along the way and set up a signal to be relayed from the bell tower of the North Church. When the troops began to march, his friend would place glowing lanterns in the tower, one if the British marched by land from Boston Neck and two if they rowed across the bay to march from Cambridge.

Although Gage had ordered guards at Boston Neck and elsewhere to prevent anyone from leaving the city, Revere slipped into a boat and pushed from shore five minutes before the order was received. Two friends rowed Revere across the Charles River, where he disembarked near the Charleston battery and obtained a horse. Richard Devens, a Whig patriot, confirmed Warren's suspicions: after sunset, nine armed British soldiers had mounted fresh horses in Charleston and headed in the direction of Concord.

At 11 P.M., Revere spotted two lanterns shining from the North Church. About nine hundred British light infantry and grenadiers were beginning to row to Cambridge. As he raced down the Mystic Road, Revere came upon two mounted British officers, their firearms visible in the moonlight. They tried to corral Revere, but he dashed past them, and they gave up the chase after two hundred yards.

Revere made the twelve-mile ride from Charleston to Lexington to find Adams and Hancock. At 2 A.M., Adams and Hancock watched the minutemen form into ranks at Lexington Common. Roll was called under the direction of the Reverend Clark. Captain John Parker walked up and down the ranks, ordering every man to load with powder and ball. Nevertheless, Adams stressed that the men should refrain from firing first and being responsible for triggering a civil war.[11]

A picket watch was set up, but the British were nowhere in sight. Soon the advance guard of redcoats was spotted. Townspeople urged Adams and Hancock to head for Woburn. As stars shone through the soft blue of the coming day, the first of the redcoats from Major John Pitcairn's division arrived. It was 5 A.M., about half an hour before dawn. Adams and Hancock were hiding in fields "near the scene of the action," Adams later reported in a letter to Samuel Purviance, Jr. of the Cecil County, Maryland committee of correspondence. He had only the clothes on his back. He had planned to return to Boston before leaving for Philadelphia to pack, but this was no longer possible.[12]

About seventy-five minutemen had assembled on a green near the meetinghouse. Alarm guns fired, and the beat of drums quickened heartbeats.

A shot was fired; it is not known from which side. A volley from British muskets followed, and the Americans fired a few harmless shots. Seven locals were killed, and nine more were wounded. These were the first deaths of the American Revolution. The soldiers cheered in jubilation over the easy victory.

The war for American independence had begun on April 19, 1775. Adams had believed all along that negotiations would not garner British concessions and that freedom was America's only security, and freedom seldom came without the shedding of blood. In this cause, he asserted that the British fired first, and the bloodshed fell on their hands. In a rare expression of euphoria over the goal for which he had committed his life, he exclaimed to Hancock, "Oh what a glorious morning this is."[13]

Adams and Hancock hid in Woburn at the home of a minister. From the window, they watched minutemen rush by on the way to battle. A guide took them along a cart path to nearby Billerica, where they remained in hiding, eating cold salted pork and potatoes served on a wooden tray.

Adams believed that the battle of Lexington marked the beginning of a new nation. Three months later he wrote in a letter to Boston patriot James Warren: "The battle of Lexington will be famed in the history of this country."

Adams and Hancock stayed in the vicinity of Lexington and Woburn for another few days before leaving for the Continental Congress in Philadelphia. On April 24, they arrived in Worcester and waited five days for the arrival of fellow delegates John Adams, Thomas Cushing, and Robert Treat Paine. Together they proceeded from Massachusetts, accompanied by an armed escort. In New Haven, Adams and Hancock met in secret with Connecticut governor John Trumbull and his council to help plan the invasion of Canada and an attack on Fort Ticonderoga.[14]

By May 6, Adams and the Massachusetts and Connecticut delegates reached New York, where they were greeted with great fanfare from charged-up citizens. Many carried weapons and pledged to defend

American rights by arms. City leaders turned out, riding in carriages and mounted on horses, providing a parade escort into New York. Thousands of residents lined the roads, waving and cheering, in a turnout never before seen in the city. Church bells rang in a glorious chorus. In a letter to his wife, Betsy, Adams detailed the reception: "The City of New York did great honor to the delegates of this province and Connecticut by raising their militia to escort them into the city, and we have each of us two sentinels at our respective lodgings. We intend to proceed tomorrow for Philadelphia. My great concern is for your health and safety. Pray take the advice of friends with respect to removing farther into the country."[15]

The eruption of the war brought about a change in John Adams, who until recently had supported conciliatory measures and thought it wise to patch things up with Britain. With his homeland now entrenched and blood already shed, he reluctantly agreed that a break with England was inevitable. Benjamin Franklin arrived in Philadelphia, where his hometown supporters voted him to be a delegate to the Continental Congress. He had sailed from England under the threat of being hanged as a traitor for his role in disclosing the Hutchinson correspondences. In a letter to a friend, he penned a characteristic adage: "Make yourself sheep, and the wolves will eat you."[16]

But many in Congress, including John Jay, Philadelphia's John Dickinson, and Thomas Jefferson, wanted to make another appeal to England to prevent a rupture. Dickinson drafted a petition that not only opposed taxation of America but demanded a guarantee of colonial rights and strictly prohibited any changes in provincial charters. Samuel Adams was pleased with Dickinson's statement, pronouncing him a thorough Bostonian.

Although John Hancock wanted to be named commander of the American forces, Adams was concerned over the grasping ambition of his protégé, whose behavior threatened to disrupt the delicate harmony among members. Adams thought it wise that the post should go to a Virginian, George Washington. Adams met with delegates from several colonies and rounded up support to nominate Hancock president of the Continental Congress instead, which would leave his colleague in a prestigious but relatively powerless position.

General Gage offered pardons to any colonists, except Adams and Hancock, who renewed their loyalty to Britain. Both men were riding a wave of popularity due to the recently announced proscription. As Benjamin Harrison welcomed Hancock to the president's chair, he said, "We will show Britain how much we value her proscriptions." On the same day, Ethan Allen and Benedict Arnold captured Fort Ticonderoga and its rich arsenal of military supplies in the attack that Adams and Hancock had helped plan.[17]

Adams closely monitored news of the situation back in Boston. A letter from Dr. Warren explained that the troops involved in the siege of Boston—a hodgepodge of commanders and soldiers from several provinces—lacked cohesion. Coordinating such a splintered force was proving impossible. The Massachusetts provincial Congress requested that the Continental Congress provide some regulation to prevent anarchy. Adams and Dr. Warren both wanted leaders in Philadelphia to adopt the makeshift army and "take the command of the army by appointing Washington as its generalissimo."[18]

Samuel Adams' consistent policy was to push Virginia into the leadership of the American cause, so that the war was not just a regional conflict, but an American one. He held numerous caucuses with Richard Henry Lee and coordinated efforts between Massachusetts and Virginia. Adams also consulted with Washington almost daily for military advice on the situation in Boston.

John Adams rose to argue the need for Congress to adopt the army around Boston. John could see a satisfied expression cross Hancock's face; he believed he was about to be nominated commander-in-chief of the continental army. When John Adams then nominated George Washington, Hancock was astonished. "I never remarked a more sudden and striking change of countenance," John remembered. "Mortification and resentment were expressed as forcibly as his face could exhibit them."[19] Samuel Adams seconded the motion.

Hancock blamed Samuel Adams for orchestrating Washington's appointment to a post he coveted. It caused a severe breach in their relationship. The Continental Congress unanimously approved of Washington's appointment on June 15. A day later, the man from

Mount Vernon left for Boston, where colonial militiamen continued the siege of Gage's hemmed-in troops.[20]

Washington and Samuel Adams were both now symbols of revolution. A piece in the *New England Chronicle* reported that babies were being named after the men:

Appleton—WE hear that Mr. Samuel Hodgdon, within a month past, had a child baptized in Boston, by the Rev. Dr. Mather, by the name of SAMUEL ADAMS; and last Sabbath was baptized, by the Rev. Mr. French, at Andover, a child of Nathanael Appleton, Esq., by the name of George Washington.[21]

Adams was impressed with another delegate from Virginia, who arrived earlier in May for his first session in Congress, thirty-two-year-old Thomas Jefferson. The young Virginian was tall and lanky with a full head of red hair. He seemed shy and reticent as he found his way around. He considered Samuel Adams, then fifty-three years old, and his fellow Virginian Richard Henry Lee as the elder statesmen of the body and himself an underclassman. "Although my high reverence for Samuel Adams was returned by habitual notices from him, which highly flattered me, yet the disparity of age prevented intimate and confidential communications," Jefferson wrote later in a letter to a friend.[22]

Meanwhile, back in Boston, a trio of British generals—John Burgoyne, Sir Henry Clinton, and Sir William Howe—had landed on May 25 with reinforcements. They had come with angling rods, expecting time to fish, but were shocked to find Gage pinned down by amateur minutemen.

On June 16, patriot militia erected a battery near Bunker Hill, on Breed Hill. The next day the British attacked. After being repulsed twice, the British forced the militia to retreat. In what became know as the battle of Bunker Hill, the British could claim victory, but they lost a third of their troops, a total of 1,150 men, compared to 441 casualties for the colonists. Dr. Joseph Warren was among the patriot dead.

News of Warren's death struck Adams hard. "The Death of our truly amiable and worthy friend Dr Warren is greatly afflicting," he wrote in a letter to his wife. "It is our duty to submit to the dispensations of heaven, whose ways are ever gracious, ever just. He fell in the glorious struggle for the public liberty."

Dr. Warren had been Adams' closest political ally in recent years, and perhaps his dearest friend outside of his family. They had written the appeal for the committees of correspondence together, and worked in concert to devise the Suffolk Resolves. Warren had tutored Samuel's son in medicine. Twenty-four-year-old Dr. Samuel Adams had since taken a position at a medical hospital in Massachusetts with the help of Warren, and attended the wounded after the battle of Lexington. He planned to join the army as a battlefield surgeon, a move that must have, in part, been inspired by Warren.

Every report of fighting around Boston left the elder Adams apprehensive about his family. To Betsy, he wrote in the days after the news of Bunker and Breed's hills: "It is painful to me to reflect upon the terror I must suppose you were under on hearing the noise of war so near you. Favor me, my dear, with an account of your apprehensions at that time, under your own hand. I pray God to cover the heads of our countrymen in every day of battle, and ever to protect you from injury in these distracted times."[23]

Adams was buoyed, however, by the courage the colonial army demonstrated at Breed's Hill. "I cannot but be greatly rejoiced at the tried valor of our countrymen, who by all accounts behaved with an intrepidity becoming those who fought for their liberties against the mercenary soldiers of a tyrant."

Although the militia and much of the populace wanted to drive the British into the sea, moderates still desperately wanted to prevent separation with Britain. Adams was impatient with petitions to the king and plans for reconciliation. In Philadelphia, hundreds of miles removed from the fighting, many of the delegates were indifferent to the suffering in Boston. Adams meanwhile was plagued with concerns about his friends. Dr. Warren's death underlined the gravity of the crisis. Information often was difficult to obtain, and rumors abounded. Some of the people Adams had dined with or shared conversations and stories about family, religion, and politics were now driven from their homes to the country, leaving their dwellings to marauders and soldiers. His family and home on Purchase Street, he knew, was a prime target. Others stayed despite the cruelties inflicted by the occupation rather than abandon their homes to looters.

Worrying was more difficult than not knowing. In a letter to his wife, he chided her for not writing more often, wondering if she was sparing him from news of unbearable grief: "If any ill accident has befallen my son or any other person dear to me, I would choose to hear it. Our Boston friends are some of them confined in a garrison, others dispersed. I know not where. Pray, my dear, let me know as much about them as you can." A day later, a letter came to provide some relief. Betsy and his son, Samuel, and daughter, Hannah, had left Boston for nearby Dedham. "It is a great satisfaction to me to be assured from you that your mother & family are out of Boston," he wrote Betsy.[24]

Many in the Continental Congress supported the war but not independence. Some who supported independence said it was too soon: America needed time. With the collapse of royal government in America, each colony not only had to write a constitution, form a government, choose leaders, and reestablish civil authority, but accomplish these feats in the midst of a war and a blockade. For the time being, members of the committees of correspondence across the colonies were the de facto government.

Many in Congress wondered if reconciliation, like discretion, was the better part of valor. Philadelphian John Dickinson was the leading moderate voice in Congress. On July 5, 1775, he introduced, and the Continental Congress approved, an "Olive Branch" petition to the King George III, asking for his majesty to intervene and resolve the differences between the colonists and Parliament. The following day, Congress adopted a statement written by Dickinson and Thomas Jefferson that explicitly rejected independence but stated that war was preferable to slavery.[25]

Jefferson was not eager to embrace independence either. He hoped the crisis would resolve itself so he could continue to lead a life of monastic contemplation at his home at Monticello. In August, Jefferson wrote to John Randolph, a loyalist who decided to migrate to England, that he was "looking with fondness towards a reconciliation with Great Britain."[26]

The Continental Congress recessed in August 1775, and Adams prepared to return to Massachusetts. Before packing for the long journey in the sultry summer heat, he wrote Betsy: "My stay with you must be short, for I suppose the Congress will meet again early in September. I have long ago learned to deny myself many of the sweetest gratifications in life for the sake of my country. This I may venture to say to you, though it might be thought vanity in me to say it to others."[27]

Adams left for Massachusetts, laden with donations from other towns and colonies amounting to several thousand pounds sterling given to help those suffering in Boston. While at home, he visited the troops and was pleasantly surprised. He wrote Elbridge Gerry, a committee man in Marblehead, that the patriot force possessed more fighting skill than previous reports had led him to believe: "Until I visited headquarters at Cambridge, I had never heard of the valor of Prescott on Bunkers Hill, nor the ingenuity of [Henry] Knox and Waters in planning the celebrated works at Roxbury. We were told here that there were none in our camp who understood this business of an engineer, or any thing more than the manual exercise of the gun. This we had from great authority, and for want of more certain intelligence were obliged at least to be silent. There are many military geniuses at present unemployed and overlooked, who I hope, when the army is new modeled, will be sought after and invited into the service of their Country. They must be sought after."[28]

At the end of August, Adams began his return trip to Philadelphia. He was desperately low on money. Massachusetts was unable to pay him salary as secretary for the provincial government or reimburse much of his expenses for his previous trip to the Continental Congress. He borrowed a suit and rode a horse on loan from John Adams. He credited the daily exercise from riding, something he had not done in several years, with controlling his palsy and improving his health.

As Adams rode past the troops stationed in Boston, many cheered and wished him safe passage. He returned to Congress on September 12. While listening to the debates in Philadelphia, his thoughts invariably turned to the men fighting in Massachusetts and Canada. To Betsy, he confided that he placed his own soul on trial and examined his motives, conscious that men often lie even to themselves about their best intentions. His thoughts always led to the same conclusion: his efforts to prod the country toward independence and a break with England were justified and righteous. The fight was absolutely necessary. He wrote: "It is an unspeakable consolation to an actor upon the public stage, when, after the most careful retrospect, he can satisfy himself that he has had in his view no private or selfish considerations, but has ever been [guided] by the pure motive of serving his country, and delivering it from the rapacious hand of a tyrant." He told Betsy that he was prepared to trust in divine providence: "The Affairs of our country are at this moment in the most critical situation. Every wheel seems now to be in motion. I am so fully satisfied in the justice of our cause that I can confidently as well as devoutly pray, that the righteous disposer of all things would succeed our enterprises. If he suffers us to be defeated in any or all of them I shall believe it to be for the most wise and gracious purposes and shall heartily acquiesce in the divine disposal."[29]

Samuel Adams did not believe that he or any person could direct history. Everyone played a role amid forces beyond human control and made choices based on the challenges history gave them. He wrote to Betsy: "Mortals cannot command success."[30]

12

INDEPENDENCE

When news reached America that King George III ignored the colonial petitions, Adams noted that they again were "treated with insolent contempt. I cannot conceive that there is any room to hope from the virtuous efforts of the people of Britain."[1]

His majesty declared the American colonies to be in a state of open rebellion. In November 1775, martial law was applied to all of the colonies, as the war spread to Maine and Virginia, and the loyalists began raising their own army on American soil. England also courted other nations, such as Russia, as well as the princes in Germany to help subdue the Americans. Samuel Adams proposed recruiting Canada and France to their cause. But he believed a treaty and alliance were not possible if Congress was unwilling to declare independence. No country would take the colonies seriously if they were still politically subordinate to England.

Yet, many in Congress still held out hope to reestablish ties. Thomas Jefferson again wrote the Virginia loyalist John Randolph in England, on November 29, 1775, saying that the colonists were deadly serious about protecting their rights even if it meant a long war. Yet he did not want independence: "Believe me, dear Sir, there is not in the British Empire a man who more cordially loves a union with Great Britain than I do."[2]

Adams, frustrated with the indecisive mood of Congress, reminded himself to be patient. Events were likely to push the country closer to independence, he knew. In a letter to James Warren (no relation to Joseph

Warren), president of the provincial government in Massachusetts, he expressed his dismay. Writing on January 7, 1776, he asked: "Are you solicitous to hear of our confederation? I will tell you. It is not dead but sleepeth."[3] James Warren had taken over as president of the Massachusetts provincial Congress after the death of Dr. Joseph Warren. He was the husband of Mercy Otis Warren and the brother-in-law of James Otis, and had risen to prominence among the Whig leadership as an organizer and member of the committee of correspondence. He quickly became Adams' closest political confidant in Boston.

In his letters, Adams set out a series of political goals for 1776: to win approval in Congress for a formal declaration of independence, to unite the colonies into a confederation, and to obtain a foreign alliance with France or another nation. He was already planning for a United States. As bitterness over the war grew, the public seemed to be leaning toward a break with England.

Adams considered the possibility of forming a confederation out of the New England states to declare independence. He met with Franklin, who only promised conditional support. In a letter to John Adams, Samuel explained Franklin's position: "I told him that I would endeavor to unite the New England Colonies in confederating, if none of the rest would join it. [Franklin] approved of it, and said if I succeeded, he would cast his lot among us."[4]

On January 24, Colonel Henry Knox showed up in Cambridge to present Washington with the forty-three British cannons and sixteen mortars that he and his men had dragged through ice and snow from Fort Ticonderoga.

Betsy wrote Samuel in February 1776 that she was staying near the American army encampment in Cambridge, four miles outside of Boston. She told him not to worry about her, that she had an escape route carefully mapped out in the event of a British attack. "I am a few stones casts of a back road, which leads to the most retired part of Newton. . . . I beg you to excuse the very poor writings as my paper is bad and my pen made with scissors."[5] She was almost penniless, and asked Samuel if he could suggest anyone to ask for money.

In early March, Washington's men captured Dorchester Heights, a vantage overlooking Boston and the harbor. The cannons brought by

Knox were hastily mounted on the heights. Peering helplessly though a spyglass, General Howe realized his army stood within range of the artillery, and he risked losing the battleships. He had no choice but to order an evacuation of Boston. The British troops scrambled aboard the ships and sailed for Halifax on March 7.

In April 1776, Samuel Adams received intelligence that redcoats were regrouping, and planned to send twenty thousand troops to target New York, Virginia, North Carolina, and Boston. Each was home to a vital American port through which supplies were channeled.

Letters to Adams from Warren and others in beleaguered Massachusetts expressed exasperation that Congress still debated independence. The general public was ahead of Congress concerning independence. Jefferson found that nine out of ten inhabitants he canvassed in Virginia supported it.[6] Yet despite the urgings of constituents, many delegates remained cautious. Adams believed delaying the decision would be catastrophic to the army, and the opportunity to break with England might vanish forever, especially if America began to suffer military setbacks.

The drive toward independence received a considerable boost in the first month of 1776 when Thomas Paine's *Common Sense* was published. The pamphlet sold 120,000 copies in just 15 days. The remarkable popularity of Paine's *Common Sense* came in part because Americans suffering hardships from the war wanted more than ever to break with England. Paine echoed many of the themes that Adams had written about before hostilities began, arguing that dependence on England was not in colonies' economic interest.

Samuel Adams praised *Common Sense,* and in response to criticism of the work by Loyalist writers he took up his pen in Paine's defense, writing an article signed "Candidus" in which he made some of the harshest statements of his writing career: "'But,' say the puling, pusillanimous cowards, 'we shall be subject to a long and bloody war, if we declare independence.' On the contrary, I affirm it the only step that can bring the contest to a speedy and happy issue."

Adams wanted to reshape the debate in a way that would appeal to the most cautious of delegates. In early 1776, he began to quietly point out to delegates in private conversation that the colonies had never ceded their sovereignty to Britain. They were free and self-governing, and always had been. Declaring independence in 1776 was not a drastic, radical step, laden with additional risks, but a plain statement of a fact already recognized by the British if not by everyone in Congress. England had lifted its protection of America. How could America's sovereignty be deferred to a nation it was at war with? Adams asked. "Is not America already independent? . . . Why then not declare it? Upon whom was she ever supposed to be dependent?" He told others in almost disbelief: "Can nations at war be said to be dependent either upon the other? I ask then again, why not declare for independence? Because say some, it will forever shut the door of reconciliation. Upon what terms will Britain be reconciled with America?"[7]

In an April letter to Reverend Samuel Cooper, a committee member in Boston, he laughed at the debate over reconciliation and independence. "Many of the leading men see the absurdity of supposing that allegiance is due to a sovereign who has already thrown us out of his protection." Adams told Cooper that he was trying to be patient, believing that he could not force fate: "Indeed I have the happiness of believing that what I most earnestly wish for will in due time be effected. We cannot make events."[8] He wrote to Joseph Hawley, a member of the Massachusetts Provincial Congress: "Sensible Tories are better politicians. THEY know, that no foreign power can consistently yield comfort to rebels, or enter into any kind of treaty with these colonies till they declare themselves free and independent." But Adams remained tactful. "I am disappointed but I bear it tolerably well," he said.

He knew that as each new provincial government opened in each colony, American independence became more entrenched and the possibility of handing the reins back to Britain became ever more remote. On April 30, 1776, he wrote, "When this is done [provincial governments are formed], and I am inclined to think it will be soon, the colonies will feel their independence—the way will be prepared for a confederation, and one government may be formed with the consent of the whole—a distinct state composed of all the colonies with a common legislature for great & general purposes."[9]

In the early months of 1776, Adams balanced his deep anxieties about his family and home with maintaining a steady, forbearing course in Philadelphia, never demanding but continuing to find ways to win converts for independence. He understood that the British would continue to galvanize the colonies.

The idea that independence was an existing fact slowly began to take hold in the minds of many delegates who previously blanched over the prospect of a decisive break with England. As provincial conventions and new constitutions began to reestablish civil government, colonies became independent states. Georgia's delegates to the Continental Congress had been given unlimited powers to vote for independence. South Carolina's government gave its representatives the authority to do the same. Virginia's provincial government supported the step, which convinced Jefferson to accept it as inevitable. Four northern states and four southern states supported the idea of a new nation. But how would the five middle states vote? Many newly christened state legislatures immediately sent authorization to their congressional delegates to endorse independence. John Adams provided an upbeat update in a letter home to James Warren: "Every day rolls in upon us, independence like a torrent."[10]

Samuel Adams canvassed delegates, pressing them to support independence and a confederation of American states, hammering home the message that they needed an alliance with France to win the war. Their best chance was to break political ties with Britain and form a united American commonwealth with a national government to make treaties and build foreign allies. He believed that much of the population was waiting to see how Congress would act, and would likely be energized by the idea of building a new nation. Adams reminded the delegates that the colonies had never ceded their independence to Britain, and that no terms for reconciliation existed any longer. A historical opportunity had been placed before them, he argued. Adams believed time could easily run out on the momentum for independence. Military setbacks or a change in fortune could place doubts in the minds of Americans who supported nationhood.

By early June, Adams and other supporters of independence decided that the time to raise the issue in Congress had arrived. To garner support from the southern colonies, Adams wanted the call to come from Virginia. The role that Samuel Adams played in triggering the call for independence cannot be fully documented because the details of

Congress's deliberations do not exist. Even if they did, Adams often chose to work behind the scenes, carefully laying out a plan that could not be detected by his rivals. Years later, Jefferson wrote of Adams' veiled control of Congress: "I always considered him more than any other member the fountain of our more important measures. If there was any Palinurus [helmsman] to the revolution, Samuel Adams was the man. Indeed, in the Eastern States, for a year or two after it began, he was truly the man of the revolution. He was constantly holding caucuses of distinguished men (among whom was R. H. Lee), at which the generality of the measures pursued were previously determined on, and at which the parts were assigned to the different actors who afterwards appeared in them. John Adams had very little part in these caucuses; but as one of the actors in the measures decided on in them, he was a Colossus."[11]

On June 7, Richard Henry Lee presented on behalf of Virginia a formal resolution calling for independence, forcing the issue to the floor of Congress. Congress passed a resolution stating that: "These United Colonies are, and of right ought to be, free and independent States, that they are absolved from all allegiance to the British Crown, and that all political connection between them and the State of Great Britain is, and ought to be, totally dissolved. That it is expedient forthwith to take the most effectual measures for forming foreign Alliances."[12] Some delegates said they needed time to consult their constituents. Congress decided to vote on the issue in three weeks but to authorize the drafting of the declaration in the interlude to avoid wasting time that might prove critical to Washington's army. The committee assigned to the task included Thomas Jefferson, John Adams, Benjamin Franklin, and Roger Sherman of Connecticut.[13]

At the time, the more complicated task was thought to be drafting Articles of Confederation that the separate states could agree on. Samuel Adams was named to a committee to create a government framework to regulate the thirteen states, authorize ambassadors, and make foreign treaties. John Dickinson was named chair of the committee.[14] In the three weeks leading up to the vote, delegates noted that Samuel Adams worked exhaustively, meeting with delegates trying to win support for independence.

Jefferson presented his unedited draft of the Declaration of Independence in late June. He produced a supremely eloquent declaration that aspired to some of the noblest instincts in man and pointed to the heavens for its authority. He said he composed the draft with "neither book nor pamphlet"[15] on hand, crafting the phrases carefully in his head. He wrote in a rented second-floor flat of a brick home on Market and Seventh streets. "We hold these truths to be self-evident: that all men are created equal," his first draft read, "that; that they are endowed by their creator with inherent and inalienable rights; that among these are life, liberty, and the pursuit of happiness."[16]

John Adams believed the declaration was a recapitulation of the Samuel Adams–authored pamphlet of 1772 for the Committees of Correspondence. George Mason wrote in the new Virginia Bill of Rights, published a month prior to the Declaration of Independence, that "all men are born and equally free and independent."[17]

Jefferson's purpose, as he said, was not to "invent new ideas altogether."[18] He took the assignment of writing a simple declaration and produced an anthem fit for the occasion of relieving a king of his duties. The colonists were not rash peasants, his words suggested, but ennobled with sublime reasoning that could scarcely be answered by any conventional political argument.

It was thanks to the decade-long efforts and writings of Samuel Adams that the colonists were already grounded in the ideas in the Declaration. They were not unfamiliar with concepts concerning "life, liberty and the pursuit of happiness" and rights endowed by their creator. They knew how these applied to their lives. Natural rights were not just erudite ideas bandied about by isolated, bookish philosophers and mountaintop sages; they were talked about in taverns, in shipyards, among planters and farmers and fishermen and freshly recruited soldiers and their families. They had been argued in newspapers and pamphlets written by Samuel Adams. The Declaration did not need to break new ground. Adams had mentally prepared America to not only embrace the ideas in the declaration but to fight for them. It is no coincidence then that Adams' litany of rights was virtually repeated in the Declaration, even if Jefferson did not directly refer to them. Jefferson did not need to lead colonists in a new direction; he merely had to give voice to their convictions.

In Philadelphia, Jefferson's work was discussed in Congress for a few days. Some minor editing occurred. Monday, July 1 was set as the day of the debate to approve or reject the Declaration. Fifty-one delegates gathered in Independence Hall that day in a meeting closed to the public. Although the windows were shut to keep out the swarms of flies that pervaded the city in summer, the muffled, percussive sounds of drums, accentuated by the shouts of military commands as American troops drilled in the sultry weather were audible within the chamber.[19]

At 9 A.M., President Hancock called the meeting to order. The first task was to read letters addressed to Congress. The contents of one gave delegates reason to wonder if it was indeed too soon to openly declare sovereignty. In it, General Washington reported that dozens of British ships had appeared on the horizon outside of New York, the vanguard of perhaps a hundred more. "I suppose the whole fleet will be in within a day or two," Washington wrote. More grave news followed. Canada was lost, and American troops were in retreat.[20]

These were the military setbacks that Adams feared could derail the momentum for independence. Losing Canada meant Britain could invade from the north or hire Native American tribes as mercenaries. Meanwhile, as Britain strengthened its hand, Washington struggled to arm his force of 7,754 men. Of these, 800 were unarmed and another 1,400 had guns in need of repair; half the infantry had no bayonets. The British strategy was to cut off any hopes for foreign supplies. Fifty-three battleships were reported off the coast near Charleston.

John Dickinson of Pennsylvania, the leader of the moderate faction, rose to oppose the call for independence: "I value the love of my country as I ought, but I value my country more, and I desire this illustrious assembly to witness the integrity, if not the policy, of my conduct. The first campaign will be decisive of the controversy." A statement of independence would be a hollow gesture that did not materially benefit the colonies, he pleaded. "The declaration will not strengthen us by one man, or by the least supply, while it may expose our soldiers to additional cruelties and outrages."[21]

John Adams rose to answer that they were already outside of British law, thrown from its protection. The Declaration did not change their situation, but allowed them the advantages of forming treaties and seeking foreign help. By remaining rebels, they lacked sovereignty. John Adams believed there was no downside. He laid out uncontested facts: the king had already broken ties with them, absolving them of any allegiance, the British initiated a war against them; a declaration of independence to the world would merely document existing conditions.

Edward Rutledge of South Carolina asked that the vote be deferred until the following day.[22] This would allow for midnight canvassing—and deal making. Samuel Adams was adept at this kind of politics; critics called it his "art."

An express rider was hired by John Adams and dispatched on a frantic, eighty-mile ride in the dead of night to reach Delaware delegate Caesar Rodney, who had been held up by illness. Rodney rose from his sickbed when he learned that his vote was urgently needed and rushed in an effort to reach Philadelphia by the next morning.

That same night Samuel Adams found that six states were for independence and six were against it. New York delegates were waiting from authorization from home to vote and therefore could not swing the decision. Adams urged the Philadelphian Dickinson to refrain from voting against independence, even if he could not vote for it. Dickinson bent to Adams' will and agreed not to attend the critical vote. This would swing Philadelphia's split delegation in favor of independence, and give the Declaration a majority of support in Congress, seven states to five.[23]

The delegates showed up Tuesday morning in a cheerful, jovial mood, fully aware that the debate was settled and the vote was a foregone conclusion. The men were giddy; it was as if a great weight had been lifted from their shoulders. Little time was wasted before twelve of the colonies voted for nationhood.[24] Although New York delegates still waited for authorization from home, it was decided, for the sake of solidarity, that the final vote should be unanimous. The Declaration then underwent two days of editing, upon which the delegates gave final approval on July 4.[25]

Word of the vote spread throughout town. A crowd gathered outside the Pennsylvania State House (now Independence Hall), waiting for the historic news to filter out. About midday, the Liberty Bell sounded, signaling that Congress had approved independence. The bell added resonance to the shouts of joy. When news reached New York, the statue of King George III was overturned, and decapitated. Later it was melted down to provide musket balls for the army.

On August 2, the delegates gathered to sign a copy of the Declaration that had been written on parchment.[26] As president of the Congress, John Hancock was the first to sign. He wrote his name large, saying that His Majesty King George III would then be able to read it without the aid of eyeglasses. Then the delegates turned to Samuel Adams and gave him the honor of signing first among them. They considered Adams the man who had "the greatest part in the greatest revolution of the world."[27] He and the rest of the Massachusetts delegation signed the Declaration on the far-right column of the document. He wrote simply "Sam Adams," in unadorned, small letters.

Samuel Adams did not take credit for orchestrating American independence. To Joseph Hawley, the Boston attorney, he reported the news of nationhood: "The Congress has at length declared the colonies free and independent states. Upon this I congratulate you for I know your heart has long been set upon it." To Richard Henry Lee, he noted that the Declaration energized the populace: "Our Declaration of Independency has given vigor to the spirits of the people." To James Warren in Massachusetts, he expressed his delight over the union between the states: "Our declaration of Independence has already been attended with good effects. It is fortunate beyond our expectation to have the voice of every colony in favor of so important a question." While the slow pace in which the Declaration came about had frustrated him, he noted that "it must be allowed by the impartial world that this declaration has not been made rashly."[28]

Adams saw American independence as a triumph for republican democracy. "New governments are now erecting in the several American States under the authority of the people," he said. "Monarchy seems to be generally exploded."[29]

Twelve years earlier, Samuel Adams set out to move America toward independence. He had persevered through discouragement and obstacles that seemed insurmountable, including shuttered legislatures, military occupation, persecution, and limited resources. As a tax collector in 1764, he had the vision to take up the fight against the most powerful country in the world, to defy a king and parliament, and split an empire. On July 4, 1776, that improbable dream came true.

13

THE TRIALS OF WAR

Adams was exhausted from his efforts to win support for the Declaration of Independence. His lifelong affliction of palsy rendered him subject to trembling spells in times of extreme stress, fatigue, heat, and overexertion. These conditions increased in the months and weeks leading up to the critical vote on independence. Adams had crowded his days and late nights with exhaustive politicking. He complained that the steamy Philadelphia summer weather did not agree with his constitution and sapped his strength. His disorder caused his hand to shake. The trembling grew worse and more unmanageable as his nervous system became overtaxed. He found it difficult to hold a teacup, a fork, and especially a pen.

Writing from Boston, James Warren urged him to take a sabbatical home to restore his strength. "I am sorry to hear your health is declining, though I can't wonder at it. Such long and intense application in a place so unhealthy must be too much for a firmer constitution than yours. I am sensible of the importance of your being in Congress at this time, and I know the reluctance you have at leaving your duty there; but your health must be attended to. We shall want you again. You must therefore take a ride, relax your mind, and breathe some of our Northern air." Adams relented and agreed to return to Boston.[1] Before leaving Philadelphia, he gave a rousing oration to citizens and fresh enlistees. A newspaper reported that Adams' words "irritated them to madness against Great Britain, and made them resolve to conquer or die in the cause they have espoused."[2]

With patriotic fervor running high, he left Philadelphia on Monday, August 12 for a seventeen-day trip back to Boston, averaging about twenty miles a day. He reached Princeton, New Jersey by Tuesday evening. The next morning, he crossed the border to the state of New York and located General Washington and the American army. "I found the General and his family in health and spirits; in deed, every officer and soldier appears to be determined [to fight]," he wrote to John Adams.[3] The soldiers were building entrenchments and fortifications and bracing defenses. The British forces that fled Boston earlier in the year for Nova Scotia were expected to return with reinforcements. Some ships had already arrived. As Adams watched the solemn soldiers at work, he marveled at how the army was its own self-supporting city. "They carry on all kinds of business within themselves," he wrote to John Adams. "Smiths, armorers, carpenters, turners, carriage-makers, rope-makers, &c., &c. they are well provided with."

Samuel Adams had advised Congress that the key to building a strong army was increasing bonuses and inducements. Because he recognized that the longer soldiers remained in the army, the more professional and experienced the force would become, he suggested offering a hundred acres of land in exchange for a three-year enlistment.[4]

Adams reached war-torn Boston on August 29. His hometown was unrecognizable, buildings reduced to rubble. Homes that were once the pride of his neighbors were ransacked and abandoned, left scarred and exposed to the elements. His family was still in Dedham, ten miles from Boston, and his home on Purchase Street was abandoned and vandalized. Boston was trying frantically to prepare its defenses and rebuild.

Unfortunately for Adams, the family reunion in Dedham was cut short by pressing duties. Among his elected posts, Adams still bore the duties as secretary of Massachusetts. By returning home, he merely replaced congressional obligations with state chores. After spending a few days with his family, he tended to a long list of military appointments that came across his desk and tried to settle disagreements that were holding up a consensus on a new state constitution. Without a government framework, courts and civic offices were closed throughout Massachusetts; the potential for lawlessness was very real.

While Adams remained in Massachusetts, Lord William Howe, the head of British forces in America, reached out to Congress with a proposal for peace talks. John Adams, Benjamin Franklin, and Edward Rutledge were chosen to meet with the British commander.[5] John Adams wrote his cousin on September 8 to assure him that Congress was resolved to remain independent: "Do not imagine from this that a panic has spread to Philadelphia."[6] Samuel meanwhile was writing John with his concerns. He did not believe the British were willing to recognize American sovereignty. Nothing short of that would lead to peace, he believed. Three hundred miles removed from the conference, Adams' anxiety grew. He believed, however, that his cousin John and the other peace commissioners were capable of handling negotiations and equally committed to American independence. "We have a report that a committee is appointed (as the expression is) 'to meet the Howes,' and that you are one," he wrote John. "This, without flattery, gave me pleasure."[7]

Samuel, however, was clear about his opinion. "It would be ridiculous indeed, if we were to return to a state of slavery in a few weeks, after we had thrown off the yoke and asserted our independence. The body of the people, I am persuaded, would resent it. But why do I write in this style? I rely upon the Congress and the committee." To his great relief, the conference fizzled. The commissioners stated unequivocally that American independence was not negotiable. Howe could offer pardons only for those who laid down their arms and renounced independence. Although the conference had been fruitless, Samuel Adams believed it had served as a critical test. "In my opinion, the independence of America stands now on a better footing than it did before," he wrote his cousin.[8]

Congress acted on Samuel Adams' calls to pursue an alliance with France. In September, Benjamin Franklin and Silas Deane, a delegate from Connecticut, were among the envoys appointed as diplomats to the royal court in Paris.[9]

Adams' visit home was short. He returned to Congress in Philadelphia in October, choosing again to make the trip on horseback. He hoped the exercise would once again improve his health. Upon arriving at his lodgings, he wrote Betsy that he felt better than he had in years and playfully poked fun at his outlaw image. Lord Howe publicly issued a proclamation that Britain's latest "most wanted" list included Adams as well as Franklin, John Adams, Hancock, and Richard Henry Lee. "I am not certain of the truth of this report," he wrote her. "If it be a fact, I am greatly obliged to his lordship for the flattering opinion he has given me of myself as being a person obnoxious to those who are desolating a once happy country for the sake of extinguishing the remaining lamp of liberty, and for the singular honor he does me in ranking me with men so eminently patriotic."[10]

In his letters to his wife, Samuel Adams could express his doubts and anxiety over the ultimate success of the revolution. To all others, he maintained an air of confidence. During the discouraging months of late 1776, the British reeled off a string of impressive victories. In September, at New York, the British launched the most impressive amphibious assault ever seen before in history. In October, American forces in Canada under Benedict Arnold were trounced at Lake Champlain. Washington was forced to evacuate Manhattan on October 23. The British scored another decisive triumph by capturing Fort Washington in New York, taking 2,818 prisoners on November 16. Three days later, British Lieutenant General Cornwallis forced American troops in New Jersey to evacuate Fort Lee and abandon precious ammunition vital to Washington's army.

In December, Washington gave a brutally honest assessment: "I think the game is pretty near up."[11] Thomas Paine wrote: "These are times that try men's souls."[12]

Adams realized that the Declaration of Independence had won approval just in time. Had the vote and state ratification been delayed by just weeks, the military losses likely would have made its adoption impossible.

To add to Adams' dismay, British troops were closing in on Philadelphia. Congress decided to flee to Baltimore on December 12.[13] "Although the enemy is within forty miles of this city [Philadelphia]," Adams wrote Betsy, "I do not regret the part I have taken in a cause so just and interesting to mankind."[14] He braced himself for the setbacks looming. He was the chair of the committee for the Northern Army as well as a member of several other committees addressing concerns of the war. More than anyone in Congress, he knew just how precarious the military situation had become.

With matters so urgent, Congress decided to give George Washington dictatorial powers for six months to demand enlistment and seize supplies needed to maintain the war effort. Adams disagreed with this in principle but accepted it in practice, based in part on his faith in Washington's character. "It became in my opinion necessary," he said.[15]

General Washington gave the American cause renewed life by crossing the Delaware River with 2,400 men on Christmas Day, 1776, to capture in a single hour more than 1,000 Hessian mercenaries hired by Britain.[16] Adams applauded the victory, believing America needed to take a bolder stance against the British. He and many other Americans in the early years of the war were unhappy with Washington's strategy of avoiding a pitched battle. Washington himself was unhappy with the strategy and longed for the chance to go on the offensive, but his only hope was to avoid losing his army and to outlast the British. Adams, however, believed time did not necessarily favor the American cause. British supplies were endless, given its fleet of merchant and military vessels.

Adams soon saw the wisdom of a war of attrition, however, and applauded Washington's foresight. In June 1777, he wrote James Warren: "I confess I have always been so very wrong headed as not to be over well pleased with what is called the Fabian War in America. I conceive a great difference between the situation of the Carthaginian & the British generals. But I have no judgment in military affairs, and therefore will leave the subject to be discussed, as it certainly will be, by those who are masters of it."[17]

When the threat to Philadelphia passed in March, Adams and the rest of Congress returned from their temporary home in Baltimore.[18]

Because of Adams' position on several key committees that oversaw the war effort, his political adversaries wondered if he had too much power. In England, observers speculated whether the same man who split the empire and seemed to control Congress was driven by personal ambition and would ultimately emerge as a dictator. A loyalist newspaper called him the "Cromwell of New England." According to a correspondent for a newspaper in London, others in Congress feared to contradict Adams. On his work on the Articles of Confederation, it was reported that "Adams had himself prepared almost a complete code of laws; but many were rejected, though with great caution, and an explanation of each particular impropriety, from a dread of too much offending that great man, who, to make use of an expression in a letter received some time since in America, was 'so clever a fellow, and so dangerous, that it was no man's interest to quarrel with him.'"[19]

But Adams did not ache for power. By 1777, he was already thinking about retirement. In a June letter to Richard Henry Lee, he confessed: "May I live to see the public liberty restored and the safety of our dear country secured. I should then think I had enjoyed enough and bid this world adieu."[20] Hundreds of mundane administrative tasks for his work in Congress pushed larger issues from the forefront of his thoughts. He was sure many others could perform these administrative duties equally well. In his mind, the more urgent issues included establishing an alliance with France and getting the Articles of Confederation ratified. France's help was critical to winning the war. Adams also worried that the war effort was the only tie binding the disparate states. If the Articles remained unratified, peace could threaten the union more than England.

As to his personal ambition, he coveted neither power nor fame. One day John Adams watched his cousin cut up copies of his letters with scissors, shredding correspondence that would have documented for posterity his role in events and issues critical to the birth of a new nation. John urged Samuel to preserve all his correspondence, but Samuel merely shrugged and said he was more concerned about preventing his letters from falling into hostile hands and endangering friends.[21]

Samuel downplayed his role in events in a letter to James Warren: "I recollect however that Shakespeare tells us, there is a tide in human affairs, an opportunity which wise men carefully watch for and improve, and I will never forget because it exactly coincides with my religious opinion and I think is warranted by holy writ, that God helps those who help themselves.'"[22]

The war continued to close in around Adams. In July 1777, General Howe launched a campaign to seize Philadelphia. He set sail from New York with fifteen thousand men, with a stop along the Chesapeake Bay, forcing Congress to consider another flight for safety. "Matters seem to be drawing to a crisis," Adams wrote to Betsy on September 17. That same day, he reported: "Both the armies are about 26 miles from this place."[23]

At 1 A.M. on Friday, September 19, an express rider arrived at Congressional President John Hancock's home with a letter from General Washington's aide-de-camp, Colonel Alexander Hamilton, warning Congress to flee Philadelphia. Hamilton had frantically scrawled the dispatch after his horse was shot from under him. As Hamilton crossed the Schuylkill River, one of his oarsmen was shot and killed and another was wounded. The British had gained possession of the ford to cross the Schuylkill, which was abating after days of swelled waters from a violent storm. British troops commandeered boats along the river and could reach the city by morning.[24]

Hancock sounded an alarm to members of Congress, and Samuel Adams was roused from his bed. Between 2 and 3 A.M., members of Congress formed a steady stream leaving town, each delegate choosing his own path of flight. The previous week, the body had voted to reconvene in Lancaster, Pennsylvania, if forced to flee. Adams joined a group of congressmen who boarded a ferry to cross the Delaware to New Jersey. They stayed in Trenton for a day, then proceeded to Easton, and made it to Bethlehem by Monday, September 21. Both Samuel and John Adams attended a worship service in German. Neither spoke the language, but Samuel never missed church.[25]

The transient national government continued on to Lancaster. After assessing the site, they decided it was too vulnerable to an attack, even from a light party of loyalists or British troops, so they proceeded to Yorktown. The trip was taxing on the fifty-five-year-old Adams. To avoid British lines, they traveled an evasive, circuitous 180-mile journey to reach Yorktown, Pennsylvania, which was only 88 miles directly from Philadelphia.[26]

In temporary quarters at Yorktown, attendance in Congress began to dwindle. As few as twenty members were present to continue business. Adams grew concerned with the mood in Congress, which was spiraling downward: men's posture was defeated, their faces anxious, and their voices lacked confidence. The prospects, which had looked so promising the previous year, now seemed to have melted away. New York was still in British hands. Howe seized Philadelphia on September 26 and continued to feign strikes on patriot storehouses around the city. This tactic kept Washington's troops constantly on the march to protect their munitions. Washington waited for reinforcements from Virginia, Pennsylvania, and Maryland. His men were inadequately fed. About 500 were barefoot, and winter was approaching. About 1,500 men under General Anthony Wayne were forced to abandon their blankets as they fled from the enemy.[27]

Samuel Adams believed that Americans would view the desperation evident in men of Congress as a telltale barometer of the American cause. He attended a closed-door meeting called to frankly discuss the faltering war effort. Adams was silent for much of the meeting, then spoke in a surprisingly enthusiastic tone, encouraging members that "the darkest hour was just before the dawn of day."[28]

Adams wanted to inspire courage in his colleagues. "Gentlemen, your spirits appear oppressed with the weight of the public calamities," he told them. "Your sadness of countenance reveals your disquietude. A patriot may grieve at the distress of his country, but he will never despair of the commonwealth. Our affairs, it is said, are desperate! If this be our language, they are indeed. If we wear long faces, long faces will become fashionable. The eyes of the people are upon us. The tone of their feelings is regulated by ours. If we despond, public confidence is destroyed, the people will no longer yield their support to a hopeless contest, and American liberty is no more."[29]

A quick reversal of fortune came in October with the stunning victory by American general Horatio Gates over British general John Burgoyne's troops at Saratoga, New York.

For years, Hancock had blamed Adams for orchestrating Washington's appointment as commander-in-chief of the American army, a post he wanted for himself. Many conflicting beliefs as well as widely differing perceptions of their roles in the revolution divided the two estranged friends. By 1777, Adams wondered if he had dismantled Governor Hutchinson's career only to replace him with an equally ambitious political personality. Hancock was less interested in republican ideals than in becoming the first governor of an independent Massachusetts. After rising to the presidency of the Continental Congress, Hancock, whom critics unfairly accused of being a mindless pawn with more money than brains, a puppet of Samuel Adams, no longer needed Adams' help and wanted to step outside the shadow of his mentor.

In 1777, Hancock saw his star rising higher than he had ever imagined. After Congress approved the Declaration of Independence on July 4, 1776, it was sent to newspapers up and down the continent. The formal signing by most of the delegates was almost a month later; when the Declaration originally arrived at newspaper offices, it bore only two names. "Signed by order and in behalf of the Congress, John Hancock, President: Attest, Charles Thomson, Secretary." Congress did not distribute authenticated copies of the Declaration of Independence with the signatures of the rest of the delegates until January 18, 1777.[30] It was only natural for many readers to assume that Hancock either wrote the Declaration or was its leading proponent.[31]

Tories were delighted at the break between Adams and Hancock. According to one newspaper account, Hancock was "indebted to Adams for the promotion to the president's chair" but was then disregarded when the object of independence was achieved."[32]

Hancock found the daily tasks of Congress tedious and often was absent. Delegates passed a resolution requiring the president to attend sessions for business to proceed. Although elected as a delegate each year throughout the war, Hancock never attended a session after October 29, 1777, when he stepped down as president to return to Boston and run for governor. Hancock announced that he would make a departing address.[33] He knew this would trigger a customary resolution of gratitude for his service, which would be useful to his political ambitions. Both Samuel and John Adams and the rest of the Massachusetts delegation opposed the resolution praising his service. Hancock was infuriated. Hancock further drew the ire of Adams by demanding that General Washington provide him with a full military escort for his trip back to Boston. Washington complied. Hancock arrived in impressive fashion to adoring crowds back in his hometown. "Mr. [Hancock] came to this town with great pomp, and was received by the military and naval gentlemen, as I am informed, with equal ceremony," Samuel Adams reported from Boston to John Adams.[34]

John Adams, who traveled the same road home from Yorktown, Pennsylvania, a few days after Hancock's entourage passed that way in late 1777, noted his diary: "The taverners are all along are complaining of the guard of light horse which attended Mr. H———. They did not pay, and the taverners were obliged to go after them to demand their dues."[35]

In Yorktown, Pennsylvania, Congress approved the Articles of Confederation. Congress endorsed the framework for a national government in November and sent it to the thirteen former colonies for ratification. Adams had worked on the Articles for seventeen months. "The Articles of Confederation seem to be well liked," Adams wrote to Richard Henry Lee on the first day of 1778.[36] The previous month, his other major goal had also been accomplished. The victory of General Gates over Britain's General Burgoyne at Saratoga convinced French leaders that Americans might just win the war, and they decided to formally recognize American independence, opening the door for an alliance.[37]

Samuel Adams spent the winter and spring in Boston in 1778, too sick to travel to Yorktown. He decided not to return to Congress until his health was restored. He was also needed to attend to state matters, including deliberations over a state constitution. In April, Adams was overjoyed when news arrived that France recognized the United States as a sovereign nation, and an alliance that might help end the war was now possible. "France has acted with magnanimity; while Britain continues to discover that meanness and poverty of spirit," Adams wrote to Richard Henry Lee.[38]

While Adams remained in Boston, a group of congressional delegates tried to replace General Washington as head of the army with Gates in December 1777. The conspiracy, called the Conway Cabal, failed when a majority of the army pledged to serve under no one but Washington. Those who tried to depose the general became political outcasts.

In 1778, Hancock saw an opportunity to cripple Adams politically by spreading the rumor that he was behind the Conway Cabal. According to these rumors, Adams was motivated by jealousy of Washington, whose star now eclipsed his own. The whispers claimed that Samuel Adams had from the outset opposed Washington's nomination as commander of the army, that he believed a New England commander should lead New England troops. Adams said of Hancock's misrepresentation: "The man who fabricated that charge did not believe it himself."[39]

The roads improved by April, and Adams left Boston for the trip back to Yorktown, Pennsylvania to join Congress. As he rode along the muddy thoroughfares, he passed bands of American soldiers, many heading to Valley Forge or on their way home on furlough. The clothes of many of the troops had become rags, and several men traveled barefoot. Many did not have coats or blankets. In the distance, he spotted a familiar figure; it was his son. Unfortunately for Adams, he and the young man were heading in opposite directions and had only a minute to embrace. He offered his son advice, and then felt a deep longing as he watched him disappear in the distance with the troops. He wrote Betsy from the town of Palmer, about 84 miles outside of Boston: "I was sorry I could not have the pleasure of conversing with him. I parted with him with great regret. May heaven bless him! Tell him I shall never think him too old to hearken to the advice of his father. Indeed I never had reason to complain of him on that Account. He has hitherto made me a glad father."[40]

During the trip, Adams was uplifted by newspaper reports that France had formally agreed to an alliance with America. This was the foreign help he had advocated since the beginning of the war. The news had been announced in Congress on May 3 that the French had agreed to a treaty on February 6, setting off celebrations across the country. Congress ratified the treaty a day later. Washington ordered reports of the treaty in the *Pennsylvania Gazette* to be read to the troops, and cannon to be fired in salute.[41]

When Adams took his seat in Congress on May 21, he was pleased to see the frantic activity as delegates prepared for the alliance. Delegates debated the reorganization of the army and the instructions for the American commissioners in Europe.

In Philadelphia, British General Henry Clinton took command of the army, replacing General Howe. Clinton received intelligence that a French fleet was on the way to Philadelphia, and ordered his men on June 18 to evacuate the city and march to New York. Adams received news of the city's liberation a day later. Along with the rest of the delegates, he made his way back to Philadelphia, where Congress convened on July 2. The effects of occupation were evident. Buildings had been torched, and warehouses demolished. The British had destroyed many of the supplies in the city and anything that might be useful to an army.

On Saturday, July 11, as Adams and the delegates discussed routine matters such as whether bills of exchange should read "the United States of North America," news arrived that the French fleet of 18 ships carrying 10,000 troops was spotted off the Pennsylvania Coast and anchored at the Delaware Capes. It was impressive show of naval power that included a ship of 90 guns, four of 80 guns, two of 74 guns and five of 64 guns along with four huge frigate battleships as well as transport vessels. The French had come ready to drive the British out of Philadelphia, but were too late.

A letter from Silas Deane, one of the American diplomats to France, arrived with word that he was with the fleet aboard the *Languedoc* with the new French ambassador to the United States, Conrad Alexander Gerard. Pilots were immediately sent to bring them up the river, and a dispatch was sent to General Washington to prepare for a joint American-French military campaign. Delegates learned that France had declared war on Great Britain on May 19.[42]

Adams, Richard Henry Lee, and New York's Gouverneur Morris were chosen to decide the proper protocol for the United States to receive its first-ever foreign ambassador. Despite his long advocacy for a French alliance, Adams thought he had been an odd choice to decide diplomatic decorum: "Would you think that one so little of the man of the world as I am should be joined in a committee to settle ceremonials?" he wrote in a letter to James Warren. But Adams realized the importance of etiquette in setting future precedents to receive diplomats and that the committee must "agree upon forms that are adapted to the true republican principles." Unlike most nations, the United States was without a monarch and a royal court to receive foreign dignitaries. The American ceremonies to receive Gerard needed to be dignified, yet not extravagant, and convey the message that congressmen were not set apart from the people they represented—the farmers and laborers, the soldiers and merchants and clergy. They were not nobles or courtiers.[43]

Adams, as a member of the marine committee, worked frantically on Sunday to find water and provisions to replenish the fleet. The committee commandeered as many casks for water as they could find; many had been destroyed by the British army. They requisitioned hundreds of sacks of flour, and ordered a commissary to collect 50 head of cattle and 500 sheep, along with chickens and vegetables.[44]

A Congressional delegation was sent to meet Deane and Gerard at nearby Chester. A barge with 12 oarsmen, dressed in scarlet trimmed with silver, rowed halfway to the ship, and then held their oars silently as 15 cannon fired a booming salute. The barge then proceeded to the ship to transport the French ambassador. The same ceremony was repeated as the party neared the shore. Four coaches with four horses carried the committee, Deane, and Gerard into Philadelphia, where the Frenchman was given temporary lodgings at the apartment of General Benedict Arnold.

Adams and the Massachusetts delegation paid a visit to Gerard on Monday. The French minister appeared to be about 50 years of age, and talked in a serious but friendly manner. He praised the Bay Colony men for their struggle for liberty. Adams thought Gerard was "not wanting in political finesse, and therefore not to be listend to, too implicitly."[45]

August 6, 1778, was the day appointed to receive Gerard in Congress. At noon, Adams and Richard Henry Lee arrived at his lodging riding a coach of six horses. The men escorted Gerard to the coach, Adams sat in the front seat and Lee on the ambassador's left. Gerard's secretary followed in a carriage. They talked about affairs in Europe, and the American ambassadors in Paris. Shortly before 1 P.M., they arrived at the State House, where a crowd waited outside. Adams and Lee announced Gerard to the mass of people as they made their way to door of the House. In Congress, Adams and Lee stood to the left of Gerard, who had been provided a chair directly opposite President Henry Laurens. One small concession had been made to give the president's chair the elevated status of a throne of a nation. His mahogany armchair had been placed on a two-foot high platform that was draped in green cloth. Gerard sat, and handed his secretary his credentials as "Minister Plenipotentiary of his most Christian Majesty the King of France" to present to Laurens. These were read aloud in French and then English. Lee then introduced Gerard to the delegates. After ceremonial bows, Gerard read a speech to Congress in French, pledging friendship between the two nations.

In the evening, a dinner was held and bands played. Cannon were again fired in salute.[46] Adams began to feel that all his major goals in Congress had been accomplished, and his presence was no longer critical in Philadelphia. Ten states had ratified the Articles of Confederation. Maryland, New Jersey, and Delaware were the remaining holdouts. To the Reverend Samuel Cooper, he wrote in December: "I intend to get myself excused from further public service here."[47]

He received a letter from Hannah in September saying that Betsy had been ill but the doctor said she was recovering, and her health would be restored in a day or two. "She is exceedingly loth to give me the least Pain," Hannah wrote to him. "She begs of me not to make myself very anxious for her." Hannah conveyed her love for her father, for which he thanked her, but he also wrote: "Be equally attentive to every relation into which an all-wise Providence may lead you, and I will venture to predict for my dear daughter an unfailing source of happiness in the reflections of her own mind. If you carefully fulfill the various duties of life from a principle of obedience to your Heavenly Father, you shall enjoy that peace which the world cannot give nor take away."[48]

He wrote Betsy in March 1779: "After near five years absent from my family, and in a climate unfriendly to my health, I have reason to expect I may be permitted to spend the remainder of my days in my native place and enjoy the pleasures of domestic life." To Betsy, he claimed that the attacks of political rivals did not bother him, and only made him more circumspect in his behavior: "I do not think my countrymen are ungrateful; but I am afraid there is a faction among them, consisting of a few men, who are under the dominion of those passions which have been the bane of society in all ages—ambition and avarice."[49]

He returned home in the summer of 1779 and spent a year in Boston, tending to local affairs, drumming up support for the army, and playing a key role in getting a state constitution ratified.

Adams was elected to the Massachusetts Constitutional Convention, which convened on September 1, 1779. Debates continued for a week before Samuel and John Adams and James Bowdoin, a wealthy merchant who served on the executive council of the provincial government, were chosen to draft the constitution. No record of their discussions was preserved, but several of the articles contained in the declaration of rights were stated earlier in works by Samuel Adams, such as the 1765 Massachusetts Resolves and the 1772 plan for the Committees of Correspondence. Many of the principals laid down in the draft were born out of his struggles and those of other Whig leaders, including the fights to prevent random searches such as those under the "writs of assistance," as well as the shuttering of the legislature by the royal governors under the Charter, the military occupation of Boston, the fight against royal prerogative, the taxation battles, and the freedom to meet and protest their grievances.

From his earliest public writings, Samuel stated that residents should be loyal to a constitution and its laws, not to leaders. John Adams agreed. He had coined the term "a government of laws, not men," in his 1774 *Novanglus Papers,* printed in Boston newspapers. The phrase was repeated in the Massachusetts Constitution and became a cornerstone of American jurisprudence. In the Declaration of Rights, they stated that all men were "born equally free and independent." They drafted a Declaration of Rights with an article protecting free speech and prohibiting random property searches by requiring a probable cause affirmed by oath. Samuel Adams' struggles to prevent the king and royal governors from interfering with the colonial assembly inspired the provision for a separation of powers between the branches of the state government, which read: "In the government of this Commonwealth, the legislative department shall never exercise the executive and judicial powers, or either of them: The executive shall never exercise the legislative and judicial powers, or either of them: The judicial shall never exercise the legislative and executive powers, or either of them."

To prevent another military occupation, the constitution prohibited the quartering of troops except in a manner approved by representative lawmakers. The draft was presented to the convention in later October for revisions.

John Adams left the convention for a diplomatic trip to Paris, boarding the frigate *The Sensible* out of Boston on Saturday, November 13. Samuel Adams helped guide the draft through the convention, which gave its approval to send to voters in March. To become law, the constitution needed two-thirds of the votes cast in the May referendum. Although many residents were mistrustful of placing power in a government after the struggles with royal authority, Adams believed the constitution provided safeguards to keep government officials in check.

"A government without power to exert itself is at best but a useless piece of machinery," he told residents at a Boston town meeting on May 3, 1780. "It is probable that, for want of energy, it would speedily lose even the appearance of government, and sink into anarchy. Unless a due proportion of weight is given to each of the powers of government, there will soon be a confusion of the whole. An overbearing of any one of its parts on the rest would destroy the balance, and accelerate its dissolution and ruin; and a power without *any* restraint is tyranny. The powers of government must then be balanced."

Voters gave their approval of the constitution in May, which provided Massachusetts with a permanent state government. Other state constitutions at the time called for a partial separation of powers, but the Massachusetts article erected the strongest framework for each branch to be able to check and balance the power of the other two divisions of government. It became a model for the design for the U.S. Constitution. The separation was further strengthened by the innovation of making the tenure of judges permanent to limit the influence of the state governor or legislature. The Massachusetts Constitution also served as a model for the Federal First Amendment.[50]

Samuel wrote to John Adams in Paris: "Never was a good Constitution more wanted than at this juncture."[51]

While in France as an American diplomat in 1780, John Adams read reports that English and Irish leaders had followed Samuel Adams' example and formed committees of correspondences to fight for their civil rights. To his cousin, John reported: "You will see by the public papers that your committee of correspondence is making greater progress in the world and doing greater things in the political world than the electrical rod ever did in the physical; England and Ireland have adopted it, but, mean plagiaries as they are, they do not acknowledge who was the inventor of it."[52]

Francis Dana, who, along with John Adams, was a member of the American diplomatic delegates in 1780, wrote Elbridge Gerry about the success of such committees in England. "The [committees of correspondence] were engines which operated with more energy and constancy than any others which were put in motion in the commencement of our opposition. They may be called the corner-stone of our Revolution or new empire. Little, I believe, did our friend, the first mover and inventor of them, expect to see this masterly stroke of policy so soon adopted by the people of England to effect the redress of their own grievances."[53]

But Dana wondered if this political tool could achieve much without the guidance of someone like Samuel Adams: "They want the sage counsel of our said friend in conducting the affairs of their committees of correspondence to the proper point."

Samuel Adams returned to Congress in June 1780. But his longing to be home was stronger than ever. "I am very solicitous to know how it fares with you and my dear connections in Boston," he wrote Betsy. "Our friends at that distance may be in their graves before one may even hear of their previous sickness. You cannot wonder then that I am in anxiety every moment. Upon this consideration alone, the public service so far from one's family must be conceived to be a sacrifice of no small value. The man who has devoted himself to the service of God and his country will cheerfully make every sacrifice."[54] In response to a letter from her in October, he wrote Betsy: "You did not expressly tell me that you [are] well, a material circumstance, which you must never omit to mention."[55]

Hancock was elected the first governor of the new state of Massachusetts in October 1780. Adams was skeptical: "They have been influenced to this choice by the pure motives of public affection. A due attention to the administration of government, I fancy, will soon determine whether they have acted with wisdom or not."[56]

Meanwhile, *Rivington's Royal Gazette* publicly reported that the Adams–Hancock split was due to Hancock's loyalty to Washington and Adams' disloyalty to the commander-in-chief of the American army. In a letter to Betsy, Adams explained the false rumors: "This is an old story which men have believed and disbelieved as they pleased, without much concern of mine. It was a pitiful contrivance to render me obnoxious to the general & our common friends. If there has been any difference between Mr. H. and me, Rivington knows not the origin of it. Mr. Hancock never thought me an enemy to Gen. Washington. He never thought that I was desirous of his being removed, & therefore could

never treat me with acrimony on that account. I never wished for the removal of General Washington."[57]

Adams served on a variety of committees that oversaw the war effort.
He believed that even complex departments should be run by elected
representatives rather than delegated to professionals. The French minister Anne-Cesar de la Luzerene, who replaced Gerard in 1779, wrote to
his government, that Adams' views hindered the war effort: "Samuel
Adams, whose obstinate, resolute character was so useful to the revolution at its origin, shows himself so ill-suited to the conduct of affairs in
an organized government."[58]

Adams not only opposed the formation of a war department, but
balked at the idea of a foreign office and a department of finance.

Samuel Adams' last official act in Congress was to sign his approval
to the Articles of Confederation, which had finally been ratified by all
the states on February 24, 1781.[59] He had spent four and a half years
guiding it from inception to adoption and was the lone remaining member of the committee originally assigned to draft the document who still
attended Congress. With his work done, he was ready to return home,
never again to depart. He resigned from Congress a month after signing
the Articles.

For several years, James Otis had been under the care of family in
Andover, Massachusetts. He would often turn to his sister Mercy and say
that "I hope when God Almighty in his providence shall take me out of
time into eternity, it will be by a flash of lightning!" On May 23, 1783,
a fierce thunderstorm characteristic of the early summer season in New
England descended to darken the skies. Otis struggled to the door to be-
hold the clashing elements and the exploding thunder, reminiscent of
the cannon fire of the revolution. Between loud thunderclaps, a bolt of
lighting, which Mercy thought appeared like a darting serpent, struck
Otis in the chest. Electricity shot through his body, and he fell to the
floor, dying instantly. She found no mark left on his body. His features
appeared angelic and placid. The following day his body was taken to
Boston and lay in state at the home he once opened in hospitality after
the repeal of the Stamp Act. Samuel Adams grieved the death of his old
friend. It had been sixteen years since they worked in concert to bring

the colonies together at the Stamp Act Congress. Now the colonies stood united as a new nation.[60]

On September 28, 1781, General Washington fired the first gun to begin the siege of Yorktown, Virginia, as an army of nine thousand American and seven thousand French soldiers hemmed in British forces. A French fleet cut off their access to the sea. The Americans bombarded the British for three weeks. At 2 P.M. on October 17, Lieutenant General Cornwallis surrendered, ending serious hostilities of the war. Britain was forced to concede American sovereignty.[61]

When British troops first arrived to occupy Boston in 1768, Samuel Adams had pledged to make American independence his life's mission. As he read the news of Cornwallis' surrender, he knew his mission had been fulfilled. American liberty had been secured.

14

A CONSTITUTION

Adams returned to Boston in the spring of 1781 homeless and with very little money. He had not received much of his salary from Massachusetts in years. The house that his father had purchased nearly seventy years earlier was damaged beyond salvage, the victim of British soldiers during the occupation. It was the home of his childhood memories, the dwelling in which he had raised his children.

Others in Boston had profited from the war, but Samuel Adams had sacrificed everything he owned. Commenting on Adams' homecoming, his friend Edward Everett said: "Hancock served the cause with his liberal opulence, Adams with his incorruptible poverty. His family, at times, suffered almost for the comforts of life, when he might have sold his influence over the counsels of America for uncounted gold, when he might have emptied the royal treasury if he would have betrayed his country. Samuel Adams was the last of the Puritans."[1]

His wife had heroically held the family together with almost no means of support in his absence. Adams applied for the accumulated back pay owed him as clerk of the Massachusetts House. His salary had gone unpaid since 1774. Rather than reimburse him in cash, the legislature allowed him to buy a home confiscated from a former Tory for 92 pounds and 7 shillings of the amount owed to him. He agreed.

Adams had persevered in Congress during the discouraging years when attendance had dwindled to a few diehards. Meanwhile, back in Boston, political enemies took aim at his reputation. During the war, a third of the population of Massachusetts remained loyal to Britain. They blamed Adams for much of their misery. Indeed, he opposed recognition of their legal rights to vote or reattain the property they owned before the war; he even supported hanging some Tories on the grounds that they had betrayed their countrymen. Adams believed the loyalists could undermine the fragile new government. But the Treaty of Paris, which officially ended the war in 1783, "earnestly recommended" that individual states recognize the political and property rights of American Tories who had been loyal to Britain during the Revolution.[2]

Adams was also a target of Hancock supporters who continued to spread the rumor that he had been disloyal to George Washington, now the most venerated man in America. Adams, however, still had a large body of admirers, and was elected to the Massachusetts Senate as its president. He had long wished for a public office in his hometown, where he could again enjoy the fellowship of family and friends. The workload and weather were more conducive to his health and tolerable to his nervous condition.

Shortly after his return home, he attended the wedding of his daughter, Hannah, to Thomas Wells, brother of his second wife, Betsy. Adams was pleased with the marriage but could not help but offer the wisdom of his years to his son-in-law. In a letter to Wells, he advised toleration even in small matters. "Of what consequence is it, whether a turkey is brought on the table boiled or roasted? And yet, how often are the passions suffered to interfere in such mighty disputes, till the tempers of both become so soured, that they can scarcely look upon each other with any tolerable degree of good humor."[3]

He also pointed out what he felt were the keys to a successful marriage: "I cannot however help repeating piety, because I think it indispensable. Religion in a family is at once its brightest ornament & its best security."

Adams, deciding that Hancock was an able leader of Massachusetts, agreed to serve on his governor's council. The two men pledged to work together, remembering their earlier days of unity and adventure. The Copley portraits of Hancock and Adams again hung prominently in Hancock's mansion.

Although Adams' life was more tranquil than it had been in decades, America was again veering toward turmoil. After the war, the unity between the states that Samuel Adams had always envisioned began to unravel. Petty rivalries between the states threatened to split the fragile alliance of divergent sovereignties, each with its own culture, religious allegiances, institutions, leaders, and interests. The bonds of camaraderie established during the war years vanished. Instead of one nation, America seemed on the verge of splitting into divergent regions and boundaries similar to the mosaic of Europe. The pendulum swing away from big government during the Revolution created an imbalance toward anarchy in peacetime.

Under the Articles of Confederation that Adams had helped draft, the national government was too weak to be effective. Congress could not regulate trade or settle disputes between states. It could not commit to treaties to protect American interests. Foreign markets barred American imports without fears of reprisals. Without the power to establish trade restrictions, Congress could not ban imports from uncooperative nations.

In order to protect Nova Scotia businesses, for instance, Britain prohibited American imports of oil, fish, lumber, potash and pearl ash to anywhere in the empire. Without a strong navy, American ships traveling to foreign markets were vulnerable on the high seas to pirates or seizure by Britain and other nations. Sailors were pressed into service of the British navy. The economic instability caused high inflation. Soldiers returned from the Revolution only to face poverty, debts, and heavy taxes. Americans at home and abroad were victims to their own passive national government under Adams' Articles of Confederation.[4]

A culture of counterrevolution began to emerge, equipped with political tools Samuel Adams had used: committees of correspondences and quasi-legal conventions. Adams believed these movements were misguided and unjustifiable. These men were not rebelling for their civil rights but rather threatened democratic institutions of their own making, bypassing legal means of redress.

In a letter to John Adams in 1784, Samuel wrote: "Now that we have regular and constitutional governments, popular committees and county conventions are not only useless but dangerous. They served an excellent purpose, and were highly necessary when they were set up, and I shall not repent the small share I then took in them."[5]

He was opposed to the Society of Cincinnati, an exclusive group whose membership was restricted to war veterans and their heirs. Adams was among those who viewed the society as the beginnings of martial nobility in America, akin to feudal lords and knights. As he wrote Elbridge Gerry in 1784: "Even patriots & heroes may become different men when new & different prospects shall have altered their feelings & views; and the undiscerning people may too late repent that they have suffered them to exalt themselves & their family upon the ruins of the common liberty."[6]

From Paris, Thomas Jefferson, the U.S. Minister to France, noted that many Europeans believed America's experiment with self-government was on the verge of collapse. A nation could not survive without the steadying hand of a king and an aristocracy. In a pure republican form of government, the masses ruled, buffeted about by passions and ignorance and a kind of national schizophrenia. In a letter to James Madison, Jefferson reported in September 1785 that foreign newspapers depicted America as ready to implode: "They supposed everything in America was anarchy, tumult, and civil war."[7]

On August 31, 1786, crowds of debt-ridden farmers in rural Massachusetts began storming county courts to prevent their land from being foreclosed. A month later, five hundred renegades under Daniel Shays, a former captain in the Revolutionary War and veteran of Bunker Hill, stormed the state supreme court to keep it closed.

At the Annapolis Convention, called in September 1786 to discuss the crisis, Congressman Alexander Hamilton proposed another convention in May to revise the Articles of Confederation. Congress endorsed the idea in February.

Across the nation, eyes turned toward the civil unrest in Massachusetts, which had already sparked one revolution. Many wondered if the state would indulge the radical spirit and if leaders would be timid in dealing with unrest. John Hancock stepped down as governor, citing poor health and chronic gout, leaving his replacement, James Bowdoin, to deal with the crisis. At a Boston town meeting in December 1786,

Adams publicly supported Governor Bowdoin's decision to call out four thousand state militiamen under the command of General Benjamin Lincoln. Local businessmen and concerned citizens had to donate funds toward the effort; the state was bankrupt. The troops were hastily sent to protect the federal arsenal at Springfield from an expected attack of twelve hundred of Shays' men. Adams had little patience with the rebellion. As president of the Massachusetts' Senate, he drafted a statement declaring the unrest a rebellion.[8]

A battle erupted on January 25, 1787, and Shays was forced to retreat to Petersham, where he was captured by Lincoln's force on February 4. Shays was tried and sentenced to be hanged but was later pardoned along with several other leaders of the rebellion. Adams advocated hanging him. The rebellion forced many across the country to demand that the Articles of Confederation be changed to give the national government the power needed to stabilize the economy. As Congressman Alexander Hamilton put it, "If Shays had not been a desperate debtor, it is much to be doubted whether Massachusetts would have been plunged into a civil war."[9] The U.S. Constitutional Convention ended in September 1787, and a new framework based on the novel idea of "federalism" was sent to the states for ratification.[10]

As Massachusetts Senate president, Samuel Adams supported a motion for each town to send delegates to a state ratifying convention. Adams was chosen as a representative, and the convention was slated to be held in Boston, beginning in January 1788.

His longtime ally, Richard Henry Lee, who remained a member of the Confederation Congress, wrote Adams in fierce opposition to the proposed constitution. "Having long toiled with you my dear friend in the vineyard of liberty, I do with great pleasure submit to your wisdom and patriotism, the objections that prevail in my mind against the new Constitution proposed for federal government." Lee called the proposed constitution "elective despotism" and commented that "[c]hains being still chains, whether [they were] made of gold or iron." The Virginian believed the proposed constitution was the work of ambitious lawyers who sought personal power. He wrote up a list of amendments, a bill of rights.[11]

Adams answered that he was shocked by the new framework for government, which would replace the Articles of Confederation that he had helped draft: "The idea of sovereignty in these states must be lost." He spent days going over the proposed constitution line by line, reading numerous essays and pamphlets arguing its merits and shortcomings. In October 1787, newspapers had begun to carry the Federalist articles arguing in favor of the constitution, authored by James Madison, Hamilton, and John Jay, as well as anti-Federalist writings.

When the Massachusetts' ratifying convention opened on January 9, 1788, only five states had approved the constitution so far: Delaware, Pennsylvania, New Jersey, Connecticut, and Georgia. Massachusetts' decision was expected to tip the balance between approval and rejection. Writing to George Washington, James Madison predicted that New York's decision hinged on Massachusetts. If the Bay State rejected the plan, he believed, anti-Federalist forces in Pennsylvania would try to regain the upper hand there as well. Rhode Island and New Hampshire appointed delegates to attend the Massachusetts convention; both states would accept the constitution if adopted in Massachusetts. The Bay State's decision would likely swing three other states. If it rejected the constitution, the plan would almost certainly be defeated.[12]

"The event in Massachusetts lies in greater uncertainty," wrote Madison in a letter to Jefferson. The anti-Federalists could count on support from separatists in Maine, who never accepted their territory's annexation to Massachusetts. They wanted their own state and believed a strong constitution threatened their cause. In addition, eighteen former Shays insurgents were elected to the ratifying convention along with many sympathizers among the poor farmers and debtors. In addition to these opponents, many of the uneducated inhabitants feared that the proposed constitution was the work of conspiratorial lawyers who wanted to erect an aristocracy.[13]

Samuel Adams took his place among the 330 delegates with several doubts about the proposed constitution. John Hancock, at home and still suffering from ill health, was chosen president, and a delegation was sent to inform him. Hancock and Adams were the two most influential men in Massachusetts. John Adams was in London as Minister to England.

As he had done at other conventions, Samuel Adams made a motion on the first day that the convention open with a prayer each morning. Twenty ministers from various faiths had been elected as delegates, and Adams suggested that clergy from each denomination take a turn in leading the morning grace. Then, for the next week, Adams listened to the debates in silence. The first divisive issue was sparked by the constitution's provision for biennial elections for representatives to the U.S. House. Adams believed that "where annual elections end, tyranny begins."[14] Fisher Ames of Dedham argued that national issues were too complex to be dealt with by an endless stream of freshmen congressmen.[15]

Adams listened to several members in support of biennial elections, and then rose, announcing that he had been convinced. He was satisfied with the propriety of elections every other year. The Federalists were stunned. They asked if he could kindly repeat his statement, perhaps even louder this time. He stated once again that he was satisfied that elections held every two years were acceptable. His words put the issue of elections to rest.[16]

But the majority of delegates appeared to oppose the constitution on other grounds. Rufus King, a constitution advocate who also attended the Philadelphia convention, wrote Madison from Boston: "Our prospects are gloomy, but hope is not entirely extinguished."[17]

On January 25, Amos Singletary, a farmer, rose to address the convention, expressing the thought on many minds: "These lawyers, and men of learning, and moneyed men, that talk so finely, and gloss over matters so smoothly, to make us poor illiterate people swallow down the pill, expect to get into Congress themselves."[18] His speech was applauded loudly, especially by farmers from the outlying counties, men who had marched with Shays.

Then Jonathan Smith, a farmer from rural Berkshire, stepped forward to reply. Berkshire had been ravaged during Shays' rebellion. He said that he had felt in danger during the rebellion. "I have lived in a part of the country where I have known the worth of good government by the want of it. There was a black cloud that rose in the east last winter, and spread over the west."[19]

An outcry erupted, especially among Shays' sympathizers. Smith was on the verge of being shouted down. Adams rose and said, "The gentleman is in order; let him go on in his own way."[20]

"You may see why I wish for good government," Smith continued, growing more impassioned. "People, I say, took up arms; and then, if you went to speak to them, you had the musket of death presented to your breast." Smith said that a strong government was better than anarchy: "When I saw this Constitution, I found that it was a cure for these disorders."[21]

The Federalists worked behind the scenes to win support from critics. A secret caucus was put together; among its members were Adams, Hancock, and Governor Bowdoin. Hancock stayed out of the debate and wanted to leverage his support for votes in the upcoming gubernatorial election. The Federalists agreed to his deal.[22]

The mechanics, a faction of silversmiths, cobblers, engravers, and other artisans, meanwhile, hatched a plan they hoped would secure Samuel Adams' support. They held a meeting at the Green Dragon Inn on Union Street, their usual meeting place, and passed resolutions in favor of the constitution.

Paul Revere, a silversmith representing the mechanics, was sent to present the resolutions to Adams. News of the meeting took him by surprise. Who had called and attended the meeting? he wanted to know. Revere told him the town's mechanics were behind the resolutions.

"How many mechanics were at the Green Dragon when the resolutions were passed?" Adams asked.

"More, sir, than the Green Dragon could hold."

"And where were the rest, Mr. Revere?"

"In the streets, sir."

"And how many were in the streets?"

"'More, sir, than there are stars in the sky.'"

Adams asked why he had not been invited. Revere explained they wanted to hear the voice of the people. Adams decided to throw in his support for the constitution.[23]

With the approval of Hancock and Adams in hand, the Federalists regained their momentum.

Adams addressed the convention and surprised many listeners with his support of the constitution: "There are many parts of it I esteem as highly valuable, particularly the article which empowers Congress to regulate commerce, to form treaties. For want of this power in our national head, our friends are grieved, and our enemies insult us. Our ambassador at the court of London [John Adams] is considered as a mere cipher, instead of the representative of the United States. Therefore it appears to me, that a power to remedy this evil should be given to Congress, and the remedy applied as soon as possible."[24]

The news that Adams and Hancock supported the new government uplifted its supporters across the nation. Madison wrote to Washington on February 11: "We flatter ourselves that the weight of these two characters will ensure our success, but the event is not absolutely certain."[25]

Massachusetts ratified the U.S. Constitution in a narrow 18-vote margin of 187 to 169. Adams and Hancock both voted in favor of ratification. Once the outcome was decided, the rivalries in the convention magically vanished. Church bells and artillery rang in chorus and thunder from Boston. "The Boston people have lost their senses with joy," Henry Knox noted.[26]

Adams was sixty-six years old in 1788 when the U.S. Constitution was passed. His health worsened, and he wanted to play a role in local issues only. The demanding years from 1764 to 1781 in which he had worked incessantly for the national cause had exhausted his health and taxed his fragile nervous system. The national leaders of the new federal government, chosen in April 1789, were at least a decade younger than he. Washington was fifty-six years old; John Adams was fifty-three; Thomas Jefferson was forty-five; Henry Knox was thirty-eight; and Alexander Hamilton was just thirty-one. But the aging man who was lauded as the "Father of the American Revolution" could take personal satisfaction in bringing together much of this extraordinary group to the American cause.

The first two political parties in the United States formed under the banners of Federalists and Republicans. Washington, John Adams, Hamilton, and Knox were among the Federalists, while Jefferson and Madison emerged as the leaders of the Republicans.

In the bitter rivalry, even a hint of reservation over the constitution was viewed as sufficient evidence to tar someone as a subversive enemy of the government. Even though Samuel Adams had voted in favor of the constitution and had helped guide it through the state convention, his enemies viewed his earlier criticisms as evidence of his true feelings. A rock was tossed into his garden, wrapped in paper that carried an assassination threat.

During the debate over the Bill of Rights, Adams voiced his frustrations with the factions emerging in a letter to Richard Henry Lee. He believed the Bill of Rights was needed to protect state governments from being overrun: "Should a strong Federalist as some call themselves see what has now dropped from my pen, he would say that I am an anti-fed, an amendment monger &c; those are truly vulgar terms."[27]

Adams wanted to maintain a delicate balance: "I am impressed with a sense of the importance of amendments; that the good people may clearly see the distinction, for there is a distinction, between the federal powers vested in Congress, and the sovereign authority belonging to the several states, which is the Palladium of the private, and personal rights of the citizens."

The claims that Adams was less than enthusiastic about Washington as president resurfaced when Reverend William Gordon, a historian from Roxbury, Massachusetts, published a history of the American Revolution in 1788. The book erroneously named Adams as part of the Conway Cabal that sought to place Horatio Gates at head of the Continental Army. Adams wrote to Lee, perhaps for Washington's eyes: "I need not tell you who have known so thoroughly the sentiments of my heart, that I have always had a very high esteem for the late commander in chief of our armies; and I now most sincerely believe that while President Washington continues in the chair he will be able to give to all good men a satisfactory reason for every instance of his public conduct. I feel myself constrained contrary to my usual manner to make professions of sincerity on this occasion because Dr. Gordon in his History of the Revolution, among many other anecdotes innocent and trifling enough, has gravely said that I was concerned in an attempt to remove General Washington from command."[28]

Many rank-and-file Federalists shunned Samuel Adams, considering him an apostate to American principles. But Adams was not without his supporters, who thought he should be elected to the U.S. Congress again. An article in the *Independent Chronicle* of December 1788 reminded voters of Adams' achievements: "America in her darkest periods ever found him forward and near the helm." Another paper lauded: "It has been said, he is old and anti-federal. His age and experience are the very qualifications you want. His influence caused the constitution to be adopted in this state."[29]

But Adams never campaigned for the office and likely did not want it. He lost the election to Fisher Ames, an eloquent Federalist. His last years in the Continental Congress during the revolution had proved lonely and tiresome.

Also in 1788, his son, Dr. Samuel Adams, died at thirty-seven years of age. His service as a battlefield surgeon during the revolution had exhausted him and permanently damaged his health. His early death was a devastating blow to Adams.[30]

The following year, 1789, Adams was elected lieutenant governor and Hancock was reelected Governor. In expressing his gratitude for the honor, Adams wrote the state legislature: "I am impressed with a warm sense of the honor done me, and it is a pleasing reflection, in my own mind, that I have this testimonial of the confidence of my countrymen, without my solicitation or interference in any manner to obtain it."[31]

Adams and Hancock were again chosen for the same offices in 1790. In his speech to the legislature, Adams felt the need to express his fidelity to the Constitution. His earliest writings in 1748 reflect a belief that loyalty should be directed to a constitution, not party affiliations or personal allegiances. He echoed those sentiments again forty years later. He believed state and federal power balanced the other, providing mutual checks to protect individual liberty.[32]

15

TWILIGHT

Samuel and John Adams could shake their heads in wonder at the changes the years had wrought, some marvelous and unexpected, some as predictable as advancing age. "I have not written a single line to any friend in, or out of Congress during the late session, having been prevented by my old nervous disorder [palsy], and am now dictating this to a confidential friend," Samuel wrote to his cousin on September 2, 1790. By now, he could barely hold a pen.[1]

John Adams had returned from London, where he had served as U.S. ambassador, and was elected to serve as America's first vice president. In September 1790, he stopped in Philadelphia before proceeding to the nation's capital in New York City. His time was filled searching for a house in New York. "The sight of our old Liberty Hall [in Philadelphia], and of several of our old friends, had brought your venerable idea to my mind," he wrote Samuel, referring to the idea for a continental congress.[2]

John then opened up a dialogue on government. He wondered if the French Revolution would spread American-style democracy or merely end in "a change of imposters." John wrote: "What, my old friend, is this world about to become? Is the millennium commencing? Are the kingdoms of it about to be governed by reason? Your Boston town meetings and our Harvard College have set the universe in motion."

Samuel doubted that human nature could be radically changed by an "enlightened" scheme of government. He did not believe that the

world was on the precipice of a golden age but that each generation had
to fight to preserve freedom: "The same tragedies have been acted on the
theatre of the world, the same arts of tormenting have been studied and
practiced to this day; and even religion and reason united have never
succeeded to establish the permanent foundations of political freedom
and happiness in the most enlightened countries on the earth." Samuel
agreed that a "change in imposters" was likely.[3]

John was intrigued by the discussion. The vice president believed a
political aristocracy eventually would come to dominate America government: "The nobles have been essential parties in the preservation of
liberty whenever and wherever it has existed. In Europe they alone have
preserved it against kings and people, wherever it has been preserved, or
at least with very little assistance from the people."[4] In a free land, a mer-
itocracy would allow great families to ascend in power and rank. These
families eventually would compete for control and popular esteem, John
believed, "for nobles there are, as I have before proved, in Boston, as well
as in Madrid."

John ended his letter with a comment that his views and those of his
more democratic-leaning cousin must be more similar than distinct. "It
is time that you and I should have some sweet communion together,"
the vice president wrote. "I do not believe that we, who have preserved
for more than thirty years an uninterrupted friendship, and have so long
thought and acted harmoniously together in the worst of times, are now
so far asunder in sentiment as some people pretend."

Samuel Adams, however, found several points of contention with his
cousin's letter. He wrote back: "A republic, you tell me, is a government
in which 'the people have an essential share in the sovereignty.' Is not the
whole sovereignty, my friend, essentially in the people? Is not government designed for the welfare and happiness of all the people? And is it
not the uncontrollable, essential right of the people to amend and alter
or annul their Constitution, and frame a new one, whenever they shall
think it will better promote their own welfare and happiness to do it?
That the sovereignty resides in the people is a political doctrine which I
have never heard an American politician seriously deny."[5]

He rejected John's assertion that a "natural aristocracy" would
emerge: "The son of an excellent man may never inherit the great qual-

ities of his father." Frequent elections would allow voters to throw out men unqualified for elected posts, preventing a permanent nobility to entrench itself, Samuel maintained.

As John Adams settled in as the nation's first vice president, Samuel Adams remained active in Boston politics, continuing in his post as lieutenant governor. He was disturbed by what he saw as signs of moral decay such as gambling and extravagant parties. He still hoped that Boston could become a "Christian Sparta," and was concerned that popular entertainments could erode morality and distract residents from the defense of their liberties. In 1791, the theater group appealed at the Town Meeting for Boston to lift its ban on public stages. Adams strongly objected.

When resident Harrison Gray Otis rose to protest the proposal, Adams praised him as "one young man willing to step forth in the good old cause of morality and religion." When a troupe tried to open a theater in violation of the ban, Hancock had them arrested on stage in accordance with the regulation.[6]

By 1793, Hancock's health was deteriorating, and it became clear that his life was fading away. He died on October 8, 1793, at the age of fifty-six. Samuel Adams followed the coffin as the chief mourner. Overwhelmed with emotion and fatigue, he excused himself from his place in the procession as it passed the State House, where he and Hancock had once challenged Governor Hutchinson and where they both had served in the state's two highest offices. Adams could not help but view the event as the fading echo of a bygone era. He was among the last surviving participants from those early battles of 1764 and the protests over the Stamp Act. Among the Boston radicals now departed were Oxenbridge Thacher, James Otis, Josiah Quincy, Joseph Warren, Thomas Cushing, and his own son.

Now John Hancock, who had flung open his doors and handed out Madeira wine to celebrate that first victory over the Stamp Act, had joined the list. Adams composed himself as the funeral train proceeded to Hancock's last resting place, the Granary Burying Ground.

Three months later, in January 1794, Samuel Adams became the governor of the state of Massachusetts. In his inaugural speech, he explained to the legislature and constituents that he did not believe the

state's top administrator should set the agenda. He saw himself in an almost passive role, the servant of the voters and an executive under the
direction of the state assembly. "Legislation is within your department,"
he told the state lawmakers. Adams believed that republican democracy
would spread abroad as nations followed the American example. He
was initially supportive of the French Revolution. In addressing the
Legislature, he said: "The doctrine of Liberty and Equality is an article
in the political creed of the United States." France, he believed, was on
the same path that the Americans had followed in the years leading up
to 1776. "The Republic of France have also adopted the same principle, and laid it as the foundation of their Constitution. That nation
having for many ages groaned under the exercise of the pretended right
claimed by their Kings and Nobles, until their very feelings as men were
become torpid, at length suddenly awoke, from their long slumber,
abolished the usurpation, and placed every man upon the footing of
equal rights."[7]

He remained popular and was elected governor annually again by
heavy majorities until 1796, despite the large Federalist faction in Massachusetts and throughout the North. But many people across the country and in Boston still criticized and shunned him as an enemy to the
Constitution.

His views, however, did not align with party politics. He applauded
Washington's advice, for instance, that America should stay away from
foreign entanglements and remain isolationist. Like the President,
Adams believed America's future lay westward in unchartered territory,
not east toward the Old World of Europe. But Adams was opposed to
John Jay's Treaty of 1795 between the United States and Britain. Riots
erupted in Boston when it was revealed that the treaty failed to prohibit
the British practice of impressing American sailors into servitude. In
New England port towns, this practice was deemed by many as a justification for another war with Britain. Many who had lost friends, family and loved ones to this form of slavery felt betrayed by the treaty,
which preserved peace but at a high cost. "You cannot imagine," wrote
vice president John Adams, "what horror some persons are in, lest peace
should continue." Throughout the streets of Boston rang the cry,
"Damn John Jay! Damn every one that won't damn John Jay! Damn

every one that won't put lights in his windows and sit up all night damning John Jay!"[8]

The British also refused to open their ports to American merchant ships, except in the West Indies, and only to vessels less than seventy tons, and prohibited U.S. vessels from exporting sugar, molasses, coffee, cocoa, and cotton to European ports. The significant British concession was an agreement to remove all British troops from U.S. soil by June 1, 1796. Washington believed the treaty, which was approved by two-thirds of the U.S. Senate on June 24, 1795, defused the risk of war with the British.[9]

Samuel Adams, who had been quick to help quell Shays' rebellion, did little to stop the riotous protests in Boston over Jay's treaty, calling the disorder "only a watermelon frolic." In January 1795, he voiced his disagreement with the treaty to the Massachusetts legislature: "I fear that it may restore to Great Britain such an influence over the government and people of this country as may not be consistent with the general welfare."[10]

His position drew the enmity of the Federalists, and the admiration among Republicans such as Jefferson and Madison.

In 1797, John Adams was elected the second president of the United States, and Thomas Jefferson was elected vice president. Virginia's electoral-college delegates, dominated by anti-Federalists, cast twenty votes for Jefferson and fifteen for Samuel Adams. Under the new Constitution, "electors" named by the state legislatures chose two candidates for President. The person with the most votes became president, and the runner up became vice president. Samuel Adams received the fifth most votes, finishing behind John Adams, Jefferson, diplomat Thomas Pinckney of South Carolina, and Aaron Burr, U.S. Senator from New York.

Adams, who turned seventy-five years old in 1797, retired from public life, stepping down as governor after a remarkable career. He had served uninterrupted as an elected representative for more than thirty-two years.

Adams remained a controversial figure, evoking strong feelings of admiration and antipathy. Fellow townsmen would point out the "Father of the American Revolution"[11] as he walked with his family to church. It seemed incomprehensible to many that British loyalists had

once viewed this kindly, aged gentleman of medium height, wearing a
tie-wig, buckled shoes, and knee-breeches, and wrapped in a red cloak,
as the most feared agitator in America, the would-be "Cromwell." He
was polite to people passing by, his head trembling slightly as he talked.
His eyes were dark blue under heavy eyebrows, his eyesight diminishing,
although he never wore eyeglasses in public. The air of gravity that in
younger days made his speeches so commanding was still evident, even
as he grew physically less and less forceful.

Samuel Adams was not pleased with the direction of his cousin John's
administration. Filling Washington's shoes proved an impossible task.
John lacked the power to unite the country that Washington had. He retained Washington's cabinet, most of whom had no loyalty to the new
president. An undeclared naval war with France began because the French
viewed Jay's Treaty as an alliance with Britain. French spies were known
to be operating in America. As war appeared imminent, President Adams
the passed controversial Alien and Sedition acts, which allowed him to jail
newspaper publishers who criticized his administration.

A friend of Samuel's asked him to write a personal letter of introduction to Vice President Thomas Jefferson. Jefferson responded immediately with a note of affection to Samuel: "A letter from you, my
respectable friend, after three-and-twenty years of separation, has given
me a pleasure I cannot express. It recalls to my mind the anxious days we
then passed in struggling for the cause of mankind. Your principles have
been tested in the crucible of time, and have come out pure. You have
proved that it was monarchy, and not merely British monarchy, you opposed. A government by representatives elected by the people at short
periods was our object, and our maxim at that day was, 'Where annual
election ends, tyranny begins.'"[12]

John Adams served only one term as president, ushering in the presidency of Jefferson. Samuel Adams, whose political sentiments lay more
with the new president than with his cousin, wrote Jefferson in 1801, expressing delight in his election.

As president, Jefferson wrote Samuel Adams with a rather extraordinary admission regarding his inaugural address: "I addressed a letter to
you, my very dear and ancient friend, on the 4th of March; not indeed
to you by name, but through the medium of my fellow-citizens, whom

occasion called on me to address. In meditating the matter of that address, I often asked myself, Is this exactly in the spirit of the Patriarch of
liberty Samuel Adams? Will he approve of it? I have felt a great deal for
our country in the times we have seen, but individually for no one so
much as yourself. When I have been told that you were avoided, insulted, frowned on, I could but ejaculate, 'Father, forgive them, for they
know not what they do.'"[13]

Adams answered that Jefferson's respect outweighed the scorn of critics: "I sincerely congratulate our country on the arrival of the day of
glory which has called you to the first office in the administration of our
Federal government. Your warm feelings of friendship most certainly
have carried you to a higher tone of expression than my utmost merits
will bear. If I have at any time been avoided or frowned upon, your kind
ejaculation, in the language of the most perfect friend of man, surpasses
every injury."

Then Adams offered candid advice about the pains of elected office,
telling Jefferson to brace for an onslaught from critics: "The world has
been governed by prejudice and passion, which never can be friendly to
truth; and while you nobly resolve to retain those principles of candor
and justice, resulting from a free elective representative government,
such as they have been taught to hate and despise, you must depend
upon being hated yourself, because they hate your principles." He ended
his letter to the president with a prayer: "May Heaven grant that the
principles of liberty and virtue, truth and justice, may pervade the whole
earth."[14]

As Adams' health began to fail, he no longer had the strength to
walk the streets of Boston. He enjoyed the company of his wife, Betsy,
and his close friends, especially older ones who had participated in the
revolutionary cause. His family noted that he was often reserved with
strangers, and an odd shyness surfaced. He was uncomfortable with attention when not working for a public cause. He would regale close
friends, however, with stories of the revolution, of eluding British soldiers at Lexington or intimidating the royal governor and British officers after the massacre of 1770. He could talk about the personalities
who had gained national fame: Washington, Jefferson, Henry Knox,
John Adams.

Unfortunately for posterity's sake, his anecdotes were not preserved. He seemed totally unconcerned with his historical legacy. While other Founding Fathers wrote autobiographies and penned letters with an eye on their place in history, Samuel Adams made no effort to document his role in engineering the break with England and helping set up the network for a new government to emerge. He produced no life story, no memoirs, no letters to friends chronicling his glory days.

He made no effort to collect his writings and newspaper articles, which would someday fill volumes and help illuminate some of the most critical moments in the formation of the new nation—as John Adams noted. In his final years, these were scattered and risked being lost to history.

It seemed sufficient for him that he knew the part he had played and did the duty he believed providence laid before him. Adams' satisfaction lay in the knowledge that "millions yet unborn" would enjoy a freedom that without his efforts may have been lost. His last known letter was dictated in October 1802 and addressed to Thomas Paine, whose latest work attacked religion. Still combative, Adams wrote: "Do you think that your pen, or the pen of any other man, can un-Christianize the mass of our citizens, or have you hopes of converting a few of them to assist you in so bad a cause?"[15]

By September 1803, those around him began to realize the end was near. Samuel spoke less, and his mind began to wander. He insisted that no elaborate plans be made for his funeral. He wanted no parade and only the most simple, plain, plank-board coffin.

On Saturday, the first day of October, difficulty in breathing interrupted his sleep. The next day, the family doctor was called. He told Betsy and Samuel's relatives that it was time to pay their last respects. As they gathered around Samuel's bed, his daughter quietly leaned over him as he tried in vain to speak. Samuel Adams was born on a Sunday, baptized on a Sunday, and had died on a Sunday, October 2, 1803.

Church bells tolled in Boston in lamentation. After some party wrangling between Federalists and Republicans, his body was provided with a military escort to his interment at the Granary Burial Ground.

Adams, a democratic-leaning Republican in the predominantly Federalist North, received muted gratitude for his life's achievements. Had he lived a few years more, while a string of Republican presidents—Jefferson, Madison, and Monroe—changed the political tide in America, perhaps he would have been elevated to a much grander status.

Upon his death, *The Independent Chronicle* in Boston observed:

SAMUEL ADAMS IS DEAD!
   We have the painful task to announce to the public, that on yesterday morning, about a quarter past seven o'clock, at his house in this town, died, in the eighty-second year of his age, SAMUEL ADAMS, late Governor of this Commonwealth, the consistent and inflexible patriot and republican. The foe of tyrants in every form; the friend of virtue and her friends, he died beloved, as he had lived respected. Admiring posterity, penetrated by a just sense of his transcendent merits, will emphatically hail him as the undeviating friend of civil and religious liberty, and the FATHER OF THE AMERICAN REVOLUTION![16]

In Congress, representative John Randolph rose before the U.S. House to propose a national mourning for Samuel Adams, calling him a "great man." Randolph said he felt inadequate to state Adams' contribution to the country: "His character and fame are put beyond that reach of time and chance to which everything mortal is exposed." The House unanimously approved Randolph's proposal that each member should wear a crape around the left arm for a month in memorial to Adams.[17]

John Adams, back on his farm in Braintree, began to collect Samuel's writings to help preserve his place in history. He commented: "It would throw light upon American history for fifty years. In it would be found specimens of a nervous simplicity of reasoning and eloquence that have never been rivaled in America." It would be impossible to understand the revolution without studying Samuel Adams' career, John wrote: "Without the character of Samuel Adams, the true history of the American Revolution can never be written. For fifty years his pen, his tongue, his activity, were constantly exerted for his country without fee or reward. During that time he was almost an incessant writer."[18]

Samuel Adams' papers were collected by his grandson, William Wells, who wrote to Thomas Jefferson, asking for his impressions. Jefferson responded, "I can say that he was truly a great man, wise in council, fertile in resources, immovable in his purposes, and had, I think, a greater share than any other member, in advising and directing our measures, in the Northern war."[19]

In 1777, during the dark and uncertain days of the revolution, Samuel wrote: "May I live to see the public liberty restored and the safety of our dear country secured. I should then think I had enjoyed enough and bid this world adieu."[20] He lived to see that dream fulfilled.

Epilogue

PATRIARCH OF LIBERTY

Samuel Adams believed the nation's founding generation fought not only for their rights but for America's future generations. "The liberties of our country are worth defending at all hazards," he admonished colonists. "If we should suffer them to be wrested from us, millions yet unborn may be the miserable sharers in the event."[1] He believed the only security for these liberties was to create a new kind of government, free of crowns and coronets, without titles or hereditary privileges. After the signing of the Declaration of Independence, Samuel Adams observed that "[m]onarchy seems to be generally exploded" in America.[2]

The world into which Adams was born and helped change was dominated by kings and courtiers. Europe's leading nations were republics only in name. In England's mixed-republic, the king shared power with nobles and the House of Commons, in which membership was limited to the affluent. Royal officials ruled under the unquestioned authority of "the king's pleasure," and most of Britain's nine million people, those working long hours on farms and in factories, textile mills, shops and shipyards, and in other laborious jobs, had no say in the laws that governed them. The English Bill of Rights of 1689 drew boundaries between the rights of the king and his subjects. But as the word "subjects" suggests, power did not stem from a mandate from British citizens.

Adams, often called a "true republican," believed that all the power should reside with a nation's people, and leaders had no authority not granted by voters. This was a radical idea at the time. In his civil rights crusade, he set out to convince colonists that their rights did not emanate from a charter granted by a king, but were ordained by providence.

All men were equal before God, he argued, and were answerable for their own choices.

Eleven years before the Declaration of Independence, he wrote that men were "unalienably entitled to those essential rights in common with all men: and that no law of society can, consistent with the law of God and nature, divest them of those rights."[3]

His words were later echoed in the national creed. These ideas were no longer radical when in 1776, Jefferson wrote: "We hold these truths to be self-evident, that all men are created equal, that they are endowed by their Creator with certain unalienable rights, that among these are Life, Liberty and the pursuit of Happiness. That to secure these rights, Governments are instituted among Men, deriving their just powers from the consent of the governed."[4]

In 1764, when Adams began to protest British authority in America, colonists thought of themselves as English citizens, and proudly sang the lyrics of the British National Anthem:

> God save the King.
> Send him victorious,
> Happy and glorious,
> Long to reign over us,
> God save the King.

Adams strove to persuade colonists to withdraw allegiance to a king and instead place their fidelity in a government founded on the ideal of individual liberty. The national consciousness could have been formed along many ideals, but thanks in large part to Samuel Adams, it centered on a belief in freedom. In the years leading up to the Revolution, he launched a one-man media blitz to forge a distinctly American mindset. He unquestionably became the most influential writer during those formative years, and the words "liberty" and "freedom" pervaded his essays and served as the foundation of all his arguments. He wanted his ideals to become characteristically American ideals.

He was remarkably successful in his efforts.

In the prewar struggle, Adams emerged as the leading patriot strategist as well as the most influential political writer on the continent. His hand was behind nearly every major protest over royal authority in America. It was Adams who, at a Boston town meeting in 1764, made the first call for the colonies to unite in opposition to British taxes, which led to the Stamp Act Congress a year later. He was the first leader to claim that Parliament had no legal authority in America. He pioneered strategies of civil disobedience such as boycotts, and united colonial legislatures with a circular letter stating colonial rights.

Adams created a committee-of-correspondence intelligence network that coordinated colonial resistance, which became a powerful engine for revolution while laying the seeds for the Continental Congress as well as the state governments to form with the collapse of royal power in America. Adams was the first major figure to publicly advocate the Continental Congress and an independent commonwealth of American states. He engineered the Boston Tea Party, which made the war with England inevitable.

He championed the Suffolk Resolves in the Continental Congress, which called for Massachusetts to erect a provincial government and cast off royal authority, a move which other colonies quickly followed. The first shots of the Revolution came when British troops who marched with orders to arrest Adams and John Hancock were intercepted by colonial militiamen. Patriots and Loyalists both credited Adams with championing the approval of the Declaration of Independence among the delegates to Congress.

Adams' influence as a writer was no less remarkable in shaping the debate in America over British policy. He coined many of the phrases that Americans shouted in defiance, and spelled out in detail the positions that were in turn dispatched in other circular letters and newspapers and heard in discussions in taverns and churches, homes, and meeting halls up and down the seacoast. He forced the British to answer his accusations, to take sides, to draw boundaries and to declare allegiances. Time and time again, Adams drew a line in the sand delineating colonial rights and British power, warning Americans well in advance to vigilantly watch for the inevitable intrusions. He sounded the alarm at each foot of ground he believed was about to be trespassed upon, and trumpeted each invasion like a vindicated prophet. Much of the debate was scripted and waged largely on his terms; he used his pen to develop opinion, lay out issues, educate colonists, form strategy, provoke debate, and force citizens and leaders to take sides. Adams laid out battle plans.

Americans of his generation came to view Samuel Adams as the "spirit of liberty," and in Jefferson's words, "the patriarch of liberty." Americans also came to identify "liberty" as the nation's cornerstone belief. It remains the nation's fundamental political ideal today.

In 1832, Samuel F. Smith wrote an American version of "God Save the King," changing the title to "My Country 'Tis of Thee," and revising the words to reflect the outlook of the young nation. Both songs are sung to the same tune, written by German composer Siegfried August Mahlmann, but the altered lyrics reflected the radical changes that Adams helped foster in the American outlook:

> My country, 'tis of Thee,
> Sweet Land of Liberty
> Of thee I sing;
> Land where my fathers died,
> Land of the pilgrims' pride,
> From every mountain side
> Let Freedom ring.

The theme of individual liberty became central to the American psyche, manifested in Jefferson's notion of the self-reliant farmer, and carried westward in the rugged individualism of the frontiersmen and pioneers. It became the underlying theme of the country's seminal literature, reflected in the works of Washington Irving, Herman Melville, James Fenimore Cooper, Ralph Waldo Emerson, Henry David Thoreau, Walt Whitman, Mark Twain, William James, and countless other writers. It was the bedrock on which Abraham Lincoln anchored his call to abolish slavery in the Gettysburg Address.

Adams not only convinced colonists of their inherent freedom; he gave them the political tools to defend it. He believed that power rested with a nation's people, not just in theory, but in public perceptions, the work that citizens produced, the way they spent their money, and their decisions to pledge or withhold loyalty. He created strategies of civil disobedience by pioneering boycotts and encouraging the use of domestic products, by setting up political networks and organizing grass-root campaigns. He used the press like no one before him to define issues and shape opinion at home and abroad, clinging to natural and legal rights to "keep and put the enemy in the wrong."[5]

These strategies have rippled throughout civil rights battles around the world. In the 1780s, British and Irish residents began to utilize methods created by Adams to fight for political power and home rule. In the twentieth century, Mahatma Gandhi used many of the same strategies to split the British Empire—the same feat Adams had accomplished almost two centuries earlier. Like Adams, Gandhi tried to keep Britain morally in the wrong, and used boycotts and the support of domestic products to put financial pressure on England to end colonial rule in India. He likewise made adroit use of the press to create sympathy abroad.

Gandhi was greatly influenced by Henry David Thoreau's *Civil Disobedience.* Thoreau grew up in Concord, Massachusetts, surrounded by Adams' legacy. In turn, Martin Luther King, Jr. was influenced by Gandhi, and the legacy of Samuel Adams can still be seen in the grass-roots efforts and civil rights battles seen today.

Adams had hoped that the ideal of liberty would spread throughout the world. As he had foreseen, fights to establish or preserve freedom would mark every succeeding generation. America, of course, has struggled throughout its history to live up to the ideal of political equality and individual liberty. Since his death, the nation witnessed the growth of slavery, a Civil War, segregation, as well as limits on political rights based on race and gender. But the ideals that Adams fought for and the tools he used to obtain his goals have likewise endured and continued to live in the hearts of future generations of abolitionists, civil rights advocates, soldiers, politicians and statesmen, and countrymen. His prayer was that liberty would continue to be cherished by "millions yet unborn."

NOTES

INTRODUCTION

1. Samuel Adams, *The Writings of Samuel Adams,* Vol. 3, ed. Harry Alonzo Cushing (New York: G. P. Putnam's Sons, 1904), online at www.gutenberg.org, letter to Richard Henry Lee, July 15, 1777.
2. George Bancroft, *History of the United States from the Discovery of the American Continent,* Vol. 3, p. 77.

CHAPTER ONE

1. Reason for Puritan Flight taken from Governor Thomas Dudley's account, quoted in Frank Halsey, *Great Epochs of American History* (New York: Funk and Wagnall's Co., 1912), Vol. 2, pp. 114–118.
2. William Jackman, *History of the American Nation* (Chicago: K. Gaynor, 1911), Vol. 8, p. 2377; James K. Hosmer, *Samuel Adams* (Boston: Houghton Mifflin, 1888), 12–13; William V. Wells, *The Life and Public Service of Samuel Adams: Being a Narrative of His Acts and Opinions, And His Agency in Forwarding and Producing the American Revolution* (Boston: Little, Brown & Co., 1865), pp. 1–2, and in Vol. 3, pp. 423–426; David McCullough, *John Adams* (New York: Simon and Schuster, 2001), pp. 29–30.
3. Wells, *Life of Samuel Adams,* p. 6; Hosmer, *Samuel Adams,* p. 15.
4. Wells, *Life of Samuel Adams,* p. 5; Hosmer, *Samuel Adams,* p. 14.
5. William Jackman, *History of the American Nation,* Vol. 8, p. 2378; Wells, *Life of Samuel Adams,* p. 5; Hosmer, *Samuel Adams,* p. 14.
6. George Bancroft, *A Plea For the Constitution of the United States, Wounded in the House of its Guardians* (New York: Harper & Bros, 1886), pp. 14–15.
7. Woodrow Wilson, *History of the American People* (New York: William H. Wise, 1931), Vol. 2, p. 145.
8. John Locke, *The Second Treatise of Government: an Essay Concerning the True Original, Extent and End of Civil Government,* cited in the American Reference Library on CD-Rom (Orem, Utah: Western Standard Publishing Company, 1998). Section 201, record 106,981.
9. Wells, *Life of Samuel Adams,* p. 10.
10. Wells, *Life of Samuel Adams,* p. 10.
11. Wells, *Life of Samuel Adams,* p. 24.

12　Hosmer, *Samuel Adams*, p. 33; Wells, *Life and Public Services of Samuel Adams*, p. 15.

13.　Wells, *The Life of Samuel Adams*, p. 16.
14.　Wells, *The Life of Samuel Adams*, p. 17.
15.　Wells, *Life of Samuel Adams*, p. 17.
16.　Wells, *Life of Samuel Adams*, p. 22.
17.　Wells, *Life of Samuel Adams*, p. 23.
18.　Wells, *Life of Samuel Adams*, p. 24.
19.　Wells, *Life of Samuel Adams*, p. 25.
20.　Bancroft, *History of the United States*, Vol. III, p. 76; Wells, *Life of Samuel Adams*, p. 27.
21.　Hosmer, *Samuel Adams*, p. 68; Wells, *Life of Samuel Adams*, p. 33.
22.　Jackman, *History of the American Nation*, Vol. 8, p. 2379; Hosmer, *Samuel Adams*, p. 33.

CHAPTER TWO

1.　John Clark Ridpath, *James Otis: Pre-Revolutionist at Project Gutenberg*, www.gutenberg.org, e-text no. 722.
2.　John Adams, Autobiography, Massachusetts Historical Society. Electronic Archive at www.masshist.org; Francis W. Halsey, *World's Great Orations* (New York: Funk & Wagnall's Co., 1906), Vol. 1, pp. 27–36; Ridpath, *James Otis*, www.gutenberg.org, e-text no. 722.
3.　Samuel Adams in ed. Harry Alonzo Cushing, *The Writings of Samuel Adams* (New York: G. P. Putnam's Sons, 1904; distributed by Fictionwise.com, 2004), Vol. 1, from document dated May 24, 1764.
4.　Franklin, *The Autobiography of Benjamin Franklin*, ed. Gordon S. Haight (New York: Walter J. Black, Inc, 1941), pp. 129–140.
5.　Wells, *The Life and Public Services of Samuel Adams*, Vol. 1, pp. 49–50.
6.　Samuel Adams, *The Writings of Samuel Adams*, in Cushing ed., Vol. 1, from document dated May 24, 1764.
7.　Samuel Adams, *The Writings of Samuel Adams*, in Cushing ed., Vol. 1, from document dated May 24, 1764.
8.　Samuel Adams, *The Writings of Samuel Adams*, in Cushing ed., Vol. 1, from document dated May 24, 1764; George Elliott Howard, *Preliminaries of the Revolution, 1763–1775* (New York: Harper & Brothers, 1905), p. 111.
9.　Samuel Adams, *The Writings of Samuel Adams*, in Cushing ed., Vol. 1, from document dated May 24, 1764.
10.　Samuel Adams, *The Writings of Samuel Adams*, in Cushing ed., Vol. 1, from document dated May 24, 1764.
11.　Howard, *Preliminaries of the Revolution*, p. 111; Samuel Adams, *The Writings of Samuel Adams*, in Cushing ed., Vol. 1, from document dated May 24, 1764.
12.　Wells, *Life of Samuel Adams*, p. 45; Bancroft, *History of the United States*, Vol. 3, p. 78.
13.　Samuel Adams in Harry Alonzo Cushing ed., *The Writings of Samuel Adams* (New York: G. P. Putnam's Sons, 1904, at www.gutenberg.org, e-text no.

2093, Vol. 3, letter of March 21, 1775; Wells, *Life of Samuel Adams,* Vol. 1, pp. 187, 215, 447, 496, and in Vol. 2, p. 44.

14. Wells, *Life of Samuel Adams,* Vol. 1, p. 149.

CHAPTER THREE

1. Wells, *Life of Samuel Adams,* Vol. 1, p. 54.
2. Bancroft, *History of the United States,* Vol. 3, p. 104.
3. Wells, *Life of Samuel Adams,* Vol. 1, p. 56.
4. Wells, *Life of Samuel Adams,* Vol. 1, p. 57.
5. Bancroft, *History of the United States,* Vol. 3, p. 109; James K. Hosmer, *Life of Thomas Hutchinson, Royal Governor of the Province of Massachusetts Bay* (Boston and New York: Houghton Mifflin and Company, 1896), p. 91.
6. Bancroft, *History of the United States,* Vol. 3, p. 112.
7. Hosmer, *Samuel Adams,* pp. 49–50.
8. Bancroft, *History of the United States,* Vol. 3, p. 120.
9. Bancroft, *History of the United States,* Vol. 3, p. 109; Franklin, *Autobiography,* pp. 129–130.
10. William Edward Hartpole Lecky, James Albert Woodburn, ed., *The American Revolution: 1763–1783* (London: D. Appleton, 1898), p. 77; Bancroft, *History of the United States,* Vol. 3, p. 120.
11. Bancroft, *History of the United States,* Vol. 3, pp. 121–122.
12. Bancroft, *History of the United States,* Vol. 3, pp. 118–119.
13. John Adams, John Adams Papers, www.masshist.org. Autobiography, entry for 1765.
14. Samuel Adams, *The Writings of Samuel Adams,* Cushing ed., Vol. 1, document dated September 12, 1765.
15. John K. Alexander, *Samuel Adams, America's Revolutionary Politician* (Lanham, MD: Rowman & Littlefield Publishers, 2002).
16. Bancroft, *History of the United States,* Vol. 3, p. 136.
17. Jackman, *History of the American Nation,* Vol. 2, p. 407; Bancroft, *History of the United States,* Vol. 3, p. 135.
18. Wells, *Life of Samuel Adams;* Samuel Adams, *The Writings of Samuel Adams,* Harry Alonzo Cushing ed. (New York: G. P. Putnam and Sons, 1904), at www.gutenberg.org, Vol. 2, from Adams' Boston Gazette article of August 19, 1771.
19. Hosmer, *Life of Thomas Hutchinson,* pp. 91–92.
20. Hosmer, *Life of Thomas Hutchinson,* pp. 92–93.
21. Wells, *Life of Samuel Adams,* Vol. 1, p. 63.
22. Wells, *Life of Samuel Adams,* Vol. 1, p. 63.
23. Bancroft, *History of the United States,* Vol. 3, p. 139.
24. Hosmer, *Samuel Adams,* p. 54.
25. Samuel Adams, *The Writings of Samuel Adams,* Cushing ed., Vol. 1, document of October 23, 1765; Wells, *The Life of Samuel Adams,* Vol. 1, pp. 71–73.
26. Samuel Adams, *The Writings of Samuel Adams,* Cushing ed., Vol. 1, document of October 23, 1765; Wells, *Life of Samuel Adams,* Vol. 1, p. 73.

27. Samuel Adams, *The Writings of Samuel Adams* Cushing ed., Vol. 1, document of October 23, 1765; Wells, *Life of Samuel Adams,* Vol. 1, p. 73.

28. Bancroft, *History of the United States,* Vol. 3, p. 153.

29. Wells, *Life of Samuel Adams,* Vol. 1, p. 50.

30. Wells, *The Life of Samuel Adams,* Vol. 1, p. 75.

31. Wells, *Life of Samuel Adams,* Vol. 1, p. 76.

32. Hosmer, *Life of Thomas Hutchinson,* p. 102.

33. Wells, *The Life of Samuel Adams,* Vol. 1, p. 76.

34. Bancroft, *History of the United States,* Vol. 3, p. 157; John Fiske, *The American Revolution* (Boston and New York: Houghton Mifflin, 1891), p. 23.

35. Lecky, *The American Revolution,* p. 83; Bancroft, *History of the United States,* Vol. 3, p. 113; Fisk, *The American Revolution,* Vol. 1, p. 18.

36. David McCollough, *John Adams* (New York: Simon and Schuster, 2001), p. 44.

37. Wells, *Life of Samuel Adams,* Vol. 1, p. 81.

38. Adam Smith, *An Inquiry into the Nature and Cause of the Wealth of Nations,* on CD-Rom, cited in the American Reference Library (Orem, UT: Western Standard Publishing Company, 1998), Book 4, Chapter VII, Of Colonies, Record, 108,730.

39. Adam Smith, *Wealth of Nation,* CD-Rom, American Reference Library, Record 108,730.

40. Samuel Adams, *The Writings of Samuel Adams,* Cushing ed., Vol. 1, letter of December 19, 1765; Wells, *Life of Samuel Adams,* Vol. 1, p. 83.

41. Samuel Adams, *The Writings of Samuel Adams,* Vol. 1, letter of December 19, 1765; Wells, *Life of Samuel Adams,* Vol. 1, p. 84.

42. Samuel Adams, The Writings of Samuel Adams, Cushing ed., letter of December 20, 1765; Wells, *The Life of Samuel Adams,* Vol. 1, p. 101.

43. William Jennings Bryan and Francis W. Halsey, *The World's Famous Orations: America,* Franklin's exam before The House of Commons (New York: Funk and Wagnall's Company, 1906), Vol. 8, p. 37.

44. Pitt quoted from America—*Great Crisis in Our History Told by Its Makers: A Library of Original Sources* (Chicago: Americanization Department of Veterans of Foreign Wars of the United States, 1925), Vol. 3, pp. 77–78; Basil Williams, *The Life of William Pitt, Earl of Chatham* (London: Longmans, Green and Company, 1913), pp. 191–193.

45. Bancroft, *History of The United States,* Vol. 3, p. 191.

46. Boston broadside from March 1766 at the Library of Congress, Collection of Broadsides, Leaflets and Pamphlets from America and Europe, Portfolio 36, Folder, electronic identification online: 14a rbpe 0360140a http://hdl.loc.gov/loc.rbc/rbpe.0360140a.

47. Lecky, *The American Revolution,* p. 94; Halsey, *Great Epochs in American History,* Vol. 3, p. 76.

48. Wells, *Life of Samuel Adams,* Vol. 1, pp. 115, 118.

49. Wells, *Life of Samuel Adams,* Vol. 1, p. 112.

CHAPTER FOUR

1. John Adams, *John Adams Papers,* diary entry of January 30, 1768.

2. John Adams, *John Adams Papers,* diary entry for December 23, 1765.
3. Bancroft, *History of the United States,* Vol. 3, p. 222.
4. Wells, *Life of Samuel Adams,* Vol. 1, p. 133.
5. Wells, *Life of Samuel Adams,* Vol. 3, p. 132.
6. Bancroft, *History of the United States,* Vol. 3, pp. 215, 465.
7. Bancroft, *History of the United States,* Vol. 3, pp. 236, 238
8. Bancroft, *History of the United States,* Vol. 3, p. 218.
9. Bancroft, *History of the United States,* Vol. 3, p. 239.
10. Wells, *Life of Samuel Adams,* Vol. 1, p. 150.
11. Wells, *Life of Samuel Adams,* Vol. 1, p. 150.
12. Wells, *Life of Samuel Adams,* Vol. 1, p. 167.
13. Adam Smith, *Wealth of Nations,* CD-Rom, Book 4, Chapter VII: of Colonies, Part 3, Record, 108,761.
14. Wells, *The Life of Samuel Adams,* Vol. 1, p. 154.
15. Bancroft, *History of the United States,* Vol. 3, p. 275.
16. Bancroft, *History of the United States,* Vol. 3, p. 275.
17. Bancroft, *History of the United States,* Vol. 3, 275–276; Wells, *Life of Samuel Adams,* Vol. 1, p. 170.
18. Colin Bonwick, *English Radicals and the American Revolution* (Chapel Hill, NC: University of North Carolina Press, 1997), p. 276; Lecky, *The American Revolution,* p. 114; Hosmer, *Samuel Adams,* p. 109.
19. Bancroft, *History of the United States,* Vol. 3, p. 284.
20. Bancroft, *History of the United States,* Vol. 3, p. 284.
21. Stout, *The Royal Navy in America,* p. 116; Bancroft, *History of the United States,* Vol. 3, pp. 276–277.
22. Wells, *Life of Samuel Adams,* Vol. 1, p. 180; Bancroft, *History of the United States,* Vol. 3, p. 284.
23. Wells, *Life of Samuel Adams,* Vol. 1, p. 180; Bancroft, *History of the United States.*
24. Hosmer, *Samuel Adams,* p. 113; Wells, *Life of Samuel Adams,* Vol. 1, p. 193.
25. Samuel Adams, *The Writings of Samuel Adams,* in Cushing ed., Vol. 2, Adams' *Boston Gazette* article of September 16, 1771; Wells, *Life of Samuel Adams,* Vol. 1, p. 171.

CHAPTER FIVE

1. Neil R. Stout, *The Royal Navy in America, 1760–1775: A Study of Enforcement of British Colonial Policy in the Era of the American Revolution* (Annapolis, MD: Naval Institute Press, 1973), p. 117.
2. Stout, *The Royal Navy in America,* pp. 117–118.
3. Herbert S. Allan, *John Hancock, Patriot in Purple* (New York: Macmillan, 1948), p. 104; Stout, *The Royal Navy in America,* pp. 118–120.
4. Stout, *The Royal Navy in America,* p. 120.
5. Stout, *The Royal Navy in America,* p. 118.
6. Thomas L. Puvis, *A Dictionary of American History* (Cambridge, MA: Blackwell Reference, 1995), Samuel Adams remark quoted in "small confidential companies."—William Gordon, *The History of the Rise, Progress, and Establishment, of the Independence of the United States of America,* Vol. 1, entry for

March 9, 1774, p. 347 (1788, reprinted 1969), cited in CD-Rom edition of the American Reference Library (Orem, Utah: Western Standard Publishing Company, 1998), record 1,317,625.

7. Woodrow Wilson, *History of the American People* (New York: William H. Wise, 1931), Vol. 2, p. 174.

8. Adam Smith, *Wealth of Nations,* CD-Rom edition of American Reference Library, Book IV, Chapter VII, Part 3, record 108,753.

9. Wells, *Life and Public Service of Samuel Adams,* Vol. 1, p. 186.

10. Allan, *John Hancock,* pp. 105–109; Mercy Otis Warren, *The Rise, Progress and Termination of the American Revolution Interspersed with Biographical, Political, and Moral Observations,* CD-Rom edition (West Roxbury, MA: B&R Samizdat Express, 2003), Vol. 1, Chapter 3.

11. Stout, *The Royal Navy in America,* p. 120.

12. Ridpath, *James Otis the Pre-Revolutionist,* at www.gutenberg.org, e-text 722; Bancroft, *History of the United States,* Vol. 3, pp. 290–291.

13. Mercy Otis Warren, *The American Revolution,* CD-Rom edition (West Roxbury, MA: B&R Samizdat Express, 2003), Vol. 1, Chapter 3; Wells, *Life of Samuel Adams,* pp. 189–190; Hosmer, *Samuel Adams,* p. 100.

14. John Adams, *John Adams Papers,* Autobiography entry for1768; Bancroft, *History of the United States,* Vol. 3, p. 292.

15. Wells, *Life of Samuel Adams,* Vol. 1, p. 167; Bancroft, *History of the United States,* Vol. 3, p. 284.

16. Hosmer, *Samuel Adams,* pp. 103, 148, 269; Hosmer, *Life of Thomas Hutchinson,* pp. 129, 220.

17. John Adams, *John Adams Papers,* Autobiography, entry for 1768.

18. Mercy Otis Warren, *The American Revolution,* CD-Rom edition, Vol. 1, Chapter 3; Wells, *Life of Samuel Adams,* p. 167; Hosmer, *Samuel Adams,* p. 136.

19. Wells, *Life of Samuel Adams,* Vol. 1, p. 196; Hosmer, *Samuel Adams,* p. 102.

20. Hosmer, *Samuel Adams,* p. 102; Wells, *Life of Samuel Adams,* Vol. 1, p. 196.

21. Hosmer, *Samuel Adams,* 102; Wells, *Life of Samuel Adams,* Vol. 1, 196.

22. Samuel Adams, *The Writings of Samuel Adams,* Vol. 2, Adams' article in *Boston Gazette,* September 16, 1771.

23. Samuel Adams, *The Writings of Samuel Adams,* in Cushing ed., Vol. 2, Adams letter to Arthur Lee, September 27, 1771.

24. Bancroft, *History of the United States,* Vol. 3, p. 297.

25. Bancroft, *History of the United States,* Vol. 3, p. 306; Hosmer, *Samuel Adams,* p. 148.

26. Bancroft, *History of the United States,* Vol. 3, p. 298.

27. Arthur M. Schlesinger, ed. *The Almanac of American History* (New York: Barnes & Noble Books, 1993).

28. Hosmer, *Samuel Adams,* pp. 117–119; Wells, *Life of Samuel Adams,* Vol. 1, pp. 209–211.

29. Stout, *The Royal Navy in America,* p. 122.

30. Stout, *The Royal Navy in America,* p. 122.

31. Wells, *Life and Public Services of Samuel Adams;* Mercy Otis Warren, *The American Revolution, CD-Rom edition,* Vol. 1, Chapter 3; Wells, *Life of Samuel Adams,* Vol. 1, p. 212.

32. Wells, *Life of Samuel Adams,* Vol. 1, pp. 212–213.

33. Wells, *Life of Samuel Adams,* Vol. 1, p. 213.

34. Wells, *Life of Samuel Adams,* Vol. 1, p. 216; Hosmer, *Samuel Adams,* p. 123. Mercy Otis Warren, *The American Revolution,* CD-Rom edition, Vol. 1, Chapter 3.
35. Bancroft, *History of the United States,* Vol. 3, p. 310.
36. Wells, *Life of Samuel Adams,* Vol. 1, p. 217.
37. Stout, *The Royal Navy in America,* pp. 123–124; Mercy Otis Warren, *The American Revolution,* CD-Rom edition, Vol. 1, Chapter 3; Allan, *John Hancock,* pp. 113–114. Hosmer, *Life of Thomas Hutchinson,* pp. 140–141; Bancroft, *History of the United States,* Vol. 3, pp. 312–313.
38. Stout, *The Royal Navy in America,* p. 124; Mercy Otis Warren, *The American Revolution,* CD-Rom edition, Vol. 1, Chapter 3; Bancroft, *History of the United States,* Vol. 3, p. 312.
39. Wells, *Life of Samuel Adams,* Vol. 1, p. 219.
40. Wells, *Life of Samuel Adams,* Vol. 1, p. 223.
41. Stout, *The Royal Navy in America,* p. 124.
42. Hosmer, *Samuel Adams,* p. 328.
43. Wells, *Life of Samuel Adams,* Vol. 1, p. 221.
44. Wells, *Life of Samuel Adams,* Vol. 1, pp. 221–222.

CHAPTER SIX

1. Bancroft, *History of the United States,* Vol. 3, p. 322.
2. Bancroft, *History of the United States,* Vol. 3, p. 322.
3. Bancroft, *History of the United States,* Vol. 3, p. 325.
4. Bancroft, *History of the United States,* Vol. 3, p. 325.
5. Bancroft, *History of the United States,* Vol. 3, pp. 323–324, 335.
6. Hosmer, *Samuel Adams,* p. 134; Wells, *Life of Samuel Adams,* Vol. 1, p. 244.
7. Hosmer, *Samuel Adams,* p. 132; Bancroft, *History of the United States,* Vol. 3, pp. 311–312; Wells, *Life of Samuel Adams,* Vol. 1, p. 237.
8. Wells, *Life of Samuel Adams,* Vol. 1, p. 203.
9. Wells, *Life of Samuel Adams,* Vol. 1, p. 224.
10. Wells, *Life of Samuel Adams,* Vol. 1, p. 226.
11. Wells, *Life of Samuel Adams,* Vol. 1, p. 238.
12. George Washington, *Writings* (New York: Library of America, 1997), p. 130; William Roscoe Thayer, *George Washington* (New York: Houghton Mifflin, 1922), p. 54; Bancroft, *History of the United States,* Vol. 3, p. 344; Kate Mason Rowland, *Life of George Mason, 1725–1792,* (New York: G. P. Putnam's Sons, 1892), p. 138.
13. Ridpath, *James Otis,* at www.gutenburg.org, e-text 772.
14. Mercy Otis Warren, *The American Revolution,* CD-Rom edition, Vol. 1, Chapter 4.

CHAPTER SEVEN

1. Mercy Otis Warren, *The American Revolution,* CD-Rom Edition, Vol. 1, Chapter 4; John Adams, *John Adam Papers,* Autobiography entry for 1770; Woodrow Wilson, *History of the American People,* Vol. 2, pp. 162–164.

2.   Wells, *Life of Samuel Adams*, Vol. 1, p. 282.
3.   Robert Middlekauf, *The Glorious Cause. The American Revolution, 1763–1789* (New York: Oxford University Press, 1985), p. 204; Bancroft, *History of the United States*, Vol. 3, p. 361.
4.   Wells, *Life of Samuel Adams*, Vol. 1, p. 288.
5.   Wells, Life of *Samuel Adams*, Vol. 1, p. 292; Bancroft, *History of the United States*, Vol. 3, p. 368.
6.   Wells, *Life of Samuel Adams*, Vol. 1, p. 292.
7.   Wells, *Life of Samuel Adams*, Vol. 1, p. 295.
8.   North Callahan, *Henry Knox, General Washington's General* (New York: A. S. Barnes and Company, 1958), p. 7; Bancroft, *History of the United States*, Vol. 3, p. 372.
9.   John Tudor, "An Eyewitness Describes the Boston Massacre," quoted in *America—Great Crisis in Our History Told by Its Makers: A Library of Original Sources*, 11 Vols. (Chicago: Americanization Department of Veterans of Foreign Wars of the United States, 1925), Vol. 3, pp. 85–87.
10. Tudor, *America*, Vol. 3, pp. 86–87; Bancroft, *History of the United States*, Vol. 3, pp. 375–376.
11. Bancroft, *History of the United States*, Vol. 3, p. 376.
12. Callahan, *Henry Knox*, p. 12; George Earlie Shankle, *American Mottoes and Slogans* (New York: H. W. Wilson Company, 1941), pp. 23–24; Hosmer, *Samuel Adams*, pp. 169, 170.
13. Mercy Otis Warren, *The American Revolution*, CD-Rom edition, Vol. 1, Chapter 6.
14. Wells, Life of *Samuel Adams*, Vol. 1, p. 323; Bancroft, *History of the United States*, Vol. 3, pp. 377–378.
15. Wells, *Life of Samuel Adams*, Vol. 1, pp. 326–327; Hosmer, *Samuel Adams*, pp. 169–170; Hosmer, *Life of Thomas Hutchinson*, pp. 161–163; Bancroft, *History of the United States*, Vol. 3, pp. 377–378.
16. Hosmer, *Samuel Adams*, pp. 173–174; Wells, *Life of Samuel Adams*, Vol. 1, pp. 326–327; Bancroft, *History of the United States*, pp. 377–378; John Fiske, *The American Revolution*, Vol. 1 (Boston and New York: Houghton Mifflin, 1891), p. 68.
17. Hosmer, *Samuel Adams*, pp. 173–174; Wells, *Life of Samuel Adams*, Vol. 1, pp. 326–327; Hosmer, *Life of Thomas Hutchinson*, pp. 162–163.
18. Richard Frothingham, "The Sam Adams' Regiments," *Atlantic Monthly* (July 1863); Jackman, *History of the American Nation*, Vol. 8, p. 2382; Hosmer, *Samuel Adams*, pp. 124, 160, 176; Oliver Morton Dickerson, *Boston Under Military Rule, 1768–1769* (Boston: Chapman and Grimes, 1936), p. 10; Wells, Life of *Samuel Adams*, p. 326.
19. John Adams, *John Adams' Autobiography*, at www.masshist.org, entry for 1770.
20. Samuel Adams, *The Writings of Samuel Adams*, Vol. 2, letter to Stephen Sayre, November 16, 1770.
21. William Jackman, *History of the American People*, Vol. 2, p. 483; Bancroft, *History of the United States*, Vol. 3, p. 406.
22. Samuel Adams, *The Writings of Samuel Adams*, Vol. 2, letter to John Hancock, May 11, 1770.
23. John Adams, *John Adams Papers*, diary entry for June 27, 1770.
24. Wells, *Life Samuel Adams*, Vol. 1, p. 335.

25. Samuel Adams, *The Writings of Samuel Adams,* Vol. 2, *Boston Gazette* article, August 13, 1770.
26. Samuel Adams, *The Writings of Samuel Adams,* Vol. 2, letter to Stephen Sayre, November 16, 1770.
27. Samuel Adams, *The Writings of Samuel Adams,* Vol. 2, document of August 3, 1770, also printed in *Boston Gazette,* August 6, 1770.
28. Wells, *Life of Samuel Adams,* Vol. 1, p. 410; Bancroft, *History of the United States,* Vol. 3, p. 406; Hosmer, *Life of Thomas Hutchinson,* p. 215; Hosmer, *Samuel Adams,* pp. 148, 191.
29. Samuel Adams, *The Writings of Samuel Adams,* letter to Benjamin Franklin, July 13, 1777.
30. David McCullough, *John Adams,* p. 68.
31. Samuel Adams, *The Writings of Samuel Adams,* Vol. 2, article in *Boston Gazette,* December 10, 1770.
32. Samuel Adams, *The Writings of Samuel Adams,* Vol. 2, article in *Boston Gazette,* December 10, 1770.

CHAPTER EIGHT

1. John Adams, *John Adams Papers,* diary entry for April 20, 1771.
2. Samuel Adams, *The Writings of Samuel Adams,* Vol. 1, letter to Arthur Lee, April 19, 1771.
3. Allan, *John Hancock,* p. 124; Bancroft, *History of the United States* (New York: Harper and Brothers, 1882), Vol. 3, p. 406; Wells, *Life of Samuel Adams,* Vol. 1, p. 420.
4. Samuel Adams, *The Writings of Samuel Adams,* Vol. 2, letter to Arthur Lee, September 27, 1771.
5. Samuel Adams, *The Writings of Samuel Adams,* Vol. 2, article in *Boston Gazette,* August 19, 1771.
6. Samuel Adams, *The Writings of Samuel Adams,* Vol. 2, article in *Boston Gazette,* October 14, 1771.
7. Bancroft, *History of America,* Vol. 3, p. 418.
8. Wells, *Life of Samuel Adams,* Vol. 1, p. 438.
9. Wells, *Life of Samuel Adams,* Vol. 1, pp. 393, 443.
10. Wells, *Life of Samuel Adams,* Vol. 1, p. 443.
11. Hosmer, *Life of Thomas Hutchinson,* p. 224.
12. Hosmer, *Life of Thomas Hutchinson,* p. 224.
13. John Adams, *John Adams Papers,* diary entry for December 29, 1772.
14. Samuel Adams, *The Writings of Samuel Adams,* Vol. 2, article in *Boston Gazette,* October 5, 1772.
15. Bancroft, *History of the United States,* Vol. 3, p. 419; Wells, *Life of Samuel Adams,* Vol. 1, p. 491.
16. Samuel Adams, *The Writings of Samuel Adams,* Vol. 2, letter to Arthur Lee, November 3, 1772; Wells, *Life of Samuel Adams,* Vol. 1, p. 495.
17. Wells, *Life of Samuel Adams,* Vol. 1, p. 496.
18. Wells, *Life of Samuel Adams,* Vol. 1, pp. 496–497.
19. Wells, *Life of Samuel Adams,* Vol. 1, p. 497.
20. John Adams, quoted in essay "Why Jefferson was Chosen to Write the Declaration of Independence," in *America,* Vol. 3, p. 180.

21. Wells, *Life of Samuel Adams,* Vol. 1, p. 500; Hosmer, *Life of Thomas Hutchinson,* p. 294.
22. Bancroft, *History of the United States,* Vol. 3, pp. 426–427.
23. Bancroft, *History of the United States,* Vol. 3, pp. 426–427.
24. Hosmer, *Samuel Adams,* p. 204; William V. Wells, *Life of Samuel Adams,* Vol. 2 (Boston: Little, Brown and Company, 1888), pp. 4–5.
25. Wells, *Life of Samuel Adams,* Vol. 1, p. 509.
26. Samuel Adams, *Writings of Samuel Adams,* Vol. 2, letter to Darius Session, January 2, 1773; Wells, *Life of Samuel Adams,* Vol. 2, p. 16.
27. Thomas Jefferson, *The Writings of Thomas Jefferson* (Washington, D.C.: Thomas Jefferson Memorial Association, 1904), Vol. 1, pp. 8–9; Thomas Jefferson, *Writings* (New York: Library of America, 1984), pp. 7–8; Woodrow Wilson, *History of the American People,* Vol. 2, pp. 181–183.
28. Wells, *Life of Samuel Adams,* Vol. 2, p. 66.
29. George Bancroft, *History of the United States* (New York: Harper & Bros, 1882), Vol. 4, pp. 124–125.

CHAPTER NINE

1. Andrew M. Allison, *The Real Benjamin Franklin* (Malta, IN: Freeman Institute and National Center for Constitutional Studies, 1982), p. 161.
2. Bancroft, *History of the United States,* Vol. 3, pp. 331–332; Wells, Life of *Samuel Adams,* Vol. 2, pp. 136–137; Hosmer, *Samuel Adams,* pp. 223, 232; Hosmer, *Life of Thomas Hutchinson,* pp. 281–283.
3. Wells, Life of *Samuel Adams,* Vol. 2, p. 25; Hosmer, *Life of Thomas Hutchinson,* pp. 249–250.
4. Hosmer, *Life of Thomas Hutchinson,* pp. 258–262; Wells, *Samuel Adams,* Vol. 2, pp. 26–28.
5. Hosmer, *Life of Thomas Hutchinson,* pp. 258–262; Wells, *Samuel Adams,* Vol. 2, pp. 26–28.
6. Wells, *Life of Samuel Adams,* Vol. 2, p. 29.
7. Samuel Adams, *The Writings of Samuel Adams,* Vol. 2, letter to John Adams, February 22, 1773; Wells, *Life of Samuel Adams,* Vol. 2, p. 31.
8. Samuel Adams, *The Writings of Samuel Adams,* Vol. 2, document of January 26, 1773; Bancroft, *History of the United States,* Vol. 3, pp. 432–433.
9. Samuel Adams, *The Writings of Samuel Adams,* Vol. 2, document of January 26, 1773; Bancroft, *History of the United States,* Vol. 3, pp. 432–433.
10. Samuel Adams, *The Writings of Samuel Adams,* Vol. 2, document of January 26, 1773; Bancroft, *History of the United States,* Vol. 3, pp. 432–433.
11. Samuel Adams, *The Writings of Samuel Adams,* Vol. 2, document of March 2, 1773; Bancroft, *History of the United States,* Vol. 3, pp. 432–433.
12. Wells, *Life of Samuel Adams,* Vol. 2, p. 45.
13. Hosmer, *Life of Thomas Hutchinson,* p. 251.
14. Hosmer, *Samuel Adams,* pp. 224, 301.
15. Bancroft, *History of the United State,* Vol. 3, p. 440; Wells, *Life of Samuel Adams,* Vol. 2, p. 75.
16. Wells, *Life of Samuel Adams,* Vol. 2, p. 77; Bancroft, *History of the United States,* Vol. 3, p. 441.

17.   Wells, *Life of Samuel Adams,* Vol. 2, p. 78.

18.   William J. Jackman, Jacob H. Patton, and Johnson Rossitter, *History of the American Nation* (Chicago: K. Gaynor, 1911), Vol. 2, p. 419.

19.   John Adams, *John Adams Papers,* diary entry for July 19 or 26, 1773.

20.   Samuel Adams, *Writings of Samuel Adams,* Vol. 2, article in *Boston Gazette,* September 27, 1773; Bancroft, *History of the United States,* Vol. 3, pp. 445–446; Wells, *Life of Samuel Adams,* Vol. 2, pp. 90–91; Hosmer, *Samuel Adams,* p. 238.

21.   Samuel Adams, *Writings of Samuel Adams,* Vol. 2, article in *Boston Gazette,* October 11, 1773; Bancroft, *History of the United States,* Vol. 3, pp. 445–446; Wells, *Life of Samuel Adams,* Vol. 2, pp. 90–91; Hosmer, *Samuel Adams,* p. 238.

22.   Hosmer, *Samuel Adams,* pp. 241–242; Wells, *Life of Samuel Adams,* Vol. 2, p. 100.

23.   Bancroft, *History of the United States,* Vol. 3, p. 443; Jackman, *History of the American Nation,* Vol. 2, p. 418.

24.   Samuel Adams, *The Writings of Samuel Adams,* in Harry Alonzo Cushing, ed. (New York: G. P. Putnam's Sons, 1904, CD-Rom edition; West Roxbury, MA: B&R Samizdat Express, 2003), Vol. 3, letter of October 21, 1773.

25.   Stout, *The Royal Navy in America,* p. 155; Benjamin Woods Larabee, *The Boston Tea Party* (Boston: North University Press, 1979), p. 104.

26.   Larabee, *The Boston Tea Party,* p. 109.

27.   Bancroft, *History of the United States,* Vol. 3, p. 448.

28.   Larabee, *The Boston Tea Party,* p. 110.

29.   Larabee, *The Boston Tea Party,* p. 110.

30.   Thomas Hutchinson's account of the "Boston Tea Party" found in *America,* Vol. 3, pp. 86–96; Larabee, *The Boston Tea Party,* p. 113; Bancroft, *History of the United States,* Vol. 3, p. 449.

31.   Larabee, *The Boston Tea Party,* p. 114.

32.   Bancroft, *History of the United States,* Vol. 3, p. 449; Larabee, *The Boston Tea Party,* p. 118.

33.   Larabee, *The Boston Tea Party,* pp. 118–119.

34.   Larabee, *The Boston Tea Party,* p. 141.

35.   Samuel Adams, *The Writings of Samuel Adams,* Vol. 3, letter to Arthur Lee, December 31, 1773.

36.   Wells, *Life of Samuel Adams,* Vol. 2, p. 122; Larabee, *The Boston Tea Party,* p. 141.

37.   Larabee, *The Boston Tea Party,* p. 141.

38.   Hutchinson, "The Boston Tea Party," in *America,* Vol. 3, p. 105.

39.   Thomas Hutchinson, "The Boston Tea Party," *America,* Vol. 3, p. 105.

40.   Samuel Adams, *The Writings of Samuel Adams,* Vol. 2, letter to Plymouth, December 17, 1773.

41.   Samuel Adams, *The Writings of Samuel Adams,* Vol. 2, letter to Arthur Lee, December 31, 1773.

CHAPTER TEN

1.   Allison, *The Real Benjamin Franklin,* p. 180.

2. Wells, *Life of Samuel Adams,* Vol. 2, p. 143; Hosmer, *Samuel Adams,* p. 265; Allison, *The Real Benjamin Franklin,* p. 184.

3. Wells, *Life of Samuel Adams,* Vol. 2, p. 143; Hosmer, *Samuel Adams,* p. 265.

4. Samuel Adams, *The Writings of Samuel Adams,* Vol. 2, letter to Arthur Lee, April 4, 1774; Hosmer, *Samuel Adams,* p. 269; Wells, *The Life of Samuel Adams,* Vol. 2, pp. 149, 150; Bancroft, *History of the United States,* Vol. 3, p. 475.

5. Mercy Otis Warren, *The American Revolution,* CD-Rom edition, Vol., 1, chapter 5.

6. Samuel Adams, *The Writings of Samuel Adams,* Vol. 2, letter to Portsmouth, New Hampshire, May 12, 1774.

7. Samuel Adams, *The Writings of Samuel Adams,* Vol. 2, letter to Philadelphia, May 13, 1774.

8. Arthur M. Schlesinger, ed., *The Almanac of American History* (New York: Barnes & Noble Books, 1993), p. 114; Bancroft, *History of the United States,* Vol. 4, pp. 14–16.

9. Jefferson, *Autobiography in the Writings of Thomas Jefferson* (Monticello edition: hereafter referred to as *Writings of Thomas Jefferson*), Vol. 1, pp. 9–10; Thomas Jefferson, *Jefferson: Writings,* ed. Merrill D. Peterson, (New York: Library of America, 1984), p. 8.

10. Jefferson, *Writings of Thomas Jefferson,* Vol. 1, pp. 9–10; Jefferson, *Writings,* p. 8.

11. Jefferson, *Writings of Thomas Jefferson,* Vol. 1, pp. 13–14; Jefferson, *Writings,* p. 11.

12. Wells, *Life of Samuel Adams,* Vol. 2, p. 177.

13. Samuel Eliot Morison, *Sources & Documents Illustrating the American Revolution, 1764–1788* (New York: Oxford University Press, 1972), p. 125; Jefferson, *Writings,* p. 103.

14. Wells, *Life of Samuel Adams,* Vol. 2, p. 193.

15. Journals of the Continental Congress, Vol. 1, pp. 34–36.

16. John Adams' diary, in Paul Smith, et. al, *Letters of Delegates to Congress, 1774–1789,* 25 Vols. (Washington, D.C.: Library of Congress, 1970; CD-Rom edition, Summerfield, FL: Historic Database, 1998), Vol. 1, p. 3.

17. John Adams' diary; *Letters of Delegates to Congress,* Vol. 1, p. 3.

18. John Adams' diary, *Letters of Delegates to Congress,* Vol. 1, p. 3.

19. John Adams, *The Works of John Adams,* Vol. 2, p. 512.

20. Galloway notes, *Letters of Delegates to Congress,* Vol. 1, p. 24.

21. John Adams' diary; *Letters of Delegates to Congress,* Vol. 1, p. 5.

22. *Journals of the Continental Congress, 1774–1789,* ed. Worthington C. Ford et al. (Washington, D.C.: 1904–37), Vol. 1, p. 14.

23. James Duane, "Notes of Debates," *Letters of Delegates to Congress,* Vol. 1, p. 30.

24. *Journals of the Continental Congress,* Vol. 1, p. 26.

25. John Adams' diary, *Letters of Delegates to Congress,* Vol. 1, p. 60.

26. John Adams to Abigail Adams, *Letters of the Delegates to Congress,* Vol. 1, pp. 49–50.

27. *Journals of the Continental Congress,* Vol. 1, pp. 27–28; John Adams letter to Abigail Adams, *Letters of Delegates to Congress,* Vol. 1, pp. 49–50.

28. *Journals of the Continental Congress,* Vol. 1, pp. 31–37.

29. Samuel Adams to Charles Chauncy, *Letters of Delegates to Congress,* Vol. 1, p. 83; Caesar Rodney to Thomas Rodney, *Letters of the Delegates to Congress,* Vol. 1, p. 77; *Journals of the Continental Congress,* Vol. 1, pp. 32–38.
30. Samuel Adams to Charles Chauncy, September 19, 1774, *Letters of Delegates to Congress,* Vol. 1, p. 83.
31. *Journals of the Continental Congress,* Vol. 1, pp. 52, 75.
32. Samuel Adams to Joseph Warren, September 25, 1774, *Letters of Delegates to Congress,* Vol. 1, p. 100.
33. Joseph Galloway notes from September 28, 1774, *Letters of Delegates to Congress,* Vol. 1, p. 120.
34. Woodrow Wilson, *History of the American People,* Vol. 2, p. 219.
35. Jackman, *History of the American Nation,* Vol. 8, pp. 2389–2390.

CHAPTER ELEVEN

1.   Samuel Adams, *The Writings of Samuel Adams,* Vol. 3, letter of May 18, 1774.
2.   Samuel Adams, *The Writings of Samuel Adams,* Vol. 3, letters of August 2, August 4, 1774, and January 9, 1775.
3.   Samuel Adams, *The Writings of Samuel Adams,* Vol. 3, letter to New York committee, January 9, 1775.
4.   Patrick Henry, "Give Me Liberty or Give Me Death," in *America,* Vol. 3, p. 118.
5.   George Reed letter to Gertrude Read, *Letters of Delegates to Congress,* Vol. 1, pp. 358–359; Richard Henry Lee to Francis Lightfoot Lee, *Letters of Delegates to Congress,* Vol. 1, p. 366; *Journals of the Continental Congress, 1774–1789,* ed. Worthington C. Ford, et al. (Washington, D.C.: 1904–37), Vol. 2, p. 75.
6.   Frank Moore, ed., *Diary of the American Revolution from Newspapers and Original Sources* (New York: Charles Scribner, 1860), Vol. 1, pp. 29–30.
7.   Samuel Adams, *The Writings of Samuel Adams,* Vol. 3, letter to Richard Henry Lee, March 21, 1775.
8.   *Diary of the American Revolution from Newspapers and Original Sources,* pp. 29–30; Wells, *Life of Samuel Adams,* Vol. 2, pp. 279–280.
9.   *Diary of the American Revolution from Newspapers and Original Sources,* Vol. 1, p. 112.
10. Paul Revere, "Deposition of Paul Revere," in *America,* Vol. 3, pp. 141–146.
11. "Account of Lexington from the Salem Gazette," in *America,* Vol. 3, pp. 119–121.
12. Samuel Adams letter to Samuel Purviance, *Letters of Delegates to Congress,* Vol. 1, pp. 361–362; Bancroft, *History of the United States,* Vol. 3, pp. 119–121.
13. Wells, *Life of Samuel Adams,* Vol. 2, p. 294; Bancroft, *History of the United States,* Vol. 4, p. 157; Hosmer, *Samuel Adams,* p. 331; William E. H. Lecky, "The *Battle of Lexington, Concord and Bunker Hill,*" in Francis W. Halsey, ed. *Great Epochs in American History, Described by Famous Writers From Columbus to Roosevelt,* 10 Vols. (New York: Funk & Wagnall's Co., 1912), Vol. 3, p. 111.
14. Wells, *Life of Samuel Adams,* Vol. 2, p. 305: Hosmer, *Samuel Adams,* p. 332.

15. Samuel Adams, *The Writings of Samuel Adams*, Vol. 3, letter to Elizabeth Adams, May 7, 1775; *Diary of the American Revolution from Newspapers and Original Sources*, Vol. 1, p. 55.

16. Benjamin Franklin to Humphry Marshall, *Letters of Delegates to Congress*, Vol. 1, p. 395.

17. *Journals of the Continental Congress*, Vol. 2, pp. 58–59.

18. *Journals of the Continental Congress*, Vol. 2, p. 91; Wells, *Life of Samuel Adams*, Vol. 2, p. 307.

19. Charles Adams and John Adams, *The Works of John Adams*, Vol. 2, p. 417; Washington Irving, cited from "Washington's Appointment as Command-in-Chief," in *Great Epochs of American History*, Vol. 3.

20. *Journals of the Continental Congress*, Vol. 2, p. 91.

21. *Diary of the American Revolution from Newspapers and Original Sources from Newspapers and Original Documents*, Vol. 1, p. 113.

22. Wells, *Life of Samuel Adams*, Vol. 2, p. 425.

23. Samuel Adams to Elizabeth Adams, *Letters of Delegates to Congress*, Vol. 1, p. 552.

24. Samuel Adams, *The Writings of Samuel Adams*, Vol. 2, letter to Elizabeth Adams, June 16 and June 17, 1775.

25. *Journals of the Continental Congress*, Vol. 2, pp. 127, 128–157; Thomas Jefferson, *Writings*, p. 11.

26. Thomas Jefferson, *Writings*, p. 749; Thomas Jefferson to John Randolph, *Letters of Delegates to Congress*, Vol. 1, p. 707.

27. Samuel Adams to Elizabeth Adams, *The Letters of Delegates to Congress*, Vol. 1, p. 683.

28. Samuel Adams, *The Writings of Samuel Adams*, Vol. 2, letter to Elbridge Gerry, September 26, 1775; Samuel Adams to Elbridge Gerry, in Ronald M. Gephart, Paul Smith, et. al, *Letters of Delegates to Congress, 1774–1789* (Washington, D.C.: Library of Congress, 1970, CD-Rom edition, Summerfield, FL: Historic Database, 1998), Vol. 2, pp. 63–64.

29. Samuel Adams to Elizabeth Adams, *The Letters of Delegates to Congress*, Vol. 2, p. 217.

30. Samuel Adams to Elizabeth Adams, *The Letters of Delegates to Congress*, Vol. 2, p. 217.

CHAPTER TWELVE

1. Samuel Adams, *The Writings of Samuel Adams*, Vol. 3, letter to James Bowdoin, Sr., November 16, 1775; Samuel Adams to James Bowdoin, Sr., *Letters of the Delegates to Congress*, Vol. 1, pp. 351–352.

2. Thomas Jefferson to John Randolph, *Letters of the Delegates to Congress*, Vol. 2, p. 403; Jefferson, *The Writings of Thomas Jefferson*, Vol. 4, pp. 32–33.

3. Samuel Adams, *The Writings of Samuel Adams*, Vol. 3, letter to James Warren, January 7, 1776; Samuel Adams to James Warren in Paul Smith, et. al, *Letters of Delegates to Congress, 1774–1789* (Washington, D.C.: Library of Congress, 1970; CD-Rom edition, Summerfield, FL: Historic Database, 1998), Vol. 3, p. 52.

4. Samuel Adams, *The Writings of Samuel Adams,* Vol. 3, January 15, 1775; Samuel Adams to John Adams, *Letters of Delegates to Congress,* Vol. 3, p. 94.

5. Samuel Adams to James Warren, *Letters to the Delegates to Congress,* Vol. 2, p. 158.

6. Thomas Jefferson to Thomas Nelson, *Letters to the Delegates to Congress,* in Paul Smith, et. al, *Letters of Delegates to Congress, 1774–1789* (Washington, D.C.: Library of Congress, 1970; CD-Rom edition, Summerfield, FL: Historic Database, 1998), Vol. 4, p. 13.

7. Samuel Adams to Samuel Cooper, *Letters of Delegates to Congress,* Vol. 3, p. 481; Samuel Adams, *The Writings of Samuel Adams,* Vol. 3, letter to Samuel Cooper, April 3, 1776.

8. Samuel Adams to Samuel Cooper, *Letters of Delegates to Congress,* Vol. 3, p. 600; Samuel Adams, *The Writings of Samuel Adams,* Vol. 3, letter to Samuel Cooper, April 30, 1776.

9. Samuel Adams to Samuel Cooper, *Letters of Delegates to Congress,* Vol. 3, p. 600; Samuel Adams, *The Writings of Samuel Adams,* Vol. 3, letter to Samuel Cooper, April 30, 1776.

10. John Adams to James Warren, *Letters of Delegates to Congress,* Vol. 4, p. 40.

11. Wells, *Samuel Adams,* Vol. 2, p. 423.

12. *Journals of the Continental Congress,* Vol. 5, p. 425.

13. *Journals of the Continental Congress,* Vol. 5, p. 431; Thomas Jefferson, *The Writings of Thomas Jefferson,* Vol. 1, pp. 26–27, 176–178.

14. Journals of the Continental Congress, Vol. 5, p. 433.

15. Thomas Jefferson, "Writing of the Declaration of Independence," in *America,* Vol. 3, pp. 167–168; Jefferson, *Writings,* p. 124; Jefferson, *The Writings of Thomas Jefferson,* Vol. 1, p. 21.

16. Thomas Jefferson, "Thomas Jefferson's Original Draft of the Declaration of Independence," in *America,* Vol. 3, pp. 171–173; John Adams, "Why Jefferson was Chosen to Write the Declaration," in *America,* Vol. 3, pp. 180–183; Thomas Jefferson, *The Writings of Thomas Jefferson,* Vol. 1, p. 29.

17. Morison, ed., *Sources and Documents Illustrating the American Revolution,* p. 149.

18. Thomas Jefferson, "The Writing of the Declaration of Independence," in *America,* Vol. 3, pp. 167–168.

19. *Journals of the Continental Congress,* Vol. 5, pp. 504–505.

20. George Washington, letter of June 29, 1776, in John C. Fitzpatrick, ed., *The Writings of Washington from the Original Manuscript Sources, 1745–1799,* 39 Vols. (Washington, D.C.: Government Printing Office, 1931–1944; reprint New York: Greenwood Press, 1970), Vol. 8, p. 203.

21. Bancroft, *History of The United States* (New York: Harper & Brothers, 1882), Vol. 4, p. 438.

22. *Journals of the Continental Congress,* Vol. 5, p. 505.

23. Moore, ed., *Diary of the American Revolution From Newspapers and Original Documents,* Vol. 2, p. 98; Wells, *Life of Samuel Adams,* Vol. 2, p. 432.

24. *Journals of the Continental Congress,* Vol. 5, p. 507; Thomas Jefferson, *The Writings of Thomas Jefferson,* Vol. 1, pp. 27–28; Jefferson, *Writings,* pp. 10, 12,18; Bancroft, *History of the United States,* Vol. 4, pp. 441–443; John Adams, *John Adams Papers,* entry for 1776.

25. *Journals of the Continental Congress,* Vol. 5, pp. 510–516.

26. *Journals of the Continental Congress*, Vol. 5, p. 626.
27. Bancroft, *History of the United States* (New York: Harper & Brothers, 1882), Vol. 5, pp. 15–16.
28. Samuel Adams to John Pitts, *Letters of Delegates to Congress*, Vol. 4, p. 417.
29. Samuel Adams to Benjamin Kent, *Letters of Delegates to Congress*, Vol. 4, p. 552.

CHAPTER THIRTEEN

1. Wells, *The Life of Samuel Adams*, Vol. 2, p. 437.
2. Moore, ed., *Diary of the American Revolution From Newspapers and Original Documents*, Vol. 1, p. 214.
3. Samuel Adams, *The Writings of Samuel Adams*, Vol. 3, letter to John Adams, August 16, 1776.
4. Samuel Adams, *The Writings of Samuel Adams*, Vol. 3, letter to John Adams, August 16, 1776.
5. *Journals of the Continental Congress*, Vol. 5, p. 738.
6. John Adams to Samuel Adams, *Letters of Delegates to Congress*, Vol. 5, p. 121.
7. Samuel Adams, *Writings of Samuel Adams*, Vol. 2, letter to John Adams, September 16, 1776.
8. Samuel Adams, *The Writings of Samuel Adams*, Vol. 2, letter to John Adams, September 30, 1776.
9. *Journals of the Continental Congress*, Vol. 5, p. 827.
10. Samuel Adams to Elizabeth Adams, *Letters of Delegates to Congress*, Vol. 5, p. 551.
11. George Washington to John A. Washington, December 18, 1776, *George Washington Papers at the Library of Congress, 1741–1799 in Washington D.C.*, at www.memory.loc.gov, Series 4, image 256.
12. Thomas Paine, *The American Crisis*, at www.loc.gov.
13. *Journals of the Continental Congress*, Vol. 6, p. 1027.
14. Samuel Adams, *Writings; Letters of Delegates to Congress*.
15. Samuel Adams, *Writings of Samuel Adams*, letter to James Warren, December 31, 1776; Samuel Adams to James Warren, *Letters of Delegates to Congress*, Vol. 6, p. 3.
16. George Washington, *Writings*, pp. 262–264.
17. Samuel Adams to James Warren, *Letters of Delegates to Congress*, Vol. 7, p. 208.
18. *Journals of the Continental Congress*, Vol. 7, p. 168.
19. Moore, ed., *Diary of the American Revolution from Newspapers and Original Documents*, Vol. 1, p. 297, Vol. 2, p. 98.
20. Samuel Adams, *The Writings of Samuel Adams*, Vol. 3, letter to Richard Henry Lee, June 26, 1777; Samuel Adams to Richard Henry Lee, *Letters of Delegates to Congress*, Vol. 7, p. 264.
21. Wells, *Samuel Adams*, Vol. 3, p. 391.
22. Samuel Adams to Richard Henry Lee, *Letters of Delegates to Congress*, Vol. 7, p. 344.
23. Samuel Adams to Elizabeth Adams, *Letters of Delegates to Congress*, Vol. 7, p. 677; Samuel Adams, *The Writings of Samuel Adams*, letter to Elizabeth Adams, September 17, 1777.

24. *Journals of the Continental Congress,* Vol. 8, pp. 742, 754; John Adams' diary, *Letters of Delegates to Congress,* Vol. 8, p. 3; John Hancock to Philemon Dickinson or Alexander McDougall, *Letters of Delegates to Congress,* Vol. 8, p. 3.

25. *Journals of the Continental Congress,* Vol. 8, p. 755; John Adams' diary, *Letters of Delegates to Congress,* Vol. 8, pp. 3, 5; John Adams to Abigail Adams, *Letters of Delegates to Congress,* Vol. 8, p. 27.

26. *Journals of the Continental Congress,* Vol. 8, p. 755; John Adams' diary, *Letters of Delegates to Congress,* Vol. 8, pp. 3, 5; John Adams to Abigail Adams, *Letters of Delegates to Congress,* Vol. 8, p. 27.

27. *Journals of the Continental Congress,* Vol. 8, p. 75; George Washington to the Continental Congress, in John C. Fitzpatrick, ed., *The Writings of George Washington from the Original Manuscript Sources, 1745–1799* (Washington D.C.: Library of Congress, Series 3a Varick Transcripts), Vol. 9, p. 2750; Samuel Chase to Thomas Jefferson, *Letters of Delegates to Congress,* Vols. 17–18.

28. Wells, *Life of Samuel Adams,* Vol. 2, p. 493.

29. Wells, *Life of Samuel Adams,* Vol. 2, pp. 492–493.

30. *Journals of the Continental Congress,* Vol. 7, p. 48.

31. Moore, ed., *Diary of the American Revolution from Newspapers and Original Documents,* Vol. 1, p. 184.

32. Moore, ed., *Diary of the American Revolution from Newspapers and Original Documents,* Vol. 1, p. 233.

33. *Journals of the Continental Congress,* Vol. 9, p. 846.

34. Moore, ed., *Diary of the America Revolution from Newspapers and Original Documents,* Vol. 1, p. 345; Samuel Adams, *The Writings of Samuel Adams,* letter to John Adams, December, 8, 1777; Samuel Adams to James Lovell, *Letters of Delegates to Congress,* Vol. 8, pp. 395–396.

35. John Adams, *John Adams' Diary,* at www.masshist.org, entry for November 17, 1777.

36. Samuel Adams, *The Writings of Samuel Adams,* letter to Richard Henry Lee, Vol. 4, letter to Richard Henry Lee, January 1, 1778.

37. *Journals of the Continental Congress,* Vol. 9, pp. 907, 932, 933.

38. Samuel Adams, *The Writings of Samuel Adams,* letter to Richard Henry Lee, April 20, 1778.

39. Samuel Adams to James Warren, *Letters of Delegates to Congress,* Vol. 12, p. 231.

40. Samuel Adams, *The Writings of Samuel Adams,* Vol. 4, letter to Elizabeth Adams, May 2, 1778.

41. *Journals of the Continental Congress,* Vol. 11, pp. 417–418; Moore, ed. *Diary of the American Revolution from Newspapers and Original Documents,* Vol. 2, pp. 39–40.

42. *Journals of the Continental Congress,* Vol. 11, pp. 683–684; Titus Hosmer to Richard Law, *Letters of Delegates to Congress,* Vol. 10, pp. 247–248; Henry Marchant to William Greene, *Letters of Delegates to Congress,* Vol. 10, p. 262.

43. Samuel Adams to James Warren, *Letters of Delegates to Congress,* Vol. 10, p. 280.

44. Marine Committee to the Comte d'Estaing, *Letters of Delegates to Congress,* Vol. 10, p. 267; Richard Henry Lee to Francis Lightfoot Lee, *Letters of Delegates to Congress,* Vol. 10, pp. 265–266.

45. Samuel Adams to James Warren, *Letters to Delegates to Congress,* Vol. 10, p. 315.
46. *Journals of the Continental Congress,* Vol. 11, pp. 688, 756–759; Moore, ed., *Diary of the American Revolution from Newspapers and Original Documents,* Vol. 2, p. 58; Samuel Holton's diary, *Letters to Delegates to Congress,* Vol. 10, p. 397; Elias Boudinot to Hannah Boudinot, *Letters of Delegates to Congress,* Vol. 10, pp. 405–406.
47. Samuel Adams to Samuel Cooper, *Letters of Delegates to Congress,* Vol. 11, p. 380.
48. Samuel Adams to Hannah Adams, *Letters of Delegates to Congress,* Vol. 10, pp. 598–599; Wells, *Life of Samuel Adams,* Vol. 3, p. 54.
49. Samuel Adams to Elizabeth Adams, *Letters of Delegates to Congress,* Vol. 12, p. 230.
50. Brook Adams, *The Emancipation of Massachusetts* (New York/Boston: Houghton Mifflin and Company, 1888), pp. 307–308; Ronald M. Peters, Jr., The *Massachusetts Constitution of 1780* (Amherst: University of Massachusetts, 1978), pp. 195–205; *U.S. Supreme Court: United States Reports: Cases Adjudged in the Supreme Court* (Washington, D.C.: U.S. Government Printing Office, 1754–1997), electronic version cited in the American Reference Library (Orem, UT: Western Standard Publishing Company, 1998), "Opinion of Felix J. Frankfurter," 1946, *Davis v. United States,* 328 U.S. 605, "Opinion of U.S. Supreme Court Justice William Rehnquist," 1990, *Spallone v. U.S.,* 493 U.S. 279; James Madison, Federalist, electronic edition, cited in the American Reference Library, No. 47, pp. 305–306; Wells, *Life of Samuel Adams,* Vol. 3, pp. 80–95.
51. Samuel Adams to John Adams, *Letters of Delegates to Congress,* Vol. 15, p. 412.
52. Wells, *Life of Samuel Adams,* Vol. 1, p. 509.
53. Wells, *Life of Samuel Adams,* Vol. 1, p. 509.
54. Samuel Adams to Elizabeth Adams, *Letters of Delegates to Congress,* Vol. 16, p. 84.
55. Samuel Adams to Elizabeth Adams, *Letters of Delegates to Congress,* Vol. 16, p. 132.
56. Samuel Adams to Elizabeth Adams, *Letters of Delegates to Congress,* Vol. 16, p. 132.
57. Samuel Adams to Elizabeth Adams, *Letters of Delegates to Congress,* Vol. 16, p. 652.
58. Wells, *Life of Samuel Adams,* Vol. 3, p. 128.
59. *Journals of the Continental Congress,* Vol. 9, p. 192.
60. Ridpath, *James Otis,* online at Project Gutenberg, www.gutenberg.org, e-text 722.
61. George Washington, *Writings,* pp. 464–465.

CHAPTER FOURTEEN

1. William V. Wells, *The Life and Public Services of Samuel Adams* (Boston: Little, Brown and Company, 1888), Vol. 3, p. 136.
2. *Journals of the Continental Congress,* Vol. 24, p. 248.
3. Samuel Adams, *The Writings of Samuel Adams,* letter to Thomas Wells, November 22, 1780.

4. Joseph A. Story, *A Familiar Exposition of the Constitution of the United States: Containing a Brief Commentary of Every Clause* (New York: Harper & Brothers Publishers, 1859; reprint Washington, D.C.: Regnery Gateway, Inc., 1986), pp. 49–51; James Madison, *Journal of the Federal Convention,* 2 Vols. (Chicago: Albert, Scott & Co, 1893; orig. published in 1840, reprint, E. H. Scott). CD-Rom edition, cited in the American Reference Library (Orem, UT: Western Standard Publishing Company, 1998), Vol. 1, pp. 189–190; Jonathan Elliot, ed., *The Debates In the Several State Conventions On the Adoption of the Federal Constitution, as Recommended by the General Convention at Philadelphia, in 178,* 5 Vols. (Philadelphia: J. B. Lippincott Company, 1901), Vol. 5, p. 206.

5. Samuel Adams, *The Writings of Samuel Adams,* letter to John Adams, April 16, 1784.

6. Samuel Adams, *The Writings of Samuel Adams,* letter to Elbridge Gerry, April 19, 1784.

7. Jefferson, *Writings,* p. 821.

8. Wells, *Life of Samuel Adams,* Vol. 3, pp. 236–237.

9. Alexander Hamilton, quoted from James Madison, Alexander Hamilton, and John Jay, *The Federalist, or The New Constitution* (Chicago: Albert Scott & Company, 1894); CD-Rom edition, cited in the American Reference Library (Orem, UT: Western Standard Publishing Company, 1998), No. 6, pp. 105–106.

10. James Madison, *Letters and Other Writings of James Madison, Fourth President of the United States,* Published by Order of Congress, (Philadelphia: J. B. Lippincott & Co.), Vol. 3, p. 586; Vol. 4, p. 380.

11. Richard Henry Lee to Samuel Adams, *Letters of Delegates to Congress,* Vol. 24, p. 465.

12. James Madison, *Writings of James Madison,* Vol. 1, p. 364.

13. Madison, *The Writings of James Madison,* Vol. 1, p. 364.

14. Jonathan Elliot, ed., *The Debates In the Several State Conventions On the Adoption of the Federal Constitution, as Recommended by the General Convention at Philadelphia, in 1787,* 5 Vols. (Philadelphia: J. B. Lippincott Company, 1901); CD-Rom edition cited in the American Reference Library (Orem, UT: Western Standard Publishing Company, 1998), Vol. 2, p. 2; Thomas Jefferson to Samuel Adams, April 24, 1801, Thomas Jefferson Papers at the Library of Congress at www.memory.loc.gov.

15. Elliot ed., *Debates,* Vol. 2, pp. 7–8.

16. Elliot, ed., *Debates,* Vol. 2, p. 11; Bancroft, *History of the United States,* Vol. 6, p. 398.

17. Madison, *The Writings of Madison,* Vol. 1, p. 373.

18. Elliot, ed., *Debates,* Vol. 2, p. 101.

19. Elliot, ed., *Debates,* Vol. 2, p. 102.

20. Elliot, ed., *Debates.* Vol. 2, p. 102.

21. Elliot, ed., Debates, Vol. 2, pp. 102–103.

22. Stephen Higginson, "How John Hancock Supported The Constitution," in *America,* Vol. 4., pp. 156–140; Francis S. Drake, *Life and Correspondence of Henry Knox* (Boston: Samuel G. Drake, 1873), p. 97.

23. Wells, *Life of Samuel Adams,* Vol. 3, pp. 260–261.

24. Eliot, ed., *Debates,* Vol. 2, p. 124.

25. Madison, *The Writings of Madison,* Vol. 1, p. 375.

26. Bancroft, *History of the United States,* Vol. 6, p. 406.
27. Samuel Adams, *The Writings of Samuel Adams,* letter to Richard Henry Lee, April 24, 1789.
28. Samuel Adams, *The Writings of Samuel Adams,* Vol. 4, letter to Richard Henry Lee, August 29, 1789.
29. Wells, *Life of Samuel Adams,* Vol. 3, pp. 278–279.
30. Wells, *Life of Samuel Adams,* Vol. 3, p. 255.
31. Samuel Adams, *The Writings of Samuel Adams,* Vol. 4, letter to the Massachusetts Legislature, May 27, 1789.
32. Samuel Adams, *The Writings of Samuel Adams,* Vol. 4, Address to the Legislative of Massachusetts, May 28, 1790.

CHAPTER FIFTEEN

1. Samuel Adams, *The Writings of Samuel Adams,* Vol. 4, letter to John Adams, September 2, 1790.
2. Charles Adams and John Adams, *The Works of John Adams* (Boston: Charles C. Little and James Brown, 1851), Vol. 6, p. 411.
3. Charles Adams and John Adams, *The Works of John Adams,* Vol. 6, p. 412.
4. Charles Adams and John Adams, *The Works of John Adams,* Vol. 6, 417, p. 420.
5. Charles Adams and John Adams, *The Works of John Adams,* Vol. 6, p. 421.
6. Wells, *Life of Samuel Adams,* Vol. 3, p. 291.
7. Samuel Adams, *The Writings of Samuel Adams,* Vol. 4, letter to the Massachusetts Legislature, January 17, 1794.
8. Charles Adams and John Adams, *The Works of John Adams* (Boston: Little, Brown, and Company, 1851), Vol. 1, p. 471; Woodrow Wilson, *History of the American People,* Vol. 3, pp. 140–141.
9. Woodrow Wilson, *History of the American People,* Vol. 3, pp. 138–140.
10. Wells, *Life of Samuel Adams,* Vol. 3, pp. 351–352.
11. Wells, *Life of Samuel Adams,* Vol. 3, p. 375.
12. Thomas Jefferson letter to Samuel Adams, February 26, 1800, from The Thomas Jefferson Papers Series 1. General Correspondence, Washington D.C.: Library of the U.S. Congress, Manuscript Division, online at www.memory.loc.gov.
13. Thomas Jefferson letter to Samuel Adams, March 16, 1801, Thomas Jefferson Papers.
14. Samuel Adams to Thomas Jefferson, April 24, 1801, Thomas Jefferson Papers.
15. Samuel Adams, *The Writings of Samuel Adams,* Vol. 4, Letter to Thomas Paine, November 30, 1802.
16. Wells, *Life of Samuel Adams,* Vol. 3, pp. 374–375.
17. Annals of Congress, 8th Cong., 2nd Session, Vol. 8, pp. 378–379; U.S. House Journal 1803, 8th Congress, 1st Session, October 19, Vol. 4, p. 410.
18. Charles Adams and John Adams, *The Works of John Adams* (Boston: Charles C. Little and James Brown, 1851), Vol. 1, pp. 673, 674.
19. Thomas Jefferson, *The Writings of Thomas Jefferson,* Vol. 1, p. 180; Jefferson, *Writings,* p. 1422.

20. Samuel Adams, *The Writings of Samuel Adams,* Vol. 3, letter to Richard Henry Lee, June 26, 1777; Samuel Adams to Richard Henry Lee, *Letters of Delegates to Congress,* Vol. 7, p. 264.

EPILOGUE

1. Samuel Adams, *The Writings of Samuel Adams,* Vol. 2; article in the *Boston Gazette,* October 14, 1771.
2. Samuel Adams to Benjamin Kent, *Letters of Delegates to Congress,* Vol. 4, p. 552.
3. Wells, *The Life of Samuel Adams,* Vol. 1, p. 75.
4. Thomas Jefferson, "Thomas Jefferson's Original Draft of the Declaration of Independence," in *America,* Vol. 3, pp. 171–173; Thomas Jefferson, *The Writings of Thomas Jefferson,* Vol. 1, p. 29.
5. Samuel Adams, *The Writings of Samuel Adams,* Vol. 3, letter to Richard Henry Lee, March 21, 1775.

BIBLIOGRAPHY

Adams, John. *Adams Family Papers including Autobiography of John Adams, Letters Between John and Abigail Adams, the Diary of John Adams.* Boston: Massachusetts Historical Society. Electronic Archive at www.masshist.org.

Adams, Brooks. *The Emancipation of Massachusetts.* Boston: Houghton Mifflin, 1887.

Adams, Charles Francis, and John Adams. *The Works of John Adams, Second President of the United States: With a Life of the Author, Notes and Illustrations.* 10 Vols. Boston: Little, Brown, 1851.

Allan, Herbert S. *John Hancock: Patriot in Purple.* New York: Macmillan, 1948.

Alexander, John K. Alexander. *Samuel Adams: America's Revolutionary Politician.* Lanham, MD: Rowman & Littlefield Publishers, 2002.

Allison, Andrew M. *The Real Benjamin Franklin.* Freeman Institute and The National Center for Constitutional Studies, 1982.

Annals of Congress, 8 Cong., 1st session. At www.memory.loc.gov.

America—Great Crisis in Our History Told by Its Makers: A Library of Original Sources. 11 vols. Chicago: Americanization Department of Veterans of Foreign Wars of the United States, 1925.

Andrews, Charles M. The Colonial Background of the American Revolution. New Haven, CT: Yale University Press, 1931.

Bailyn, Bernard. *The Ideological Origins of the American Revolution.* Cambridge: Belknap Press, 1992.

Bancroft, George. *History of the United States from the Discovery of the American Continent.* 6 vols. New York: Harper & Bros, 1882.

Bancroft, George. *A Plea For the Constitution of the United States, Wounded in the House of its Guardians.* New York: Harper & Bros, 1886.

Barzun, Jacques, *From Dawn to Decadence: 1500 To The Present.* New York: Harper Collins, 2001.

Becker, Carl, and Humphrey Milford. *The Eve of the Revolution: with England.* New Haven, CT: Yale University Press, 1918.

Berger, Carl. *Broadsides and Bayonets: The Propaganda War of the American Revolution.* Philadelphia: University of Pennsylvania Press, 1961.

Bobrick, Benson. *An Angel in the Whirlwind.* New York: Penguin, 1998.

Bonwick, Colin. *English Radicals and the American Revolution.* Chapel Hill, NC: University of North Carolina Press, 1977.

Bryan, William Jennings, and Francis W. Halsey. *The World's Famous Orations. America, vols. 8–10.* 3 vols. New York: Funk and Wagnall's Company, 1906.

Callahan, North. *Henry Knox, General Washington's General.* New York: A.S. Barnes and Company, 1958.

Carman, Harry J. *Social and Economic History of the United States: From Handicraft to Factory, 1500–1820.* Boston. D. C. Heath, 1930.

Christie, Ian R., and Benjamin W. Labaree. *Empire or Independence, 1760–1776:A British-American Dialogue on the Coming of the American Revolution.* New York: W. W. Norton, 1976.

Copeland, David A. *Debating the Issues in Colonial Newspapers: Primary Documents on Events of the Period.* Westport, CT: Greenwood Press, 2000.

Coupland, R. *The American Revolution and the British Empire: The Sir George Watson Lectures for 1928, Delivered before the University of London in the Winter of 1928–9.* London: Longmans, Green and Co., 1930.

Cushing, Harry Alonzo, ed. *The Writings of Samuel Adams.* New York: G.P. Putnam's Sons, 1904. Vol. 1, Electronic edition distributed by Fictionwise. 4 Vols. 2–4, online at www.gutenberg.org.

Drake, Francis Samuel. *Life and Correspondence of Henry Knox.* Boston: Samuel G. Drake, 1873.

Eliot, Charles W. *American Historical Documents, 1000–1904. The Harvard Classics, vol. 43.* New York: P. F. Collier and Son Corporation, 1938.

Ellis, Joseph J. *Founding Brothers: The Revolutionary Generation.* New York: Albert A. Knopf, 2000.

Elliot, Jonathan, ed. *The Debates In the Several State Conventions On the Adoption of the Federal Constitution, as Recommended by the General Convention at Philadelphia, in 1787.* 5 vols. Philadelphia: J. B. Lippincott Company, 1901.

Ferling, John. *Setting the World Ablaze: Washington, Adams, Jefferson, and the American Revolution.* New York: Oxford University Press, 2002.

Fisher, Sydney George. *The True History of the American Revolution.* Philadelphia: J. B. Lippincott, 1902.

Fiske, John. *The American Revolution.* Vol. 2. Boston: Houghton Mifflin, 1891.

Ford, Worthington, ed., et al. *Journals of the Continental Congress, 1774–1789, 34 vols.* Washington, D.C.: Library of Congress, 1904.

Franklin, Benjamin. *The Autobiography of Benjamin Franklin.* Ed. Gordon S. Haight. New York: Walter J. Black, Inc, 1941.

———. *Benjamin Franklin: Silence Dogood, The Busy-Body, and Early Writings.* New York: Library of America, 2005.

Friedman, Milton. *Capitalism and Freedom, Fortieth Anniversary Edition.* Chicago: University of Chicago Press, 2002.

Frothingham, Richard. "The Sam Adams' Regiments," *Atlantic Monthly,* July 1863.

Halsey, Francis W. *Great Epochs in American History, Described by Famous Writers From Columbus to Roosevelt.* 10 vols. New York: Funk & Wagnall's Co., 1912.

———. *World's Great Orations.* New York: Funk & Wagnall's Co, 1912.

Hosmer, James K. *Samuel Adams.* 7th ed. Boston: Houghton Mifflin, 1888.

———. *The Life of Thomas Hutchinson, Royal Governor of the Province of Massachusetts Bay.* Boston: Houghton Mifflin and Company, 1896.

Howard, George Elliott. *Preliminaries of the Revolution, 1763–1775.* New York: Harper Brothers, 1905.

Hutchinson, Thomas. *The diary and letters of His Excellency Thomas Hutchinson: Captain-general and governor-in-chief of his late Majesty's province of Massachusetts Bay.* London: Sampson Low, Martson, Searle & Rivington, 1886. Reprint from Ann Arbor: Proquest, 2003.

Jackman, William J., Jacob H., Patton, and Johnson Rossitter. *History of the American Nation*. 9 vols. Chicago: K. Gaynor, 1911.

Jefferson, Thomas. The Thomas Jefferson Papers Series, Manuscript Division, online at www.memory.loc.gov.

———. *The Writings of Jefferson:* Monticello Edition. Deposited in the Department of State and Published in 1853 By Order of the Joint Committee of Congress. 6 Vols. Washington, D.C.: Thomas Jefferson Memorial Association, 1904–1905.

———. *Thomas Jefferson, Writings*. Ed. Merrill D. Peterson.(*Autobiography, Notes on the State of Virginia, Public and Private Papers, Addresses, Letters*). New York: Library of America, 1984.

Journals of the Continental Congress, 1774–1789. Ed. Worthington C. Ford et al. Washington, D.C., 1904–37.

Ketcham, Ralph (Introduction). *The Anti-Federalist Papers*. New York: Signet Classics, 2003.

Ketchum, Richard M., ed. *The American Heritage Book of the Revolution*. New York: Simon and Schuster, 1958.

Larabee, Benjamin Woods. *The Boston Tea Party*. Boston: Northeastern University Press, 1979.

Lecky, William Edward Hartpole. The American Revolution, 1763-1783. Ed. James Albert Woodburn. New York: D. Appleton, 1898.

Locke, John. *The Second Treatise of Government: an Essay Concerning the True Original, Extent and End of Civil Government*. Cited in the American Reference Library on CD-Rom. Orem, UT: Western Standard Publishing Company, 1998.

McCullough, David. *John Adams*. New York: Simon and Schuster, 2001.

Macmillan, Margaret Burnham. The War Governors in the American Revolution. New York: Columbia University Press, 1943.

Madison, James, Alexander Hamilton, and John Jay. *The Federalist, or The New Constitution*. 2 vols. Chicago: Albert Scott & Company, 1894. Cited in the American Reference Library. Orem, UT: Western Standard Publishing Company, 1998.

Madison, James. *Journal of the Federal Convention*. 2 vols. Chicago: Albert, Scott & Co, 1893. Orig. published 1840. Reprint. E.H. Scott.

Madison, James. *Letters and Other Writings of James Madison, Fourth President of the United States. In Four Volumes*. Published by Order of Congress. 4 vols. Philadelphia: J. B. Lippincott & Co, 1865.

———. *James Madison, Writings (1772–1836)*. New York: Library of America, 1999.

Martyn, Charles. *The Life of Artemas Ward: The First Commander-In-Chief of the American Revolution*. Port Washington, NY: A. Ward, 1921.

Middlekauff, Robert. *The Glorious Cause: The American Revolution, 1763–1789*. New York: Oxford University Press, 1985.

Miller, John C. *Origins of the American Revolution*. Boston: Little, Brown, 1943.

Montesquieu, Charles De. *The Spirit of the Laws*. Cambridge: Cambridge University Press, 1989.

Moore, Frank, ed. *Diary of the American Revolution From Newspapers and Original Documents*. Vols. 1 and 2. New York: Charles Scribner, 1860.

Morgan, Edmund S. and Helen M. Morgan. *The Stamp Act Crisis, Prologue to Revolution*. Chapel Hill: University of North Carolina Press, 1995.

Morison, Samuel Eliot. E., ed. *Sources and Documents Illustrating the American Revolution, 1764–1788, and the Formation of the Federal Constitution.* Oxford: Clarendon Press, 1923.

Namier, Lewis. *England in the Age of the American Revolution.* 2nd ed. New York: St. Martin's Press, 1961.

Paine, Thomas. *Common Sense: Addressed to the Inhabitants of America.* Philadelphia: W. and T. Bradford, 1776. Cited in the American Reference Library. Orem, UT: Western Standard Publishing Company, 1998.

Parton, James. *Revolutionary Heroes and Other Historical Papers.* Reprint Edition. White Fish, MT: Kessinger Publishing, 2004.

Peters, Ronald M., Jr., *The Massachusetts Constitution of 1780.* Amherst: University of Massachusetts, 1978.

Purcell, L. Edward. *Who Was Who In The American Revolution.* New York: Facts on File, 1993.

Purvis, Thomas L. *A Dictionary of American History.* Cambridge, MA: Blackwell Reference, 1995.

Rowland, Kate Mason. *Life of George Mason, 1725–1792.* New York: G. P. Putnam's Sons, 1892.

Reich, Jerome R. *British Friends of the American Revolution.* Armonk, NY: M. E. Sharpe, 1998.

Ridpath, John Clark. *James Otis: Pre-revolutionist.* At Project Gutenberg website, www.gutenberg.org, e-text, 722.

Ritcheson, Charles R. *Edmund Burke and the American Revolution.* Leicester, England: Leicester University Press, 1976.

Schlesinger, Arthur M., ed. *The Almanac of American History.* New York: Barnes & Noble Books, 1993.

Shankle, George Earlie. *American Mottoes and Slogans.* New York: H. W. Wilson Company, 1941.

Skousen, Mark. *The Making of Modern Economics The Lives and Ideas of the Great Thinkers.* Armonk, NY: M. E. Sharpe, 2001.

Smith, Adam. *An Inquiry into the Nature and Cause of the Wealth of Nations.* CD-Rom edition. Cited in the American Reference Library. Orem, UT: Western Standard Publishing Company, 1998. Book 4, Chapter VII, Of Colonies, Record, 108,730.

Smith, Paul, ed., et al. *Letters of Delegates to Congress, 1774–1789.* 25 Vols. Summerfield, Florida: Historical Database, 1998.

Sosin, Jack M. *Agents and Merchants: British Colonial Policy and the Origins of the American Revolution, 1763–1775.* Lincoln: University of Nebraska Press, 1965.

Stark, James H. *The Loyalists of Massachusetts and the Other Side of the American Revolution.* Boston: J. H. Stark, 1910.

Story, Joseph. *A Familiar Exposition of the Constitution of the United States: Containing a Brief Commentary of Every Clause, Explaining the True Nature, Reasons, and Objects Thereof; Designed for the Use of School Libraries and General Readers.* New York: Harper & Brothers Publishers, 1859. Reprint, Washington, D.C.: Regnery Gateway, Inc., 1986.

Stout, Neil R. *The Royal Navy in America, 1760–1775: A Study of Enforcement of British Colonial Policy in the Era of the American Revolution.* Annapolis, MD: Naval Institute Press, 1973.

Taylor, Robert J. *Western Massachusetts in the Revolution.* Providence, RI: Brown University Press, 1954.

Thayer, William Roscoe. *George Washington.* New York: Houghton Mifflin, 1922.

Thoreau, Henry David. *Collected Essays and Poems.* New York: Library of America, 2001.

Tyler, Moses Coit. *The Literary History of the American Revolution, 1763–1783.* Vol. 1. New York: G. P. Putnam's Sons, 1897.

U.S. House Journal. 1803. 8th Cong., 1st session., at www.memory.loc.gov.

U.S. Supreme Court. United States Reports: Cases Adjudged in the Supreme Court. Washington, D.C.: U.S. Government Printing Office, 1754–1997. Electronic version cited in the American Reference Library. Orem, UT: Western Standard Publishing Company, 1998.

United States National Archives and Records Service. *The Founding Fathers: Delegates to the Constitutional Convention.* Washington, D.C.: www.nara.gov/ex-hall/charters/constitution/confath.html, 1998.

United States Executive Office of the President. *Weekly Compilation of Presidential Documents.* Washington, D.C.: U.S. Government Printing Office, 1994–1999.

Van Tyne, Claude Halstead. The Loyalists in the American Revolution. New York: Macmillan, 1902.

Wahlke, John C., ed. *The Causes of the American Revolution.* Revised ed. Boston: D. C. Heath and Company, 1967.

Warren, Mercy Otis. *History of the Rise, Progress, and Termination of the American Revolution.* 2 vols. CD-Rom edition. West Roxbury, MA: Samizdat Express, 2003.

George Washington Papers at the Library of Congress, 1741–1799. In Washington D.C., online at www.memory.loc.gov.

Washington, George. *Writings.* New York: Library of America, 1997.

Wells, William V. *The Life and Public Services of Samuel Adams: Being a Narrative of His Acts and Opinions, and of His Agency in Producing and Forwarding the American Revolution.* 3 Vols. Boston: Little, Brown, 1888.

Woodrow Wilson. *History of the American People.* 5 vols. New York: William H. Wise. 1931.

Woods, Gordon. *Radicalism of the American Revolution.* New York: Vintage Books, 1991.

Zobel, Hiller B. *The Boston Massacre.* New York: W. W. Norton., 1970.

INDEX

Adams, Elizabeth Checkley (first wife of SA), 27–9, 31–2

Adams, Elizabeth Wells (Betsey), 157, 204, 211, 212; courtship with SA, 36–7; marries SA, 45; SA letters to, 172, 175–6, 177, 180, 193–4, 197, 201, 204, 207

Adams, Hannah (daughter of SA), 31, 37, 70, 87, 88, 157, 204, 212

Adams, Henry, 20

Adams, John (grandfather of SA), 20

Adams, John (Second U S. President), 15, 16, 25–6, 33, 36, 37, 50–1, 78, 80–1, 113, 126, 129, 131–2, 171, 173, 177, 196, 197, 199–200, 216, 219, 227, 231; begins political career, 59; assessment of Boston politics, 65; on James Otis, 65–6; assessments of SA, 107, 231; defends soldiers after Boston Massacre, 106, 110; withdrawal from politics, 113, 126, 135; delegate in first Continental Congress, 154, 157–61, 164; attitudes toward independence, 131–2, 172; SA letters to, 180, 192–3, 199–206, 213–14, 223–5; and Declaration, 183, 184–7; and peace conference, 193; letters to SA, 193, 199–206, 223–5; drafting of Massachusetts Constitution, 204–6; elected U.S. Vice President, 223; elected U.S. President, 227–8; presidential administration, 228

Adams, John Quincy, 13

Adams, Joseph (brother of SA), 22, 30

Adams, Joseph (son of SA), 31

Adams, Joseph (grandfather of second U.S. President), 20

Adams, Mary (sister of SA), 22, 30

Adams, Mary Fifield, (mother of SA), 21–2, 30

Adams, Mary (daughter of SA), 31

Adams, Samuel (father of SA), 20–9; death of, 30–1

Adams, Samuel (first son of SA), 31

Adams, Samuel (second son of SA), 31, 37, 45, 157, 175, 201; death of, 221, 225

Adams, Samuel: accusations of treason, 84–6, 101, 103–4, 149, 193–4; ancestry, 19–20
and Articles of Confederation, 180, 182–4, 195–6, 200, 208; and Battle of Lexington, 169–171; and Boston Tea Party, 140–7; and Boston Town Meeting, 24, 33–4, 36, 38, 41–2, 47–8, 54, 55, 68, 78, 80, 85–6, 99, 103–5, 127–30, 142, 214–15, 223, 225; and Circular letter, 72–4, 81–3, 91–2, 95, 105, 115, 129, 141; and civil disobedience, 42–3, 54, 91–4, 236–7; and Committees of correspondence, 114–16, 126–7, 131–2, 140–3, 150, 151–2, 154, 156, 163–4, 166–7, 170, 174, 177, 180, 182, 205–7, 213, 235; and Hutchinson letters, 133–5, 137–8; and Massachusetts Constitution, 192, 200, 204–6;

and Stamp Act Congress, 47–51, 57, 62–3; and Suffolk County Resolves, 156, 162–3, 165–6, 175, 235; as tax collector, 34; birth of children, 31–2; calls for Continental Congress, 139–40, 235; character of, 20, 23, 27–8, 36–7, 103–4, 140, 155–6, 163, 204, 211–12, 230–1; childhood, 19–20; chosen as delegate to Congress, 154; death of, 230–1; demands lifting of military occupation in 1770, 102–5; denies Parliament's authority, 29, 32, 34, 41, 47–8, 55–6, 57–8, 114–16, 128–9, 130, 134–7, 188–9, 235; early political influences, 21–4, 26, 41; economic views, 17, 26, 40–1, 60, 68, 70–1; education, 22, 25–7; efforts to unite colonies, 13–14, 39, 41–2, 45, 47–51, 57, 63, 71–5, 80–3, 85, 91–2, 96, 105, 113–32, 139–40, 180–2; elected Lt Governor, 221; elected president of Massachusetts Senate, 212; elected to the Massachusetts House, 55; in Continental Congress, 159–64, 171–6, 179–89, 191, 193–99, 201–5, 207–8; journalism of, 16–17, 29–30, 40, 62–3, 92–5, 100–1, 108–9, 110–11, 115–27, 130, 139–40, 235–7; marriages, 31–2, 36–7, 45; on colonial independence, 13–14, 16–17, 27, 41, 49–51, 56–7, 60, 73, 78, 87, 94–5, 103–4, 106, 116, 129, 136–7, 139–40, 150, 156–9, 163, 170–1, 177–8, 179–89, 191–5, 209, 233–6; on French Revolution, 223, 226; on George Washington, 208–9, 220; and Washington Administration, 226; on John Adams' Administration, 228; on liberty of press, 94; on U.S. Constitution, 215, 218–19; opposes Boston Port Bill, 151, 156, 162–3; opposes British pay of colonial judges, 70, 127, 128–9; opposes episcopate in colonies, 72, 115, 160; opposes king's prerogative, 108–9; opposes Stamp Act, 46–51, 54–6, 62–3; opposes Sugar Act, 38–43, 45; opposes Tea Act, 140–7; opposes Townshend Acts, 69–75; proscription of, 171–3, 193; reaction to Shays Rebellion, 215; receives French minister, 202–3; statements of colonial rights, 23–7, 29, 32–3, 41–2, 51, 56–9, 63, 70–5, 81–3, 88–9, 94–6, 108, 114–16, 126–8, 134–7, 139, 166–7, 185–6, 233–4; use of boycotts, 39, 41–3, 46–7, 54, 59–63, 68, 84, 87, 91, 95–6, 107, 152, 155, 157, 162, 235, 237; views on U.S. Bill of Rights, 220; writes "True Sentiments of America," 70–3; writes Massachusetts Resolves, 57–8; writes petition to King, 70–4, 81–3, 86–9, 91–2

Albany Plan, 39, 49
Allen, Ethan, 167, 173
Allen, James, 30
Ames, Fisher, 217, 221
Anabaptists, 160
Anglican Church, England, Church of, 20, 72, 115, 160–1
Annapolis Convention, 214
Annapolis, Maryland, 95
Appleton, Nathanael, 174
Arnold, Benedict, 167, 173, 194, 203
Articles of Confederation, 184, 195–6, 200, 204, 208, 215–16; weaknesses of, 213–15
Association of Continental Congress, 167
Attucks, Crispus, 139

Baltimore, 194
Baltimore, Lord (Cecilius Calvert), 57
Bancroft, George, 15
banking, see land bank
Barnstable, Massachusetts, 35
Beaver, The, 144, 146–7

Belcher, Jonathan, 25
Berkshire Country (Massachusetts), 217
Bernard, Francis, 42, 48, 49, 52, 55, 56, 59, 62, 66, 67, 68, 69, 73, 74, 79, 80, 81, 86, 87, 92, 116; orders rescinding of circular letter, 81–2, dissolves Massachusetts Assembly, 83, advocates changes in Charter, 84; call for troops, 85, reports to British, 91; recalled to England, 96; made Baron of Nettleham, 96; leaves Boston, 97
Bill of Rights (English) 26, 233; (Virginia) 185; (U.S.) 220
Blackstone, William, 115
Boston Gazette, 42, 88, 93, 100, 101, 109, 110, 115, 139
Boston Latin School, 22
Boston Massacre, 15, 99–111, 113–14, 126, 168
Boston Port Bill, 150, 156
Boston Tea Party, 145–7; causes of 140–7; reaction in England, 149–50
Botetourt, Lord, Norbonne Berkeley, 95
Bowdoin, James, 15, 154, 157, 204, 214–15, 218
Boycott, Charles C., 42–3
boycotts, 39, 42–3, 46–62, 84, 91, 95–6, 107, 162, 166–7
Breed's Hill, *see* Bunker Hill, Battle of
British Army's occupation of Boston, 83, 87–9, 99–111, 114–15, 149, 166, 167–71, 173, 174–5
British Constitution, 30, 94, 128, 136, 138
British Navy at Boston, 78–9, 103–4, 113–14, 141, 144
Brutus, 115
Bryant, William Jennings, 15
Bunker Hill, Battle of, 174–5, 177
Burgoyne, John, 174, 198, 200
Burke, Edmund, 61, 62, 93
Burnet, William, 23
Bute, John Stuart, 46, 52

Catholics, *see* Roman Catholics

Charles I, 20
Charleston (aka Charlestown), Massachusetts, 144, 151, 155, 161, 170
Charleston, South Carolina, 186
Checkley, Elizabeth, *see* Elizabeth Checkley Adams
Checkley, Samuel, 22, 27
Choiseul, Etienne Francois, 92
Church of England, *see* Anglican Church
Church, Benjamin, 34, 128–9
Circular Letter, 72, 91–2, 95, 105, 115, 129, 150, 235; reaction to in colonies, 73–5; reaction by British leaders, 73–5; order to rescind, 81–3, vote not to rescind, 82–3
Civil Disobedience, 42–3, 54, 91–4, 237
Clarke, Jonas, 169–70
Clarke, Richard, 141–2
Clinton, Henry, 174, 201
Coercive Acts, 152, 156; *see also* Boston Port Bill
Commentaries on the Laws of England, 115
Committees of Correspondence, 114, 127–9, 137, 139–40, 150–1, 163–4, 166–7, 170, 176, 180, 182, 204–5, 206–7, 213, 235
Common Sense, 181; SA's praise of, 181
Continental Congress, *see* U.S. Congress (Continental)
Conway Cabal, 200, 220
Cook, Elisha, 23
Cooper, James Fenimore, 236
Cooper, Samuel, 102; SA's letters to, 182, 204
Copley, John Singleton, 126, 157, 212
Corner, John, 77–9, 85
Cornwallis, Charles, 195, 209
Cushing, Harry Alonzo, 15
Cushing, Thomas (employer of SA), 28
Cushing, Thomas (political colleague of SA), 34, 66, 108, 127–8, 158, 160, 171, 225; suspicions of treason, 93; chosen as delegate to Congress, 153–4

customs officials, 35, 69, 74, 84, 99,
        100, 133, 134, 137, 145

Dalrymple, William, 87, 103–5
Dana, Francis, 206–7; assessment of
        SA, 207
Dartmouth, Lord (William Legge), 140
Dartmouth, The, 143, 146–7
Deane, Silas, 193, 202–3
DeBerdt, Dennys, 59, 60, 67, 87, 109
Declaration of Independence, 14, 57,
        180, 183–9, 191, 193, 199, 226,
        233–6; Congressional vote on,
        187–8
Declaratory Act, 96, 115
Devens, Richard, 170
Dickinson, John, 172, 184; and
        reconciliation, 176; and Articles of
        Confederation, 184, 186–7;
        opposes Declaration, 186–7
Duche, Jacob, 160–1
Duke of Cumberland, The, 85
Dunmore, Lord, see John Murray

East India Company, 140–4
economic issues, 17, 26, 41, 60, 68,
        71, 78
Edes, Benjamin, 93
Edwards, Jonathan, 22
Eleanor, The, 144, 146
Emerson, Ralph Waldo, 236
English merchants, 39, 46, 62–3, 83,
        92, 106
English Society of the Bill of Rights,
        114
Evening Post, The, 93
Everett, Edward, 211

Faneuil Hall, 41, 86, 143, 151
Federalist, The, 216
Fifield, Mary, see Mary Fifield Adams
Fifield, Richard, 21
Flucker, Thomas, 155
Folsom, Nathaniel, 158
Fort Ticonderoga, 180
France, proposed alliance, 179, 180,
        183, 193, 196, 202; recognizes
        American independence, 201–2;
        sends diplomat, 202–4

Franklin, Benjamin, 16, 24, 94, 109,
        109–10, 129, 133, 137, 149–50,
        159, 172, 184, 193–4-; Albany
        Plan, 39, 49, on Stamp Act, 46,
        61
Franklin, William, 109, 159
French Revolution, 223, 226

Gadsden, Christopher, 50, 67, 158
Gage, Thomas, 74, 80, 88, 96, 149,
        151, 153–5, 161–3, 169–70, 173
Galloway, Joseph, 159, 163
Gandhi, Mahatma, 237
Gaspee, The, 130
Gates, Horatio, 198, 200, 220
George III, King (George William
        Frederick), 42, 55, 57, 62, 66, 67,
        69, 81, 91, 108, 145, 167, 176,
        179, 188
George IV, King of England, and
        Prince of Wales, 51
Gerard, Conrad Alexander, 202–3, 208
Gerry, Elbridge, 177, 206–7; SA letter
        to 214
Gettysburg Address, 236
Gill, Jonathan, 93
Gordon, William, 220
Gray, John, 101
Green Mountain Boys, 167
Greenleaf, Benjamin, 154
Grenville, George, 37–8, 39, 55, 58,
        61, 67, 92
Gridlely, Jeremiah, 59

Habersham, James, 50
Hall, James, 143
Halsey, Francis W., 15
Hamilton, Alexander, 197, 214–15,
        219
Hancock, John, 16, 34, 66, 78, 79, 80,
        105, 107–8, 113, 116, 126–8,
        134, 137, 142, 151, 153, 165,
        172–3, 186, 188, 197, 211,
        216–19, 235; background of, 66;
        plot to assassinate, 167–9;
        committee of safety, 169; at
        Lexington, 169–71; military
        ambitions, 172; political
        ambitions of, 198–9; rift with SA,

198–200, 207–8, 212;
    Massachusetts governor, 207, 211,
    212, 214, 221; death of, 225
Hancock, Thomas, 66
Harlow, Ralph V., 15–16
Harrison, 62
Harrison, Benjamin, 173
Harvard College, 20, 22–3, 25, 26, 27,
    223
Hawley, Joseph, 135, 154, 182; SA
    letter to, 188
Henry VIII, King of England, 92
Henry, Patrick, 42, 47, 115, 131, 152,
    164, 167
Hessians, 195
Hillsborough, Lord (Wills Hill), 74–5,
    82–3, 85, 96, 101, 107–8
Hodgdon, Samuel, 174
Hollis, Thomas, 73
Hood, Samuel, 77, 80, 85, 88
Hosmer, James K., 15
Howe, William, 174, 181, 196–7, 201,
    and peace conference, 193
Hughes, John, 46
Hume, David, 115
Hutchinson, Thomas 36, 39, 49, 50,
    52–4, 58; 97, 101–5, 107–10,
    144, 155–6, 168–9, 198, 171;
    receives royal salary, 69; on Whigs,
    69; seeks witnesses against SA, 84,
    93; and Boston Massacre, 101–5;
    named Massachusetts Governor,
    107; assessments of SA, 84, 116,
    126–9, 140; defends Parliament,
    134–7; letters exposed, 133–4,
    137–9, 149, 172; reaction to
    Boston Tea Party, 145–7

Independence Hall, *see* Pennsylvania
    State House
Independent Chronicle, 220–1, 231
India, 37
Irish leaders, 206
Irving, Washington, 236

Jackson, Richard, 54
James I, King of England, 136
James II, King of England, 26
Jay, John, 160, 172, 216, 226–7

Jay's Treaty of 1795, 226
Jefferson, Thomas, 14, 16, 131, 153,
    155, 174, 181, 183, 214, 216,
    219, 227–9, 231, 236; on
    reconciliation, 172, 176, 179;
    assessments of SA, 174, 184, 228,
    231–2; and Declaration of
    Independence, 184–6, 234; first
    inaugural address, 228–9; letters
    to SA, 228–9; SA letter to, 228–9

Killroy, Matthew, 110
King, Jr., Martin Luther, 237
King, Rufus, 217
Kirk, Russell, 16
Knox, Henry, 177, 180, 219, 229

land bank, 24–6, suits over, 32–3
Laurens, Henry, 203
Lee, Arthur, 113, 137–8, 147, 150
Lee, Richard Henry, 126, 131, 152,
    159, 173, 174, 184, 193–4,
    202–3; proposes Declaration, 184;
    SA letters to, 188, 196, 200, 215,
    220
Leonard, Daniel, 130
Lexington, Battle of, 169–71
Liberty Tree, 51–2, 58, 62, 142
Lincoln, Abraham, 236
Lincoln, Benjamin, 215
Locke, John, 26, 41, 89, 108, 115;
    Second Treatise on Government,
    26
Luzerne, Anne-Cesar de la, 208
Lynch, Sr., Thomas, 159

Madison, James, 214, 216, 219, 227,
    230–1
Magna Carta, 36, 57, 115, 137
Mahlmann, Siegfried August, 236
Mansfield, Lord (William Murray),
    61–2
Marblehead, Massachusetts, 166, 177
Maria, Henrietta, 20
Mason, George, 95, 185
Massachusetts Charter of 1691, 23, 30,
    70, 128, 131, 135, 156, 204–5
Massachusetts Constitution of 1780,
    192, 204–6

Massachusetts Ratifying Convention
    (of U.S. Constitution), 215–19
Massachusetts Spy, 142
Mather, Cotton, 22
Mauduit, Israel, 46
Mauduit, Jasper, 46
McKean, Thomas, 158
Melville, Herman, 236
Meserve, George, 55
Miller, John C., 16
Minutemen, 165
Mississippi, 49
mobs, 16, 50–4, 79, 80, 100–5, 142,
    145
Mohawks, 146
Monroe, James, 230–1
Montagu, John, 113, 146
Montesquieu, 115
Montgomery, Hugh, 110
Monticello, 176
Montreal, 167
Morris, Gouverneur, 202
Mount Vernon, 173
Murray, John (Earl of Dunmore),
    163–4

New England Chronicle, 174
non-importation agreements, *see*
    boycotts
North, Lord Frederick, 69, 79, 92–3,
    105, 141

Oliver, Andrew, 52, 53, 55, 133,
    137–8
Otis, Harrison Gray, 225
Otis, James, 34, 35–6, 48–51, 62, 69,
    80, 82, 85–7, 93, 97, 99, 108,
    128–9, 180, 208, 225

Paine, Robert Treat, 153–4, 158–9, 171
Paine, Thomas, 181, 194, 230
Parker, John, 170
Paxton, Charles, 66, 67, 137
Penn, William, 57
Pennsylvania Gazette, 201
Pennsylvania State House (Independence
    Hall), 186, 203, 223

Pierce, Joseph, 93–4
Pinckney, Thomas, 227
Pitcairn, John, 170
Pitt, William, 51, 67; and Stamp Act,
    61
Preston, Thomas, 102, 106, 110; trial
    of, 110
Puritans, 19–23, 130, 160–1, 211
Purviance, Samuel Jr., 170

Quartering Act, 70, 153
Quincy, Josiah, 34, 68, 225; defends
    soldiers after Boston Massacre,
    106
Randolph, John (U.S. Congressman),
    231
Randolph, John, 176, 179
Randolph, Peyton, 160
Reed, Joseph, 161
Revere, Paul, 152, 162, 163, 169–70,
    218
Rhode Island, 50, 95, 100, 130–1,
    150, 166, 216
Richmond, Virginia, 167
Rivington, James, 207
Rockingham, Marquis of (Charles
    Watson-Wentworth), 55, 61
Rodney, Caesar, 187
Rotch, Francis, 142–5
Ruggles, Timothy, 97
Rush, Benjamin, 158–9
Rutledge, Edward, 158, 160, 187,
    193
Rutledge, John, 50, 158

Sayre, Stephen, 106, 108
Scott, James, 142
Sewall, Jonathan, 78, 134
Shakespeare, William, 13, 196
Shays' rebellion, 214–17, 227
Shays, Daniel, 214–17, 227
Sherman, Roger, 184
Shirley, William, 33
Singletary, Amos, 217
Smith, Adam, 41, 59–60, 70, 78
Smith, James, 87
Smith, Jonathan, 217

smuggling, 69–70, 77, 79, 142
Society of Cincinnati, 214
Somersetshire, England, 20
Sons of Liberty, 51, 52, 53, 54, 85, 93, 94, 141, 161, 169
Squire, Edith, 20
Stamp Act Congress, 48, 49, 51, 55–8, 62–3, 114–15, 129, 139, 235
Stamp Act, 46–63, 51–5, 58–63, 67, 69, 94, 109, 114–15, 225, 235
Suffolk County Resolves, 162, 165, 174–5, 235; drafting, 156; provisions of, 156–7
Sugar Act, 38–40, 42, 43, 45, 46, 53
Sullivan, John, 158, 166
Sylvester, Richard, 84

Tea tax, 96, 106, 140–1, *see also* Boston Tea Party
Thacher, Oxenbridge, 38, 55, 225
Thompson (also spelled Thomson), Charles, 158, 199
Thoreau, Henry David, 237
Ticonderoga, Fort, 167, 171, 173
Townshend Acts, 92, 95–6, 106–7, 115–16; becomes law, 68; provisions of, 68; reaction in colonies to, 68–9; plans to repeal, 96
Townshend, Charles, 66, 67, 68, 69
Treaty of Paris, 212
Trumbull, Johnathan, 171

U.S. Congress (Continental), 152–64, 167, 171–8, 191–204, 207–8, 211, 221, 235; public calls for, 139, 152–3; First Continental Congress, 152–64

U.S. Congress, (under Articles of Confederation), 213–14, 216–21
U.S. Constitution, 206, 215–21
U.S. House of Representatives, 231
U.S. Senate, 227
United Parishes of Christ's Church (Philadelphia), 160–1

Voltaire, 116

Warren, James, 78, 179–81, 183; SA letters to 179–80, 188, 195–6, 202; letter to SA, 181
Warren, Joseph, 34, 37, 85, 105, 128–9, 153, 157, 162–3, 167–8, 169, 173, 175, 225; and Suffolk Resolves, 156, 165; death of, 174–5
Warren, Mercy Otis, 87, 97, 103, 151, 180, 208
Washington, George, 15, 16, 95, 159, 172–3, 180, 186, 192, 195, 198–202, 209, 212, 216, 219–20, 226–7
Wayne, Anthony, 198
Wedderburn, Alexander, 149
Wells, Elizabeth, *see* Adams, Elizabeth Wells
Wells, Thomas, 212
Wells, William, 231
Whatley, Thomas, 133–4
Whitefield, George, 22
William of Orange, King of England, 26
Wilson, James, 155
Wilson, Woodrow, 14
Witherspoon, John, 158
Writs of Assistance, 35–6